G000167817

Gorbachev's ex
to Eastern Europe

Manchester University Press

PERSPECTIVES ON DEMOCRATIC PRACTICE

Series editors: SHIRIN M. RAI and WYN GRANT

With the ebbing away of the 'third wave' of democratisation, democratic practice is unfolding and consolidating in different ways. While state-based representative democracy remains central to our understanding of the concept, we are also conscious of the importance of social movements, non-governmental organisations and governance institutions. New mechanisms of accountability are being developed, together with new political vocabularies to address these elements in democratic practice. The books published in this series focus on three aspects of democratic practice: analytical and normative democratic theory, including processes by which democratic practice can be explained and achieved; new social and protest movements, especially work with a comparative and international focus; and institution-building and practice, including transformations in democratic institutions in response to social and democratic forces. Their importance arises from the fact that they are concerned with key questions about how power can be more fairly distributed and how people can be empowered to have a greater influence on decisions that affect their lives.

This series takes forward the intellectual project of the earlier MUP series, *Perspectives on Democratization*.

Already published

Gorbachev's export of *Perestroika* to Eastern Europe

Democratisation reconsidered

HELEN HARDMAN

Manchester University Press

Published by Manchester University Press
Altrincham Street, Manchester M1 7JA, UK
www.manchesteruniversitypress.co.uk

British Library Cataloguing-in-Publication Data is available

Library of Congress Cataloging-in-Publication Data is available

ISBN 978 0 7190 9664 8 paperback

First published by Manchester University Press in hardback 2012

This paperback edition first published 2015

The publisher has no responsibility for the persistence or accuracy of URLs for any external or third-party internet websites referred to in this book, and does not guarantee that any content on such websites is, or will remain, accurate or appropriate.

Printed by Lightning Source

Contents

List of tables

Acknowledgements

Conducting this research was exciting at every turn, which is thanks to the generosity of individuals in Belgrade, Budapest, Cracow, Łódź, Moscow and Warsaw, who very kindly shared their views and experiences at interview. Throughout the research, I received crucial advice and help from many people and anything useful in this book reflects their input; any mistakes or misjudgements are mine.

I am very grateful to my doctoral supervisors, Richard Crampton and Elizabeth Frazer, for their support of this project in its preliminary stages, and their invaluable advice during the years that followed. As well as advising on the Russian case study and other chapters, Stephen Whitefield did a great deal to help arrange my fieldwork in Moscow. Thanks are owed to Archie Brown, Paul Chaisty, Paul Goode, Petra Schleiter, George Schöpflin, Robert Service, Edward Walker and Kieran Williams for their comments on my research at early stages. I am grateful to Archie Brown for his support of my application to the Gorbachev Foundation. For research and fieldwork funding, I am grateful to the University of Oxford's Department of Politics, St Antony's College and the Taylor Ilchester fund.

From the Bodleian Library, I would like to thank Carole Menzies and Kati Evans for their help. A number of libraries outside Oxford also very kindly granted me access to their collections during the course of this research: the Baykov Library at Birmingham University, the Biblioteka Narodowa and Biblioteka na Koszykowej in Warsaw, the British Library, Cambridge University, the London School of Economics, the School of Oriental and African Studies, Svetozar Marković University in Belgrade and University College London.

I am grateful to: the staff of the Magyar Országos Levéltár in Budapest; Csaba Varga, Ilona Kecsmer, László and János Szabó for their help arranging and facilitating interviews in the Hungarian Parliament; the Gorbachev Foundation; Aleksandr Yakovlev's Fond Demokratiia; RGANI; the staff of Russian Research and the Lukin family in Moscow. In Warsaw I owe thanks to the staff of the Archiwum Akt Nowych, to Anna Nizińska and her family and to Joanna Marciniak for their kindness and hospitality.

Jan Zielonka and Richard Sakwa made insightful comments at the doctoral viva, which helped in preparation for this book. For the great leap in editing the work into a book, a large debt of thanks is owed to the advice and help of the series editors, in particular Wyn Grant, and an enormous thank you to all involved at MUP for their patience, encouragement and advice.

Most importantly, thanks are owed to my family and friends for their support over many years: my parents Isabel and Gerald, and to John and Catherine Hardman, Michael, Annabel, Edward and William Davey, Geoffrey Greatrex, Vanessa Mathews, Jackie and the Corbett family, and Denise and the Hospitality Committee.

List of abbreviations

AAN	Archive of Modern Records (in Warsaw)
BCP	Bulgarian Communist Party
CC	Central Committee
CCC	Central Control Commission
CCRC	Central Control-Revision Commission
CEE	Central and East European
CMEA	Council for Mutual Economic Assistance (also known as Comecon)
Cominform	Communist Information Bureau (1947–56)
Comintern	Communist International (1919–43)
CoPD	Congress of People's Deputies
CPC	Communist Party of China
CPCZ	Communist Party of Czechoslovakia
CPSU	Communist Party of the Soviet Union (1952–)
FSB	Federal Security Service (Russia)
FYP	Five Year Plan
GDR	German Democratic Republic
HCP	Hungarian Communist Party
HDF	Hungarian Democratic Forum
HSP	Hungarian Socialist Party (October 1989–)
HSWP	Hungarian Socialist Workers' Party (31 October 1956–89)
HWP	Hungarian Workers' Party (1948–57)
IMF	International Monetary Fund
JNA	Yugoslav People's Army
KGB	State Security Committee (Soviet Union)
KISZ	Communist Youth League (Hungary)
KPP	Communist Party of Poland (1925–38)

KPRP	Communist Workers' Party of Poland (1918–25)
LC	League of Communists
LCP	Lithuanian Communist Party
LCY	League of Communists of Yugoslavia
MADISZ	Hungarian Democratic Youth Union
MOL	Hungarian National Archives
NATO	North Atlantic Treaty Organisation
NEP	New Economic Policy (Soviet Union)
NGO	Non-Governmental Organisation
NKVD	People's Commissariat for Internal Affairs
NPC	National Party Conference
OPEC	Organisation of the Petroleum Exporting Countries
PUWP	Polish United Workers' Party
RCP	Romanian Communist Party
RCP(B)	Russian Communist Party of Bolsheviks (1918–25)
RGANI	Russian State Archives of Modern History
RSDWP	Russian Social Democratic Workers' Party (–1918)
RSFSR	Russian Soviet Federative Socialist Republic
SD	Democratic Party (Poland)
SED	Socialist Unity Party of Germany
SI	Socialist International
SLD	Union of Left Democrats (Poland)
USSR	Union of Soviet Socialist Republics
WTO	Warsaw Treaty Organisation (Warsaw Pact)
ZSL	United People's Party (Poland)

Introduction

Liberalisation or democratisation?

This book broadly looks at what has been commonly identified as the liberalisation process across the one-party regimes
of Central and Eastern Europe (CEE) during the period 1987–
89. The focus of the work is on one particular joint initiative,
which the General Secretary of the Communist Party of the
Soviet Union, Mikhail Gorbachev, strongly encouraged his
fraternal counterparts to embrace. It examines how these
leaderships sought to work together, with varying degrees of
success, to overcome problems which were clearly systemic
and common to all these regimes at the time. The underlying
rationale which underpinned this initiative was the preserva-
tion of the socialist fraternity as a group; this was perceived as
a duty to which all these regimes were bound by the Warsaw
Pact and the Socialist International (SI). Across the fraternity
a movement (which was not publicised as such) was initiated
by Gorbachev with the purpose of maintaining the one-party
regime, much along the same trajectory which the Communist Party of China had begun in 1985.

This brief period in the transformation of the one-party
regimes of Central and Eastern Europe may be interpreted as
'history', as it were, since most of these regimes have reached
a stage of consolidated democracy and established liberal democratic institutions, which support and sustain this in practice.
But in the case of Russia, examining the transition process of
the Soviet regime during the Gorbachev era is complicated by
the fact that commentators have since queried the nature of the

emergent regime, variously describing it, since the emergence of United Russia and the Putin presidency of 2000, as a 'managed democracy', 'authoritarian', a 'kleptocracy' or a 'militocracy'. During the early Yeltsin presidency, scholars questioned the quality of the new institutions and practices, and the marginal role elections played in this process.[1] Since the Putin era, and the rise of his 'party of power', there has been a clear onslaught against the political opposition incrementally, through the law on political parties (2001, 2004),[2] and electoral reform (2004, 2006),[3] the appointment of regional governors by the President[4] and control of the media by corporations that support the Presidential administration.[5] This indicates that there has been and continues to be a significant disconnect between what the regime claims as 'democracy' and what in practice it has delivered to Russian society. We could avoid this problem by saying that the term 'democratisation' is used in the case of Russia to denote the anticipated trajectory of the regime change at the beginning of the process, rather than how it has turned out so far in practice. This in itself is problematic, however, as we could query *who* anticipated that full democratisation would occur, *who* wished to see this introduced and whether or not this contingent of the Russian electorate is represented by opposition parties that have since been successfully (and apparently irreversibly) marginalised by the Yeltsin and Putin administrations. The 'floating party system' that developed allowed strong groups to rebrand themselves and coalesce just prior to elections to guarantee the safe transfer of power, which remains within a small ruling elite.[6] This practice effectively disenfranchises large proportions of the electorate,[7] and it is not clear how the political opposition can successfully re-enter to compete in the political arena under such conditions.

This disconnect, between democratisation in theory and practice, began during the Gorbachev era when the Communist Party of the Soviet Union (CPSU) announced bold plans of '*demokratizatsiia*'. This new departure, as it was heralded by Gorbachev, has been interpreted by many as a reform process comprising radical liberalisation, which was motivated by CPSU reformists, who were led by Gorbachev, to modernise the party in the light of a sudden new 'awareness' that practices during the previous eras had been unacceptable and that consequently a clear break with the past was required. 'To make *perestroika* irreversible'[8], Gorbachev convened the Nineteenth CPSU Conference at which he publicised that the new direction of party reform would be 'more democracy' but also that the party was to achieve greater control over the state, and would increase its vanguard status in society. Between 1985 and 1991, Gorbachev's package of reforms entailed little other than modernisation to make the party more attractive and to legitimise its leading role in society, and to make the existing system more efficient through economic liberalisation. Gorbachev appealed to the Central and East European leaders, in the spirit of socialist internationalism, to modernise their regimes and parties so as to preserve the existing model of the one-party communist state throughout the region.

Aside from the issue of whether or not democratisation has taken place in Russia, the process of Russian regime 'transformation' can still be adequately explained within democratisation literature, as most agree that liberalisation does not necessarily lead to democratisation, and authoritarian regimes may liberalise to become less authoritarian, but may never reach the stage of democratisation. It follows, therefore, that leaders introducing liberalisation may simply be encouraging the reform of the existing system as a means to making it viable, rather than seeking regime change *per se*. Liberalisation has been identified as 'controlled and reversible', whereas democratisation marks a stage of regime change when a return to the *status quo ante* is no longer feasible. Although in some instances liberalisation may have been historically followed by democratisation, those leaderships that introduced liberalising reforms may not have intended the ensuing process of regime change and democratisation. The feature which distinguishes an authoritarian regime, such as the model of the one-party state of Central and Eastern Europe, from a democracy, is open contestation over the right to win control of the government, a process which is determined by free and fair competitive elections.[9]

In the context of the Soviet Union, so long as the dominant logic of reform was liberalisation rather than democratisation, then the goal was 'to reform the command economy and refound Soviet hegemony rather than to destroy it',[10] and liberalisation at this stage was reversible.[11] Therefore, what might appear as a linear transition from authoritarianism to 'democracy' was instead a more complicated process, whereby leaderships wished to liberalise without democratising, and this process was then followed by 'reluctant democratisation' as other forces gained control of the situation, ousted incumbents and forced regime change. Therefore, had *perestroika* increased efficiency enough to make the economy viable, and modernise the party sufficiently to re-establish its authority within society, then Gorbachev would have maintained, as far as possible, the one-party state. Instead, liberalisation raised expectations within the party among those who wanted more radical reform, and inevitably weakened the Union, as republics became more autonomous. Gorbachev and the All-Union Party, the CPSU, became redundant following the establishment of the Russian Soviet Federative Socialist Republic (RSFSR) party in 1990.

In the context of the Nineteenth CPSU Conference of 1988, the reforms that Gorbachev introduced were intended to consolidate the party's authority and increase its control over the state and society.[12] The intention behind introducing some aspects of the rule of law was to regulate rather than 'smash' the state and to overcome corruption within, which was grinding the system down.[13] Thus constitutional reforms were devised to kick-start the stagnant economy, which threatened to petrify political structures further. The purpose, therefore, of the reforms introduced at the Nineteenth CPSU Conference was to break the bureaucracy's stronghold over the state and its resistance to *perestroika*, as Chapter 3 will demonstrate. At the conference, Gorbachev construed himself as a centrist, shifting his allegiance between the left and right to destabilise the growth of a stable opposition to *perestroika* in either camp.[14] This victory for *perestroika* did not evolve naturally as a result of the new policy of open debate as engendered in *glasnost*, but was carefully planned in advance and to some extent staged, much in the same tradition as previous Soviet party conferences, which Chapter 2 will consider.

The dynamic which led to the spate of conferences in the fraternal states was designed as an integrated process with the CPSU Conference, intended to provide support for *perestroika* from outside, but also geared towards modernising fraternal socialism, in step with CPSU reforms, with the intention of salvaging the socialist one-party state model.

The Chinese Communist Party Conference 1985

A process of reform in this vein geared towards modernising the party and rooting out bureaucracy began in the Communist Party of China (CPC) in September 1985, when a national conference was convened for the first time in thirty years. At this conference a large number of officials from the CPC Central Committee and Politburo resigned and were replaced with younger, better-educated and more reformist officials.[15] Many of the new cohort had been trained in the Soviet Union, including one of the new Vice Premiers in the Politburo, Li Peng, who had studied at Moscow University at the same time as Gorbachev.[16] This heralded the normalisation of relations between China and the Soviet Union, although as Gorbachev advised fraternal party leaders at the Warsaw Pact meeting in October 1985, the Chinese wished to conduct these affairs clandestinely, in such a way that the West would have no idea that China was cooperating with the Soviet Union.[17] Normalisation was only officially marked in May 1989, just after the Tiananmen Square massacres, during Gorbachev's visit to China as the first Soviet General Secretary to visit since Nikita Khrushchev in 1959.[18]

Prior to this, relations between the CPC and the fraternal parties of Central and Eastern Europe were also normalised for the first time in decades, which the acting General Secretary of the CPC, Zhao Ziyang, marked with a visit to Poland, the German Democratic Republic (GDR), Czechoslovakia, Hungary and Bulgaria between 4 and 20 June 1987.[19] In each of these states, the visits were described in the press as momentous for both party and state, and resulted in bilateral agreements to secure effective technology transfer and improved trade relations.[20] During Ziyang's visit to Poland, which was the first on his grand tour, the First Secretary of the PUWP, General Wojciech Jaruzelski announced in his speech the importance of cooperation among the socialist states as a way to combat the threat of Western imperialism.[21] The Hungarian press declared that the CPC's economic reforms were designed to strengthen the leading role of the party in society.[22] This suggests a common purpose to the economic liberalisation, one that both Gorbachev and Ziyang anticipated would secure better party control and influence over society. The CPC's first major step in beginning this reform process was to make far-reaching personnel changes at their party conference in 1985. It would seem logical to assume, therefore, that Ziyang would have raised this issue with the fraternal party leaders during his visits, and is quite likely also to have recommended the convention of conferences across the Central and East European space, for the same purpose of replenishing personnel and modernising the party. The CPC Conference is the most likely blueprint for the Gorbachevian conference. Moreover, since the common aim of all conferences was to strengthen the leading role of the party through a series of modernising reforms, including economic liberalisation, there appears to be a certain concerted effort across socialist parties in achieving this, with the aim of securing the future of the communist party model.

A few days after Ziyang's visit to the fraternal leaders, János Kádár, the aged Hungarian leader, addressed a meeting of the Central Committee (CC) of the Hungarian Socialist Workers' Party (HSWP) on 23 June 1987 and raised the issue of adopting 'the capitalist model' to solve the country's economic crisis, which he attributed to sudden changes in the world economy resulting from the energy crisis. In defence of the solution of marketisation, Kádár explained that the capitalist states of the West had reached a critical stage in overcoming the crisis in their own economies, but that Hungary did not have the necessary energy resources and efficiency to cope in the new world economy.[23] He stated that similar debates were taking place among the Chinese and Soviet leaderships, and Kádár concurred with both in wanting 'more rather than less socialism'.[24] Although willing to salvage the system through economic liberalisation, Kádár refused to acknowledge the need for his own resignation. At the end of his speech, Kádár stated that a 'Chinese colleague' had informed him of the plan that the long-standing Chinese leader, Deng Xiaoping, should resign from two of his three official posts. Kádár then unequivocally stated that his own resignation was not, however, necessary, because his own situation was not analogous with Deng's, who at eighty-three was ten years older than Kádár.[25] As will be discussed in Chapter 5, at this meeting in June 1987 a number of HSWP CC members advocated Kádár's resignation. Between 1987 and 1989, there appears to have been a two-pronged attack by both China and the Soviet Union against the aged regimes of the fraternal Central and Eastern European parties, to secure leadership change to modernise these parties and encourage market liberalisation to compete with the global economy. This book focuses on Gorbachev's role in this movement, those Soviet domestic factors that favoured and necessitated such a movement, and fraternal party leaderships' responses to this initiative.

CEE conferences 1987–89 held in the spirit of 'socialist internationalism'

As Chapter 4 will discuss, Gorbachev tried to establish a new socialist order on the basis of peaceful relations, whereby Soviet military intervention in Central and Eastern Europe would no longer be used to maintain the ageing regimes of the fraternal states. Gorbachev encouraged fraternal leaderships to convene their respective conferences as part of this initiative. This step implicitly required the ouster of old regimes that had been established under the auspices of Soviet military intervention, as these leaderships' legitimacy was entirely underpinned by the 'Brezhnev Doctrine'. As Chapters 5 and 7 will examine, individuals in these leaderships had requested Soviet military intervention to maintain their regimes, but this factor was conveniently omitted from these fraternal states' narrative of events. This 'myth' helped construe these leaderships as having been forced to comply with the Soviet Union, and only collaborating under duress to protect their states from Soviet aggression. By the time Gorbachev came to power as General Secretary in 1985, military intervention had already been eschewed by the Soviet Union during the Polish crisis between 1980 and 1981. As Chapter 7 will show, Gorbachev was eager to dissociate the CPSU from those fraternal leaders who had personally benefited as a result of Soviet military intervention or the justification of domestic regimes' use of force as the lesser evil to the imminent threat of Soviet intervention.

The renunciation of the Brezhnev Doctrine has been popularly attributed to Gorbachev and generally dated from March 1988. At one level, rejection of the Brezhnev Doctrine implicitly promised that the CPSU would not use force against Central, Eastern and South-eastern European states. On another level, it claimed that the fraternal parties were no longer obliged to follow the lead of the CPSU in managing their domestic policies and that Soviet pressure would not be applied to this effect, as Karen Dawisha has defined the term:

The Brezhnev Doctrine as it was known in the West or 'socialist internationalism' as it was sometimes called in the Soviet bloc, had been enunciated after the Soviet invasion of Czechoslovakia in 1968 and was taken to mean that each communist party was responsible not only to its own people but also to all the socialist countries that the sovereignty of individual socialist countries was of lesser importance than the interests of world socialism, and that it was not only the right but also the positive duty of all socialist countries to come to the aid of any socialist state where socialism was threatened... Soviet insistence that bloc parties adhere to the principle of socialist internationalism had been one of the keys to Soviet ideological control in Eastern Europe.[26]

As Chapter 4 will discuss, between 1987 and 1989 Gorbachev appealed to communist party leaders of the fraternal states of Central, Eastern and South-eastern Europe to call their respective party conferences for the purpose of modernising their parties to make them viable. Gorbachev called on the fraternal leaderships to act together in the spirit of socialist internationalism to reshape their regimes for the sake of preserving the existing model. There is evidence of some pressure having been brought to bear by Gorbachev in securing the fraternal parties' compliance with this, which may be interpreted as his continuing application of the Brezhnev Doctrine. Although there was certainly no threat of military intervention, the Soviet Union was still in a strong position with respect to the leaderships in these states, and so Gorbachev was able to exert influence, with varying degrees of success, over the fraternal leaderships.

Soviet political and economic 'control' over fraternal states

In the context of the period in question – just before the end of Soviet hegemony over Central, Eastern and South-eastern Europe – the nature of the research begs the question: to what extent *could* the Soviet Union still practicably exert 'control' over its 'outer empire' at this time? 'Control' is the term that has been coined to describe influence exerted by more powerful states over weaker ones as a causal factor in explaining their regime transition[27] or, in the context of this book, liberalisation. Scholars commonly agree that the nature of Central and East European dependence on the Soviet Union was variable in 1987, as was Soviet political leverage over these states.[28]

Nonetheless, the significant CPSU influence over Central and East European transitions has been widely stressed, albeit to varying degrees.[29] Although the Soviet Union's relations with the fraternal regimes had evolved by the late 1980s, which had further increased the variance among the relationships between the Soviet Union and different fraternal regimes, fraternal compliance with Soviet policy was still expected at this time:

> As the system grew older the room for diversity and domestic autonomy progressively expanded. (In fact such 'autonomy' was indispensable for the bloc's smooth functioning in an increasingly complex and more peaceful environment.) Both the satellites and the Soviet center learned to coexist in a mutually satisfactory way without the need for direct rigid controls and constant use of overt force, and the political and economic conditions in each satellite grew more divergent and varied depending on each country's political culture and level of development. This progressive maturing eventually brought about a transformation of the early rigid 'satellite system' into an inherently looser and more complex Soviet 'solar system'. Under the looser system, each bloc member was able to develop its distance from the Kremlin, but also by diverging ever more from the paths taken by the other constituent countries (by increasing the variety in specific domestic conditions). This disintegration of early uniformity, however, did not mean (at least until 1989) that orbiting around the Kremlin was not a must or that domestic conditions were permitted to alter beyond the limits drawn by the Kremlin.[30]

Scholars have noted that certain factors still served as Soviet leverage over the 'outer empire', but during the time in question the effects of these levers can be identified by their systematic removal, rather than their application. Soviet foreign policy towards Central, Eastern and South-eastern Europe was characterised, at this time, by the overt reduction in Soviet hegemonic power to interfere in the domestic policies of these regimes. The existing literature depicts a linear trajectory, which can be summarised briefly as follows. Soviet liberalising policies facilitated transition from authoritarianism in these regimes by removing the following levers: the Brezhnev Doctrine of limited sovereignty, economic dependence via the Council for Mutual Economic Assistance (CMEA) and the presence of Soviet troops in Central Europe. Traditionally, foreign policy towards the fraternal states had always been one of keeping these regimes in step with the pace of CPSU 'thaws' or 'freezes'. This policy of 'limited sovereignty' was one that had been spelled out through experience: at times of reform, fraternal regimes were expected to liberalise to the same extent as the CPSU, but not beyond – the penalties for such transgressions had been learned through the bitter experiences of the GDR in 1953, Poland and Hungary in 1956, and Czechoslovakia in 1968. Within the sphere of this policy, in the context of the late 1980s, the liberalisation of the Soviet political system after 1986 implicitly demanded a commensurate step by these regimes, and to many fraternal leaders, *perestroika* represented a challenge to their authority.[31] However, on the basis that the Soviet Union had not intervened militarily during the Polish Solidarity crisis of 1980–81, there is reason to believe that the Soviet Union had renounced the right to intervene militarily in its 'Outer Empire' long before 1988, as Matthew Ouimet has argued, showing that before Gorbachev, preceding CPSU general secretaries Konstantin Chernenko, Yurii Andropov and Leonid Brezhnev had already clearly conveyed this to fraternal party leaders.[32]

In this light, returning to Dawisha's definition of the Brezhnev Doctrine as constituting both military and political interference, we may conclude that the only vestige of the doctrine in 1987–88 was possible Soviet political interference. As will be argued in Chapter 4 and in the case study chapters on Hungary, Yugoslavia and Poland, this aspect of the Brezhnev Doctrine was still very much operational between 1987 and 1989, although not supported by the threat of Soviet military intervention. Most of the fraternal party leaderships had legitimised their regimes and enforced social compliance by the threat of Soviet invasion in the event of social unrest. Therefore, the Soviet renunciation of military intervention would consequently have been unwelcome to these leaderships. At the same time, economic dependence on the Soviet Union for heavily subsidised energy imports (the CMEA six and Yugoslavia) continued to act as cement binding these states together, albeit within a framework of voluntary dependence; by the late 1980s, the fraternal states were heavily reliant on Soviet subsidies as their economies foundered.

Case selection

To understand better what Gorbachev hoped to achieve at the Nineteenth CPSU Conference and how the choice of institution was perceived by leaders as crucial to bringing about the desired outcome, this book concentrates on fraternal parties that used their respective conferences to align their parties with Gorbachevian *perestroika*: the HSWP, the League of Communists of Yugoslavia (LCY) and the Polish United Workers' Party (PUWP). These cases are clearly quite disparate as these states were and still are very different in terms of culture, history and language; any other assessment would require a great stretch of the imagination. What the Soviet Union and Yugoslavia, as federal states, seemed to have in common in 1988 were problems of rising nationalism, outbreaks of violence and issues of 'stateness'[33] among their constituent republics. However, non-aligned Yugoslavia in 1988 had for a number of decades been considered practically 'Western' by other communist states and was granted benefits by the West for this. Hungarians, as the 'happiest barracks in the camp', enjoyed a higher standard of living than any of the other communist states. Poland was, arguably, the most advanced of these regimes with an established and well-supported opposition, in the form of the Solidarity movement. In 1988, what these regimes shared in common was that they were the most reform-oriented of all the states and therefore would be most likely to align politically with Gorbachev at their conferences. Therefore we would expect these cases to confirm that the most reformist regimes convened Gorbachevian conferences. As the case study chapters will show, there was collaboration between the leaderships over their respective conferences, although Poland surprisingly proves the exception in terms of both timing and outcome. This suggests that other factors were at work, which determined fraternal party leaderships' responses to Gorbachev's request.

Historical institutionalism

The theoretical framework underpinning this research is twofold. Firstly, within the democratisation literature, the research indicates that there was continued CPSU 'control'[34] over fraternal party policy-making later than is commonly held in the literature and that conferences were convened with the purpose of consolidating the party's power through modernisation and controlled regime liberalisation. Evidence is shown that conferences were convened across the fraternal parties as a show of 'communist solidarity' with the CPSU in their implementation of *perestroika*, to keep apace with Soviet reforms and to affirm to dissenters both in the party and beyond that the future of the one-party system was secure. Hence, in keeping with historical precedent, the conferences were convened in response to a Soviet call for action.

Secondly, applying institutional approaches to researching the phenomenon of the conferences in 1987–89 helps explain *why* Gorbachev and other leaders chose to convene a conference *when* they did so. According to the Party Rules of all the communist parties of Central and Eastern Europe, there were two (or arguably three) all-party meetings, which the Central Committee could convene to elicit the views of the party membership. The first was the congress, which, as stipulated in the Party Rules, was convened regularly, in practice usually every five years, where policy was formed and the election of the leadership took place. Between congresses, 'extraordinary' congresses or conferences could be convened. Extraordinary congresses shared the same powers as the congress, the only difference being the earlier scheduling of the event, before the end of the five-year period. Afterwards, however, an 'extraordinary' congress was simply described as a 'congress', and was incorporated into the same numbering sequence as preceding and succeeding regular congresses. Alternatively, there was provision in the Party Rules for the Central Committee to convene instead an all-party conference. Unlike the congress, the powers of the conference were not described in the Party Rules. Instead, there was a simple, open-ended provision stating that between congresses the Central Committee could convene a conference. In practice, most of the fraternal parties very rarely did so.

To understand better, therefore, the party conferences of 1988–89, three different institutional approaches have been applied in the case study chapters. Institutionalism has been criticised for focusing on institutions as constraints, which inevitably leads to the self-fulfilling prophecy of explaining continuity rather than change, and in concentrating on exogenous factors the approach fails to examine endogenous processes, which may prove crucial to understanding events. Practitioners have therefore identified the heuristic value of combining these structural approaches with analysis of discourse between actors to temper the rigidity of the research, and to more thoroughly examine the way in which actors themselves operate within these constraints, how they interpret institutional rules and bring about change. This approach has been termed 'discursive institutionalism'.[35] The research in this book combines historical and rational choice approaches with analysis of archival materials, stenographic reports, memoirs and interviews with key actors. While the dominant focus of this book is discourse-based evidence and therefore could be described entirely as 'discursive institutionalism', the book shows how those institutional theories that have been criticised for their exogenous and superficial approach, appear equally helpful in explaining events and usefully supplement and support this research.

Historical institutionalism argues that over time informal institutional rules develop, and stay in place to shape future outcomes; these 'informal constraints' are as 'sticky' as formal rules.[36] On this premise, each case study reconstructs the conference's 'informal constraints' by tracing common features in conference organisation and outcome across the twentieth century, which helps to clarify what conferences generally entailed and therefore what actors anticipated in advance of the conferences of 1987–89. Secondly a rational choice approach is applied, which examines how the conference represented to actors a different policy choice from the choice of a congress. This is based on the premise that people select institutions in the knowledge of which ones are most advantageous to them in securing their desired outcome; therefore their choice of institution may be interpreted as synonymous with a specific policy choice.[37] As will be illustrated in Chapters 1, 2, 5, 6 and 7 the 'policy choice' which the conference traditionally entailed was a purge of the opposition and a consolidation of the General Secretary's power. In the fraternal parties, convention of the conference had other connotations as well, as it often traditionally comprised a Soviet clampdown on errant fraternal parties and marked the beginnings of normalisation following a brief spell of liberalisation. The main body of the research, which supports these two arguments with empirical evidence, is drawn from analysis of discourse from archives, interviews, published memoirs and textual analysis of the conference stenographic reports.

Methods and data collection

Data was collected through interviews with key players at these conferences in Belgrade, Budapest, Moscow and Warsaw, and archival research in all of these cities, with the exception of the Serbian national archives in Belgrade, to which I was not granted access. Before the fieldwork stage, with the exception of the Polish case, a preliminary textual analysis of the published stenographic reports from each of the conferences was conducted. In-depth analysis of these reports was performed in the event that interviews were not forthcoming, or access to archives proved restricted and hence limited as a means of relevant data collection.

Textual analysis

Ostensibly, the purpose of these conferences was to solicit the wider opinion of party members, at an all-party meeting, to find solutions to the problems these states faced. Since these regimes had begun liberalising to a limited extent, it was anticipated that debate at these meetings would display a range of different preferences. The aim of the textual analysis was to reveal nuances in delegates' speeches at a time when officially 'monolithic unity' in the party required members to express general support for their leaderships' policies, while at the same time these regimes were in the process of liberalising, and party members had begun expressing their own preferences. But, the very few speakers at these meetings that advocated far-reaching changes often chose to allude to taboo subjects in a coded way, while their hardline, conservative superiors sprinkled their speeches with terms that are traditionally associated with liberal democracies. Interpretive coding of text enabled recording of a more fine-grained reading of these minutes, while the application of grounded theory provided a *tabula rasa* which generated a model common to all three cases.

I chose a grounded theory approach to analyse the published minutes of the three party conferences because the meetings had not been systematically and comparatively examined before, and secondary literature concerning them was sparse. A content analysis of the minutes – that is, employing quantitative methods to test hypotheses deductively – seemed too narrow a research design in the case of the research, and, as described later, particularly inappropriate to the data; for example, scouring the text for instances of speakers advocating the introduction of a multiparty system or not, and on that basis asserting that the conferences were (or were not) democratising forums, would have shifted the focus away from the real reason these conferences were held, and left many interesting and important features in the minutes unearthed. Similarly, although a powerful tool, discourse analysis of the minutes would have focused more on speakers' use of language than on speech content, on how their language was used to exert influence and how it codifies power relations. This would make a fascinating research project, and could yield some very interesting results, but there were concerns that such a study might be too interpretive, and difficult to support with evidence from interviews and archival material.

Grounded theory
The mechanics of the method can be briefly summarised as follows. Firstly, transcripts of text are read through, possible analytical categories are identified and any potential arising themes noted. As the categories emerge, all data from these groups are collated and compared, and preliminary ideas are noted down that suggest how categories might be linked together. The relations among categories are used to build theoretical models while the researcher can continue to verify and modify these as new interpretations of the constantlydata come to light. Results of the analysis are presented using exemplars – that is, direct quotations from the text that illustrate the theory.

The philosophy underpinning the method is that research should be grounded in the textual articulation of reality through analysis of field notes, interviews and other field data. The method is therefore primarily inductive, drawing from the data to form theory, and eschews imposing on the analysis any pre-structured categories at the beginning of the analysis.[38] Later, however, once the project has begun to take shape and patterns have begun to emerge, the analysis becomes more deductive, testing for other incidences of emergent features, and refining the model further to draw these out. It thus attempts to interpret the actions of those under examination within the context of the given situation while acknowledging the subjective, qualitative nature of the examination and hence, as far as possible, tries to control for the author's subjectivity through the methods employed. By generating substantive theory through comparative analysis and coding of data, the method builds a theory from the pool of categories created in relation to the data under scrutiny.

Conducting the analysis using QSR N6
Textual analysis of the conference minutes was performed using QSR N6. The software facilitates the storage, coding, retrieval and analysis of text, and was designed to promote theory-building by allowing the function of making links between designated coded categories (termed in the software as 'nodes') and the option of classifying codes within a structured hierarchy using the terminology associated with a tree.[39] N6's theory-building facility, which allows relations between categories to be examined, is what makes it more powerful than the majority of textual analysis software packages that simply permit code and text retrieval.[40] QSR N6 was selected over NVivo for the project, which to a large extent was a matter of personal preference. Although NVivo's flexibility and the wide range of word processing tools it offers are very appealing, my impression, on comparing the two, is that NVivo's strength lies in micro analysis, which is better for discourse analysis, and parsing. I was concerned I would get lost in the mass of data (900 pages) that needed analysing within the time frame, and could encounter difficulties drawing out the bigger picture. I preferred, therefore, to begin with a macro study, which is N6's strength, as it encourages a more structural approach with hierarchies and tree building. It does, however, have other features that can be used for fine-grained analysis, which, although not as visually attractive and interactive as NVivo, serve the purpose well.

Because of its theory-generating capacity, grounded theorists tend to use this software. The successive versions of QSR NUD*IST and NVivo that have come out on the market are evidence that the software has developed into a tool geared towards grounded theorists. For example, NVivo, the sister software to NUD*IST, has been named after the term Anselm

Strauss uses in his open coding system, 'in vivo' – a function in the software which allows the practitioner to generate a code directly from the text – and N6 also has a function 'in vivo' which allows the creation of a coding category taken directly from the text. While this marriage of theory and software has been well received by many, some worry that this may stifle the necessary creativity required for theory-building. Others question the explanatory force of theories generated by this method and doubt whether a theory 'generated' from the particular context can be generalised to other cases.

The full texts of the minutes of the conferences held in 1988 by the CPSU, HSWP and LCY were imported into N6 and coded electronically. The texts comprised four published monographs.[41] For reasons of compatibility of fonts and software, I translated the CPSU conference minutes into English before importing as text files into N6, although other software now supports different fonts. Although not an ideal solution, this certainly ensured very good familiarity with the text. Serbo-Croatian texts (in Roman script) were scanned from the hard copy into text files and imported directly. In the case of the LCY conference, where instead much fewer and longer reports were published on behalf of their republican parties, sources are referred to in the textual analysis in Chapter 6 by the name of the republican party.

The coding frame
The first stage of analysis comprised coding, which is the process of categorising and sorting data. These codes then serve as shorthand to label content and the relations between data, and any emergent patterns. The coding system adopted was Anselm Strauss's, which constituted firstly 'open coding' – a stage of scrutinising the text closely, from which provisional concepts or categories that seem to fit the data emerge.[42] In terms of the software terminology, this was the process of creating 'nodes' in the three QSR projects. Secondary to this was 'axial coding', whereby emergent categories in turn become the focus of the analysis, with the purpose of drawing any links between the category under examination and other categories. Axial coding was performed when subcategories (or 'child nodes' according to the QSR terminology) were generated by cutting and pasting a node and appending it to another, which resulted in altering the hierarchy between the coded categories.

Finally, the analysis becomes more deductive at the 'selective coding' stage, when the main core categories were picked out and on this basis a hierarchy was formalised, appending sub-categories to the designated core categories. Selective coding occurs to some extent simultaneously with open and axial coding, although much more systematically in the later stages of the coding. It is a process of creating codes relevant to the topic under research, for example, using the jargon, concepts and axioms of the categories under study and making them relevant to the existing literature of that subject, which in this case was the democratisation literature. My core category in each project was 'democratisation' or 'liberalisation' versus evidence to show that conferences were trying to approve policies that would maintain the *status quo*. The three sets of conference minutes were coded independently of one another, but useful categories were 'borrowed' where evidence of similar patterns occurred. Common core categories emerged – for example, in the evidence of discussion of perceived irregularities surrounding delegate-selection to the conference (who was selected and why), who was selected to speak, policies approved and whether they were legally binding, and references to how the conference was prepared.

Within each speech all text was coded thematically; hence text expressing a particular viewpoint on an issue is tagged and collected together with all such other incidences of the view or topic at a specific 'node' – a label identified by a topic-related 'coding stripe'. N6 software stores all coded text from each speech at the relevant 'node'; hence once text in each speech has been coded, every incidence of a feature in the conference minutes is attached to a specific 'node' and retrievable in its entirety. At the most superficial level, this provides an exhaustive report of all viewpoints on issues expressed at the conference, revealing trends of opinion and helping identify how well 'represented' the different 'factions' were at the conference. This provides a valuable quantitative report of viewpoints expressed. The software facilitates comparison of these categories through Boolean searches of nodes and documents. Moreover, the categorisation of opinions and topics discussed at the conference helped in distinguishing genuine debate or spontaneous discussion from material which appeared artificially staged.

Codes are designed that are appropriate to the text under analysis; this procedure has been described by textual analysts as eliciting 'inferred' categories from the text itself, as opposed to devising 'assumed' categories in advance of analysing the text, and then imposing a framework *a priori* on the data.[43] The rationale behind this approach is that if categories are devised with reference to the text, then this will enable theory-building from the data itself, so the theory must necessarily be salient to the text; this was preferred over 'testing' a hypothesis on the basis of the presence or absence of a variable. For example, absence or presence of words commonly associated with the vocabulary of a liberal democracy did not necessarily correlate with a speaker's expression of liberal democratic ideals in the case of these conference minutes, as the same terms carried different connotations in different contexts. Devising a coding frame from the text itself empowers the coding frame to meet the goodness of fit criterion for the model; 'saturation' of that model, however, by including all variables in a perfect description of the text, amounting to its replication, is avoided by coding at a level that transcends the unit of individual words (instead sentences or paragraphs were coded). However, where individual words did bear significance (such as individuals' names referred to in speeches), these were coded separately also. Choice of categories came in the first instance from the text of the conference minutes; speeches largely included a certain number of points which were easily categorised according to theme.

As themes recurred or different views were expressed, different codes were devised and a coding frame was developed in the form of a tree structure; certain coding patterns emerged around different speakers and the views they expressed. Once these patterns began emerging, the analysis shifted to a deductive process, focusing on how the rest of the text related to these common features. Some text was coded more than once, as relevant to more than one code.[44] This sometimes later resulted in the merging of these codes if one code was clearly a subset of another. Some text coded was of peripheral value to the research and was not reported. This text remained coded, but just did not appear of significant value to the overall pattern which emerged and was not discussed in the textual analysis reports. For example, in the Moscow project, each time another speaker or another person was cited (in whatever capacity – whether to agree or disagree with another speaker at the conference, or to cite poets, such as Alexander Pushkin or Vladimir Lenin for the sake of dramatic effect), these persons were listed as a new 'child node' under the top level tree node 'Citation', resulting in sixty-three child nodes. Most of these appeared of little consequence, with one or two references to a person made usually in agreement with another speaker to endorse a view they had expressed. References to Gorbachev and Lenin were numerous and all positive, so again were not reported, as they did not appear particularly significant. However, interestingly, in the cases of a couple of individuals, citation was heavy and negative. So, for example, in the case of the node 'Citation', only references to the Director of the Institute of Economics, Union of Soviet Socialist Republics (USSR) Academy of Sciences, Leonid Abalkin, came to be of importance for the textual analysis report. References to Boris Yeltsin were also significant – so much so, in fact, that a new 'top-level node' (of which there are only fifty-three in the entire Moscow project, whereas there are over a thousand lower-level nodes) was created for 'Yeltsin', as speakers expressed a wider range of views about Yeltsin and devoted more time to this.

It was anticipated that in the context of the material, some interpretation would be required, as although these parties were in the process of liberalising and individuals in these regimes had developed different preferences by this time, the leadership still expected party unity. Dissenters under these conditions were likely to remain guarded in what they said and how they expressed opinions that deviated from the party line.

Interpretive coding and maintaining validity and reliability
This phenomenon of self-restraint is generally referred to as 'self-censorship' and denotes an individual's perception of operating limits and the practice of using restricted speech to voice opinions, for fear of uttering something potentially impolitic which might be penalised. Soviet-era citizens dealt with this by using ambiguous language or even non-reference, or in other cases completely redefined words to convey the desired meaning so that they could communicate on taboo subjects and promote forbidden ideals without being open to the accusation of breaking the rules.[45] In instances where speakers' discourse may be constrained, therefore, interpretive coding is helpful as a means of picking up nuance.

At the other end of the spectrum, speech at the conference that could have been interpreted as advocating full-scale regime change had to be treated with some degree of scepticism. As noted earlier, textual analysts have pointed out the methodological flaws of over-interpreting the significance of presence or absence of words. Commonly, words or phrases lose their force and meaning through overuse; this phenomenon has been termed 'semantic satiation': when a phrase or word is used by a speaker to convey the effect of endorsing a value, but is perhaps received by the speaker's audience as insincere. Symbols of democracy occur less frequently where democratic procedures are accepted than where they are in dispute.[46] In the context of the conference minutes, for example, use of the term *'perestroika'* in a positive context was not necessarily an indication of the speaker's full affirmation of Gorbachev's policy of *perestroika*. János Kádár, the Hungarian First Party Secretary in 1988, freely used the word in his speech without in any sense expressing a desire for change in keeping with Gorbachev's policy, which instead promoted personnel change via the removal of the aged party elite, including Kádár's own removal. So, the presence of such apparently 'liberalising' terms may not necessarily be evidence of an alignment of policy with Gorbachev. This is borne out by a comparison of the presence of such words in delegates' speeches. Kádár was one of the speakers least in favour of Gorbachevian alignment at the Hungarian conference, and yet he mentioned in his speech the word *perestroika* three times, democracy four times and *glasnost* four times; he quoted a church leader and Margaret Thatcher in positive terms.[47] In contrast with this, some of the most reformist speakers did not use any of these words, perhaps because they had become perceived as meaningless through overuse, as is well illustrated by the speech of one of the most reformist speakers at the Hungarian conference, who did not express herself using words which, if applying a content analysis dictionary, would indicate a reformist position. However, interpretation can lead us to infer that she was the only delegate speaker who promoted the introduction of a multiparty system.[48] Thus only by examining what is said on the level of sentences and paragraphs and in context can the language be 'unpacked' and adequately coded. For example, reference to the need for personnel changes would be an indication of a speaker's desire for *'perestroika'* in the sense that Gorbachev meant it.

Similarly, some delegates made very conflicting statements over policy which required interpretation during the coding process. For example, in the case where there was incidence of, say, a vacuous reference in favour of more 'democratisation' in conjunction with a demand that the Communist Party increase its 'vanguard status in society', this was interpreted as paying lip service to the rhetoric of 'democratisation' though not advocating the introduction of a multiparty system, as instead the strengthening of the CPSU's role in society was proposed. So, 'democratisation' in this context may be better interpreted as 'greater mobilisation of the people in favour of the CPSU'. This is how such conflicting statements were interpreted during the coding procedure, for example, of the speech made by Sapamurat Niyazov, the First Secretary of the Turkmen Communist Party, who is well known for the very repressive authoritarian regime which he maintained as President of Turkmenistan until 2006. Thus coding relied to a large extent on interpretation of delegates' speeches in the context of what they said. Clearly, the need to maintain consistency when undertaking interpretive coding in this way is essential to ensuring the reliability of the coding frame and the ensuing results.

Reliability testing comprised checking the consistency of my own coding ('intra'-coder reliability), which was performed through the simple mechanism of checking previous codes created during the next session and on subsequent occasions. There may have been a tendency to err on the side of a rather conservative coding of the text, as my concern was to ensure that my own interpretation of the text shaped the coding frame as little as possible. Nonetheless, the results enabled a subsequently richer discussion with interviewees present at these conferences, and emerging patterns that would not otherwise have been brought to light were confirmed at interview.

The results of the textual analysis
This textual analysis was conducted before the interview and archival stages of the research into the conferences, and the results which were drawn indicated a common effort by leaderships in these states to broadcast a common message, which they achieved by selecting individuals known to favour the centrist-reformist policy of *perestroika*. These events were carefully staged to show all-party approval of a centrist line of

reform, which was not necessarily embraced by the majority of these parties. As one delegate at the Soviet conference quipped:

> Comrade communists, delegates of the party conference, I will not keep you for long. I am already the fourth metallurgist and worker that has been allowed to speak today. This fact could serve to show really, either the extent to which the situation in metallurgy has become very problematic, and throws up a lot of issues, or the fact that we are speaking out more heatedly in favour of *perestroika*.[49]

As detailed in the case study chapters, data from archival documents and interviews confirmed the results of the textual analysis, which in turn validates the method applied.

With respect to the question of reproducibility – that is, the validity of the theory generated and whether it is generalisable to other cases – the answer is yes and no. Clearly the theory does not apply generally, for example, to any conference or meeting. However, the research shows that the theory generated works for the particular institution of the Communist Party Conference during the Gorbachev era. Moreover, it is likely to generalise to the conference as an institution throughout the twentieth century in that the meeting was unrepresentative, and conference outcomes suggest that it was commonly convened, in certain states, to align fraternal party policy with Soviet policy. Generically, as an institution the conference (across the fraternal socialist states of Central and Eastern Europe) was described in similar, open-ended terms, which essentially granted the leadership of these parties the right to convene the conference between five-yearly congresses, to discuss pressing issues, as Chapter 1 will discuss. The lack of formal rules defining the conference leaves open to question how this meeting differed in terms of its organisation and representation from the other all-party meeting, the congress, which is defined in more concrete terms and had a decentralised process of delegate selection through regional organisations. Textual analysis revealed clear patterns that views expressed appeared unrepresentative of the party membership's different preferences at this time. Delegates who spoke at these meetings conveyed a clear message supporting the centrist-reformist leaderships and expressed the need to consolidate the party's power to maintain the *status quo* of the party's leading role in the one-party state. Moreover, Hungarian and

Yugoslav conferences indicated a clear policy alignment with Gorbachev's *perestroika*.

An example of how this model extends to other cases from the Gorbachev era is that of the PUWP conference, held a year after the three meetings in Hungary, the Soviet Union and Yugoslavia in May 1989. Since the Polish conference was convened a whole year later, we might expect that this conference would have proved an exception to the rule. Archival and interview research into the case of Poland was conducted after the main body of research had been completed. In the case of the Polish fraternal party, delegates' speeches were not published in their entirety; only a pamphlet containing a few speeches was issued. The full report of the conference was available in the Archive of Modern Records (AAN) in Warsaw and comprised more than 500 pages of documentation. Computer-assisted textual analysis performed in the same way as the other cases was therefore not feasible in this instance, and instead required reading the stenographic reports in the archives and taking notes. I was more reliant, therefore, on interview and other archival data. On reading the text there appeared a similar homogeneity with the other conference records, which again suggested speakers were chosen to convey a specific message. Similarly, the message appeared particularly anachronistic in the context of Poland in May 1989, by which time semi-free elections to the Parliament had already been organised for the next month, and the party had already begun negotiating with the opposition the terms of power sharing. Although unable to examine the stenographic report with the same rigour as the Hungarian, Soviet and Yugoslav conferences, and evaluate views expressed with the same accuracy, a similar picture emerged. The vast majority of speakers at the conference rallied around First Secretary Wojciech Jaruzelski, advocating that the party retain its leading role. Although round-table negotiators had already agreed and arranged semi-free elections to the Parliament at which members of Solidarity would stand as candidates in opposition to the party, speakers at this conference still queried the party's recognition of Solidarity in this way, advocating that the party retain its leading role and consolidate its power.[50]

As one interviewee confirmed, delegate selection for the Polish conference was controlled by the leadership, whereas delegate selection to the other all-party meeting, the five-yearly congress, was a more decentralised process. The leadership chose, therefore, to convene the party conference, as they had more control over its outcome.[51] The evidence strongly suggested that the theory generated from the textual analysis of the other three cases would apply equally to the Polish case, as Chapter 7 will demonstrate.

With respect to evaluating the method of textual analysis, the validity of its application in this instance and whether the theory it generates has a predictive value, the research confirmed to me that it does have this capacity. This suggests that in instances where fieldwork or archival research is not feasible, or access is limited, the analysis of relevant published text is a valid and worthwhile exercise, and moreover may present patterns that interviewees themselves might not be forthcoming about, or even aware of.

Interviews and archival research

Semi-structured questionnaires were designed for the interviews, and certain key questions were included in all interviews, while supplementary questions were geared towards individuals and their particular roles at the time of the conferences. Follow-up questions and discussions during the interviews often ensued. I conducted the majority of interviews with conference delegates who were in the leadership or who attended as rank-and-file party members. Supplementary interviews were also conducted with social scientists or party members from these states who did not attend the conference but who were informed of these meetings. Some thirty interviews were conducted in total and these were with a mixture of individuals: some still serving in government or in opposition, others that had retired to become academics. In each case interviewees were very generous with their time, and very patient with my questions.

To a certain extent responses to the core questions differed, although these differences depended on the viewpoints of respondents, which varied significantly. There was a particular consistency among former high-ranking CPSU delegates to portray a rose-tinted view of the conference, and they strenuously denied any collaboration between party leaderships over the conferences. This may be best explained by two factors: either they were not aware, or did not want to challenge the widely held assumption that Gorbachev renounced the Brezhnev Doctrine of interference in other states' domestic affairs before these conferences were held. Challenging this assumption would be perceived as impolitic, therefore, especially as this collaboration was part of a joint initiative to preserve the one-party state. Other respondents from different states preferred not to answer such questions, which they considered still sensitive, and advised consulting instead the archives for the relevant evidence. This suggests that some participants shared concerns over imparting such information. In any event, archival sources indicated that Gorbachev strongly encouraged these fraternal party leaderships to convene their conferences with the aim of strengthening the one-party model across the fraternal states and that there was collaboration between the leaderships in some states in engineering a desirable Gorbachevian outcome at the conference.

In Moscow I was granted access to the Gorbachev Foundation archives, and to the Russian State Archives of Modern History (RGANI). There were a number of restrictions on the material which was made available to me in RGANI, and I was permitted to see very few relevant Politburo documents. At the Gorbachev Foundation, in contrast, access to the documents listed in the catalogue was very good, although there was a proviso that no photocopies could be made of the materials, and computers were not allowed in the reading room. Therefore, the only way to copy relevant sections of these materials for use in the research was to make handwritten notes, verbatim, which was rather time-consuming.

In Budapest, access to documents in the Hungarian National Archives (MOL) was very good, and I was granted access to stenographic reports of the Politburo, Central Committee and other meetings, of which I was allowed to order photocopies. In the Archive of Modern Records (AAN) in Warsaw, access was fairly good, although I was not granted admittance to all materials I wished to see, in particular stenographic reports from Politburo meetings from the late 1980s. In the case of all archival research, there was a good deal of serendipity as to whether the materials would contain the relevant discussions, and these were not always located where expected. In some instances, relevant materials appeared in other fonds (archival sources).

Some interpretation was required with the archival transcripts in some instances, as speakers did not always elaborate fully on topics with each other, for there was a good deal that would have been mutually understood and discussions between a couple of individuals held *in camera* were clearly not intended for third parties. Some of these transcripts indicate very frank exchange, which does not always portray interlocutors in a good light. This suggests that participants at these meetings did not anticipate the fall of the regime, nor that these documents would therefore be declassified so soon.

Conclusion

This research explains change during this period not as a process of liberalisation leading to 'reluctant democratisation', but rather how parties sought to reclaim their legitimacy and reassert their leading role over both state and society, through a process of 'reluctant liberalisation'. Instead of being an enlightened step on the part of Gorbachev, this initiative was rather a desperate attempt to consolidate the party's power. In all of the fraternal regimes, to varying degrees, the party's authority over the state and society had significantly weakened over time and party decisions increasingly remained unimplemented. This strongly suggests that by the late 1980s, the party across the fraternity was no longer in control of state resources, both politically and, we must therefore conclude, materially. This research therefore agrees with those accounts that argue the primary cause for the liberalisation process in CEE was changes in the global economy, placing these with Latin America and Southern Europe in the third wave of 'democratisation' or regime change.

The fraternal party leaderships were all aware of common problems that their regimes shared, and the conference was the means by which a decisive party line could be broadcast as having been reached 'unanimously' at an all-party meeting. The extent of the threat to socialist one-party regimes was such that non-aligned China and Yugoslavia overcame their differences with Warsaw Pact member states to communicate and work together in finding solutions. In 1985, China had already begun a significant and effective modernisation process, and by 1987 the Soviet Union and Central and Eastern Europe were lagging behind, unable to galvanise similarly the needed support for the party in society, nor able to exert power over society to implement reforms, which would introduce efficiency into the economy.

This book explores the phenomenon of the conferences in CEE, and interprets conference outcomes as indicative of the lengths to which these parties, or at least the General/First Secretary and his supporters, were willing to go in changing their regimes to make them viable. At each conference, those with a voice at the meeting made it clear that the introduction of a multiparty system was unthinkable, and that the leading role of the party must be retained. As Chapter 1 will discuss, the choice of institution – a conference – rather than a congress was what facilitated such a unanimous and decisive stance on the limits of the reform process.

Notes

1   S. Saari, 'European democracy promotion in Russia before and after the "colour" revolutions', *Democratization* 16:4 (2009), pp. 632–55.

2   K. Wilson, 'Party-system development under Putin,' *Post-Soviet Affairs* 22:4 (2006), pp. 314–48.

3   V. Gel'man, 'Political opposition in Russia: a dying species?', *Post-Soviet Affairs* 21:3 (2005), pp. 226–46.

4   R. Sakwa, *Russian Politics and Society* (London: Routledge, 4th edn, 2008), pp. 275–8.

5   S. Oates, 'The neo-Soviet Model of the Media', *Europe-Asia Studies* 59:8 (2007), pp. 1279–97.

6   R. Rose, 'How floating parties frustrate democratic accountability: a supply-side view of Russia's elections' in A. Brown (ed.) *Contemporary Russian Politics: a reader* (Oxford: Oxford University Press, 2001), pp. 215–23.

7   S. Whitefield, 'Mind the representation gap: explaining differences in public views of representation in postcommunist democracies', *Comparative Political Studies* 39:6 (2006), pp. 733–58.

8   CPSU, *XIX Vsesoiuznaia konferentsiia kommunisticheskoi partii sovetskogo soiuza, 28 iiunia-1 iiulia 1988 goda: stenograficheskii otchet*, vol. 1 (Moskva: Izdatel'stvo politicheskoi literatury, 1988), Gorbachev's speech, p. 19.

9   J. Linz and A. Stepan, *Problems of democratic transition and consolidation: Southern Europe, South America and Post-Communist Europe* (Baltimore MD: The John Hopkins University Press, 1996), p. 3.

10   L. Whitehead, *The International Dimensions of Democratization: Europe and the Americas* (Oxford: Oxford University Press, 1996), p. 362.

11   S. Whitefield, *Soviet Industrial Ministries as Political Institutions, 1965–1990* (D.Phil. thesis, University of Oxford, 1991), p. 190.

12 R. Sakwa, *Gorbachev and his Reforms, 1985–1990* (New York NY: Philip Allan, 1990), p. 129; B. Hazan, *Gorbachev and his Enemies: the Struggle for Perestroika* (Boulder CO: Westview, 1990), p. 185.

13 Sakwa, *Gorbachev and his Reforms*, p. 132.

14 G. Breslauer, *Gorbachev and Yeltsin as leaders* (Cambridge: Cambridge University Press, 2002), pp. 79–107; B. Hazan, *Gorbachev's Gamble: the 19th All-Union Party Conference* (Boulder CO: Westview, 1990), pp. 1–64; Hazan, *Gorbachev and his Enemies*, pp. 166–290.

15 L. Ladany, *The Communist Party of China and Marxism, 1921–1985: a self portrait* (London: C. Hurst & Co., 1988), pp. 498–502.

16 *Ibid.*, p. 503.

17 P. Dybicz and G. Sołtysiak, *Rozmowy dyplomatyczne polityków państwstron Układu Warszawskiego* (Warszawa: Wyd. MAG, 2009), p. 15.

18 *History of the Chinese Communist Party: a chronology of events, 1919–1990* (Beijing: Foreign Language Press, 1991), p. 500.

19 *History of the Chinese Communist Party*, p. 477.

20 *Rudé Pravo*, 12 June 1987, p. 1; *Neues Deutschland*, 6–7 June 1987, p. 6.

21 *Życie Warszawy*, 5 June 1987, p. 2.

22 *Népszabadság*, 15 June 1987, p. 1.

23 Magyar Országos Levéltár, KB 288 f.4 225 23 June 1987, p. 72.

24 *Ibid.*, pp. 73–4.

25 *Ibid.*, pp. 80–1.

26 K. Dawisha, *Eastern Europe, Gorbachev and Reform: the Great Challenge* (Cambridge: Cambridge University Press, 2nd edn, 1990), p. 219.

27 Whitehead, *The International Dimensions of Democratization*, pp. 8–15.

28 A. Pravda, *The End of Outer Empire: Soviet-East European Relations in Transition 1985–90* (London: RIIA, 1992), pp. 10–11.

29 Whitehead, *The International Dimensions of Democratization*, pp. 363–66; see also A. Brown, 'Transnational Influences in the Transition from Communism', *Post Soviet Affairs* 16:2 (2000), p. 185; Dawisha, *Eastern Europe*, pp. 127–53; J. Elster and C. Offe, *Institutional Design in Post-Communist Societies: Rebuilding the Ship at Sea* (Cambridge: Cambridge University Press, 1998), pp. 2–3; Pravda, *The End of Outer Empire*, p. 15; Linz and Stepan, *Problems of Democratic Transition and Consolidation*, pp. 236–54.

30 V. Sobell, *The CMEA in Crisis: Toward a New European Order?* (New York NY: Praeger, 1990), pp. 25–6.

31 Pravda, *The End of Outer Empire*, p. 10; see also, Dawisha, *Eastern Europe*, pp. 20–1.

32 M. Ouimet, *The Rise and Fall of the Brezhnev Doctrine in Soviet Foreign Policy* (Chapel Hill NC: University of North Carolina, 2003), p. 255. Ouimet argues that the Soviet invasion of Afghanistan depleted Soviet resources, reducing their capacity for military intervention elsewhere.

33 Linz and Stepan, *Problems of Democratic Transition and Consolidation*, p. 366.

34 Whitehead, *The International Dimensions of Democratization*, pp. 8–15.

35   V. Schmidt, 'Taking ideas and discourse seriously: explaining change through discursive institutionalism as the fourth new institutionalism', *European Political Science Review* 2:1 (2010), pp. 1–25.

36   D. North, *Institutions, Institutional Change and Economic Performance* (Cambridge: Cambridge University Press, 1990), pp. 44–5.

37   G. Tsebelis, *Nested Games: Rational Choice in Comparative Politics* (Berkeley CA: University of California Press, 1990), p. 98.

38   B. Glaser and A. Strauss, *The Discovery of Grounded Theory: Strategies for Qualitative Research* (Chicago IL: Aldine Pub., 1967); B. Glaser, *Theoretical Sensitivity: Advances in the Methodology of Grounded Theory* (Mill Valley CA: Sociology Press, 1978).

39   E. Frazer, 'Probably the Most Public Occasion the World Has Ever Known: "Public" and "Private" in Press Coverage of the Death and Funeral of Diana, Princess of Wales', *Journal of Political Ideologies* 5:2 (2000), pp. 201–23.

40   E. Weitzman and M. Miles, *Computer Programs for Qualitative Data Analysis: a Software Sourcebook* (London: Sage, 1995), pp. 238–56.

41   CPSU, *XIX Vsesoiuznaia konferentsiia KPSS*; Hungarian Socialist Workers' Party (HSWP), *A MSZMP országos ertekezletének jegyzőkönyve 1988. május 20–22* (Budapest: Kossuth Kiadó, 1988); League of Communists of Yugoslavia (LCY), *Konferencija SKJ, Beograd, 29–31 maj 1988: Jačanje vodeće idejno-političke uloge, jedinstva i odgovornosti Saveza komunista u borbi za izlazak iz društveno-ekonomske krize* (Beograd: Izdavački Centar Komunist, 1988).

42   A. Strauss and J. Corbin, *Basics of Qualitative Research: Grounded Theory Procedures and Techniques* (London: SAGE, 1990), p. 31.

43   R. P. Weber, *Basic Content Analysis* (London: Sage, 2nd edn, 1990), p. 37.

44   This did not affect the results of the analysis, as the quantity of text units coded was not used as a measure as in a content analysis.

45   Á. Horváth and Á. Szakolczai, *The Dissolution of Communist Power: the Case of Hungary* (London: Routledge, 1992), pp. 217–19.

46   K. Krippendorf, *Content Analysis: an Introduction to its Methodology* (Beverly Hills CA: Sage, 1980), p. 41.

47   HSWP, *A MSZMP országos ertekezletének jegyzőkönyve*, pp. 231–9.

48   *Ibid.*, pp. 85–9.

49   CPSU, *XIX Vsesoiuznaia konferentsiia KPSS*, vol. 1, p. 337.

50   See, Chapter 7, pp. 245–7.

51   Interview with former Polish Prime Minister, Leszek Miller, Warsaw, 30 September 2010.

1

The conference as an institution

Introduction

This chapter explains the different institutional approaches used in the case study chapters, which help us to understand the nature of the national party conference generically, to contextualise the conferences held in 1988–89. The main body of the work comprises research drawn from archives, interviews, published sources and textual analysis of the conference stenographic reports, which loosely falls into the category of 'discursive' institutionalism.[1]

The aim of this chapter is to explain the purpose of the supplementary historical and rational choice institutional analysis, which provides background information in the case study chapters. To get a clearer picture of how and why leaderships in these regimes convened conferences requires some understanding of what they might have anticipated these meetings would bring, although clearly the Party Rules give little away in this respect. Some commentaries on the Nineteenth All-Union CPSU Conference have therefore been prefaced by brief historical surveys of the conference,[2] as commentators logically look to previous meetings to find a pattern that might act as a precedent.

The current chapter therefore compares the rules guiding conference convention across the fraternal parties of CEE, identifies an absence of formal rules and outlines the empirical method that will be used in the case studies to reconstruct a blueprint for the anticipated 'informal' rules that governed this institution. This historical institutional approach identifies the 'informal' constraints that had been crystallised as conference procedure over the preceding decades and helps to clarify what the conference represented to these leaderships in 1988. It helps explain why leaderships unusually selected a conference, over, say, an extraordinary congress. As subsequent chapters will demonstrate, this decision to convene a conference constituted a specific policy choice. To contextualise this approach, the next sections outline some generic definitions of the concept of 'institutions', which are helpful for identifying what kind of dynamic we might expect to operate under institutional conditions where very few regulations constrain actors.

Defining institutions

Conceptualising institutions as enforced by a 'third party'

Definitions of the term 'institution' are vast in number and semantically diverse within the social sciences alone. A helpful way to conceptualise institutions, and to distinguish them more generally from simple social conventions, is with a narrow focus on the normative function that institutions serve in terms of structuring how individuals should act in a context where legal or other mechanisms operate to ensure compliance with these norms.[3] This presupposes that enforcement of these rules or norms will be made by a third party who 'will predictably and reliably come to the support of actors whose institutionalised and therefore legitimate normative expectations have been disappointed'.[4] Needless to say, we could question the 100 per cent 'predictability' and 'reliability' of impartial third-party enforcement in any regime. So to a certain extent this proviso is perhaps best understood as an 'ideal type' defined according to how it was designed in theory rather than evaluated *post facto* on the basis of practice. In its perfect form this condition of obligation is helpful for regimes governed by the rule of law, and offers a good working definition for the comparative study of institutions in established democracies and the new democracies of CEE. However, in the context of one-party state-era institutions, this may be perceived as more problematic.

Institutions governed by 'reciprocal accountability'

In one-party regimes there is little, if any, separation of powers as the state has been moulded to buttress the party's power, which means that the state's ability to intervene in party politics is inevitably curtailed, if not precluded. In theory these third parties existed, but in practice they did not operate as such. State bodies with the constitutional power to act as a third-party 'enforcer' against the CPSU were the Supreme Soviet and Council of Ministers. However, these institutions have been described as rather ineffectual in terms of their autonomy from the party, in that both were heavily populated with members of the Politburo and CC, ensuring homogeneity in decision-making between the highest party and state organs.[5] So, as we might expect, after the CPSU Conference of July 1988, the legislative changes proposed in the conference resolution were simply endorsed by a special session of the Supreme Soviet in November 1988.[6]

Although the party retained a firm grip, therefore, over policy-making, it remained reliant on state organs to execute these decisions, and there was in practice some independence of state power, albeit ill-defined. The system of 'reciprocal accountability' that had evolved effectively intertwined state and party structures to interlink them, so that broadly speaking, policies were formally approved at party level, but implementation was effected by the state. This afforded the bureaucracy significant power as to how, and to what extent, policy was implemented. In terms of party policy-making, though, the bureaucracy's influence was somewhat limited and indirectly applied, as officials could only make proposals within their own realm.[7] However, influence was brought to bear more directly (by individuals) as party officials needed to retain good relations with the bureaucracy that supported them politically and materially. Ultimately, ministries' power to pass their own legislation and implement it endowed them with considerable influence.[8] As early as 1941, the administrative structures of the Soviet state had grown powerful enough that even Stalin had to struggle to gain the advantage over state ministries and sometimes without success.[9]

Although the Soviet state bureaucracy's power rivalled and sometimes surpassed that of the party's, the Soviet state did not act as a counterweight to the Communist Party's power in the same way as the rule of law to government structures in liberal democracies. Influence or pressure brought to bear by state officials on an institution such as the party conference could only have been via those party members who were also state officials, or party members whose interests coincided with those of state officialdom, or who sought to defend bureaucratic interests for whatever reason. Since the vast majority of those that worked full-time for a state ministry were also party members, and the leading officials of governmental agencies were not only members of the party but also of the leading party organs, implicit state influence over party policy would have been considerable, and vice versa. Therefore, while the concept of 'third-party enforcement' of an alternative line of action in the context of CPSU institutional outcomes certainly existed, these would have been applied from within by individuals not always declaring their interests to be those of the 'state' and would have been applied on an ad-hoc basis. So, third-party intervention was not performed 'reliably' or 'predictably'.

By the time Gorbachev became CPSU General Secretary, the state ministries still enjoyed considerable power at the party's expense. One of the main impetuses for Gorbachev's *perestroika* was to break the power of the bureaucracy,[10] as well as oust those party members resistant to reform. Since state interests were entrenched to maintain the *status quo*, efforts were deployed by such individuals to slow down or stop reforms that jeopardised the future of their paymasters, the ministries, or more broadly, the state bureaucracy. Significantly, as is detailed more in Chapter 3, Gorbachev sought to recruit as many delegates as possible to the conference who would be supportive of *perestroika* and denounce the bureaucracy's resistance to reform. Thus in selecting delegates who were supportive of his policies, Gorbachev sought to minimise the possible constraints that could have been brought to bear on him at the conference, such as delegates speaking out against his reforms. Similarly, the HSWP, LCY and PUWP leaderships carefully chose delegates for their respective conferences, as detailed in Chapters 5, 6 and 7, to improve the odds of a favourable outcome.

So, although theoretically there was provision for third-party intervention on behalf of a disappointed contingent, no such intervention occurred *post facto* in the case of the CPSU

Conference, nor is there any evidence of this in the case of the other fraternal parties' conferences. There is another more concrete reason for this other than the argument that the party always 'got its own way', which as has been discussed was not always guaranteed, because of rival state powers. In the context of the Communist Party conferences, what would ultimately have precluded 'enforcement', by a third party, of proper procedure and outcome was that the Party Rules defining the conference do not specify procedure, as will be discussed in this chapter. Since there were few, if any, expectations of a procedure to be followed in terms of formal regulations, how could anyone object *post facto* and claim that they had been disappointed? This would suggest that any disagreement over conference procedure would have to be raised and resolved before the meeting took place, in the form of debate over the rules, or debate over the choice of institution; for example, was there another institution that would be more likely to favour the outcome of the prospective 'disappointed' contingent?

As the case study chapters will show, there was indeed such debate over the choice of institution between 1987 and 1989, as those pushing for more significant reforms advocated the convention of an extraordinary congress instead of a conference. This suggests that although there were few if any apparent 'formal constraints', certain individuals already perceived that their preferences were more likely to be disappointed at a conference. From this we may infer that conferences traditionally did not favour this contingent's preferences and that in spite of the lack of formal constraints, party members anticipated *a priori* that they would be disappointed. We can logically infer from this that apart from 'formal constraints', actors must have been aware of some other factor at work at conferences, which they predicted would not favour their preferred outcome. Since these are not 'formal' constraints, and yet they were anticipated, this suggests that actors perceived that certain 'informal' constraints would be operative. We may identify these as comprising procedures which had been internalised through past practice.

Historical institutionalism

The durability of 'informal' constraints

Counter-intuitively, perhaps, scholars from different branches of the social sciences agree that those institutional constraints, which prove the most 'sticky' (that is, resistant to change) are those which have developed through practice over time rather than those enshrined in written rules. Formal regulations may be amended overnight, on paper, but informal practices and unwritten procedures tend to persist stubbornly, regardless of changes made to the formal rules.[11]

The collective memory of institutional outcome acquires a force of its own, over time, beyond the power of individual agents, thus shaping future outcomes; once this common perception of how the rules govern the game through past experience has been established, outcome becomes path-dependent on this understanding. The key to the durability of institutions thus lies in this shared memory of previous rounds of the game regardless of how these may correspond to the formalised written rules guiding them.[12]

This habitual practice from past experience – that is, the routinisation of the game – acquires its own influence over players' expectations of future outcome and thus shapes outcome; hence the formal written rules may come to signify a good deal more than is precisely conceptualised in words. This dichotomy has been expressed as 'rules versus routines'.[13] So, under conditions where formal rules do not adequately describe the activities and powers of an institution (as is the case with the conference), we need to look at the invisible guiding-hand processes. As mentioned earlier, given the paucity of formal rules that defined and shaped these conferences, we must conclude that informal constraints were at work, and seek to identify them.

Douglass North proposes a simple solution for this: where formal constraints have remained static over time, informal constraints – including any changes to these – can be deduced from the outcome.[14] As the case studies in this book will show, the empirical evidence supports North's claim that informal constraints are at least as sticky as 'formal constraints' governing actors' behaviour within institutions. From this, North argues that informal procedures can be even more powerful than written rules, since what is repeatedly done in practice tends to act as a precedent for future procedure.[15] This is well illustrated, for example, by the interpretation of law in UK courts by reference to practice in past cases. Institutions are shaped by actors and these informal constraints, once crystallised, then come to guide future actors.[16]

Returning to the issue of the debate between different factions within the party over the convention of a conference or an extraordinary congress, the fact that this took place indicates a common awareness across the different parties that a conference favoured a certain kind of outcome. This may be distilled further to a common perception that outcome is dependent on the choice of institution. Where different institutions clearly favour particular outcomes, we may infer that the choice of institution is, broadly speaking, synonymous with a particular policy choice, as the next section discusses.

Institutions as a policy choice

According to a rational choice institutional approach, where actors have knowledge of formal and informal institutional constraints, these individuals will evaluate *a priori* the likely success of their desired outcome within the constraints of different institutions, so that ultimately they will select or lobby for institutions they consider more likely to yield their preferred outcome.[17] As George Tsebelis has suggested, ultimately actors come to choose a certain institution on the grounds that it will produce a specific type of outcome. Once institutional constraints are known to actors, the choice of institution in itself becomes a specific policy preference.[18] Hence an actor's choice of institution becomes synonymous with a specific policy choice, and the decision-making process over this institutional choice assumes great significance, as different individuals or groups lobby for their preferred policy by means of different institutions.[19]

According to this explanation, Gorbachev would have weighed up which institution was most likely to yield his preferred outcome. Some commentators have suggested that the feature of the conference which was particularly attractive to Gorbachev was that the Party Rules did not define the conference's procedural rules or powers. These had been intentionally left unspecified by Lenin and his successors, for the purpose of endowing leaderships with a flexible decision-making body to deal with unforeseen circumstances or crises.[20] Certainly the unprecedented timing of the conference in 1987, decades after the last one was convened by Stalin in February 1941, suggests a sense of crisis management, and raised speculation over why Gorbachev chose the conference and what he hoped to achieve by it.

What policy choice was the conference for Gorbachev?

One reason why Gorbachev chose to convene a conference was to overcome resistance to *perestroika* within the CPSU at all levels,[21] which was manifested in continued economic inefficiency and corruption. Between autumn 1987 and April 1988, the *perestroika* campaign came to a halt. This was mainly as a result of the growing bureaucratic resistance to *perestroika* and the open attack by Gorbachev's opponents against key elements of *glasnost*. In April 1988, Gorbachev began a counter-offensive against his opponents.[22]

However, this resistance to *perestroika* in the CC was apparent to Gorbachev before autumn 1987, as he had begun taking steps to overcome this opposition as early as January of that year. Scholars agree that it was to combat this resistance by removing or neutralising opponents in the CC, and to discuss the impending economic crisis, that Gorbachev proposed holding the Nineteenth Party Conference.[23] Gorbachev first raised this at the January 1987 Plenum, but the motion to hold a conference was only approved later, at the June 1987 Plenum. At this meeting, Gorbachev tentatively suggested that personnel changes take place at the conference.

What Gorbachev initially wanted to achieve from the conference, therefore, was personnel changes to the CC in a bid to increase support for *perestroika* within the CC.[24] Secondly, he needed a high-profile public display of support for his reforms[25] 'to make *perestroika* irreversible'.[26] One of Gorbachev's close aides, Georgii Shakhnazarov, confirms this hypothesis. The only party organ, apart from the party congress, that had the power to re-elect the CC was the 'emergency' or 'extraordinary' congress. According to Shakhnazarov, however, convening an emergency congress would have raised a state of alarm, which Gorbachev wished to avoid. Shakhnazarov has stated that Gorbachev specifically chose to convene the conference because he believed that the Party Rules were open-ended enough to attribute to the conference the powers of the congress, which would thus enable the desired personnel changes.[27]

By the time of the conference, however, Gorbachev had already successfully eliminated much of the 'ballast' he wanted removed from the CC by means of early retirement.[28] This gave him the opportunity to use the conference to promote *perestroika* and denounce any remaining party members who still resisted. At the conference he proposed controversial laws designed to declaw the upper echelons of the bureaucracy in an attempt to break the ministerial stronghold over resources that had eluded party control. By combining the posts of First Party Secretary and Regional Head of the Soviets, Gorbachev sought to impose party power over the regional bureaucracies. Similarly his creation of the new parliament, the Congress of People's Deputies (CoPD), essentially disenfranchised the ministries and the Council of Ministers was liquidated.[29]

What policy choice for fraternal party leaderships?

In the interim, however, before the CPSU Conference was held, between November 1987 and June 1988, National Party Conferences (NPCs) were held in Albania, Romania, Bulgaria, Hungary and Yugoslavia. In each of these states' languages, the term may be translated as it is above, with the exception of Yugoslavia, which translates as 'Yugoslav' party conference, in order to distinguish the federal from the republican conferences. Soviet commentators from 1988 (Khizhniakov and Solov´ev) referred to '*obshchepartiĭnye konferentsii*' – 'general party conferences' when discussing the term generically.

To avoid confusion, reference will be made to the Albanian, Bulgarian, Hungarian, Polish and Romanian conferences both generically and specifically as 'NPCs'. Yugoslavia's will be referred to as the 'LCY conference' and Soviet ones as the 'CPSU conference'. In all of these regimes, with the exception of Albania and Romania, the main theme of each respective conference was how to better implement *perestroika* and liberalise the economy to extricate the country from economic crisis. Instead of proposing like-minded systemic reforms, Romania's conference concentrated on which economic goals needed to be met and how to improve worker discipline to increase economic productivity.[30] What is common, therefore, to Bulgaria, Hungary, Romania, the Soviet Union and Yugoslavia, in the period 1987–88, is that all convened their respective NPCs to discuss future economic and political policy as a matter of some urgency before their next respective planned congresses. In Poland the conference was convened a year later in May 1989. However, although every party (except in the case of Albania) convened the conference for nominally the same reason, some regimes pursued very different goals at their respective conferences, as is detailed in Chapter 4.

Of particular interest here, however, is the timing of the conferences. Firstly, the CPSU took the decision in June 1987 to hold its conference before the other parties decided to convene their respective meetings, and yet the CPSU conference was the second to last of these meetings held, in July 1988, as Table 1 shows. Secondly, this was a party body which the Soviet Union had not convened since 1941. Unlike the party congress convened regularly every five years, the conference, as similarly stipulated in the Party Rules of all communist countries, *can* be convened between congresses, should the CC deem it necessary. This apparently leaves the decision to the discretion of each respective country's CC. Since no other guidelines appear in the Party Rules, it is inevitable that we are drawn to look backwards to see whether a pattern of outcomes emerges.

The length of time that had elapsed since the conference had last been convened varied from country to country. As Table 1 shows, the last time the conference had been convened preceding that of 1987–88 was 1985 in Albania, 1984 in Bulgaria and Poland, 1973 in Yugoslavia, 1957 in Hungary and 1941 in the Soviet Union. From the disparate dates there seems to be little in common between the last respective conferences. This then throws up two questions.

Firstly, under what conditions did leaderships choose to call the conference? When looking at these conferences as unrelated events, one realises how much *circumstantial* evidence there is pointing towards a link between them. The fact that all parties chose to convene their conferences within a few months of one another, when they had not done so for between four and forty-five years, could be ascribed to coincidence, but this appears highly unlikely. As briefly explained above, Gorbachev's main reason for convening the CPSU conference at that specific time was to try to overcome resistance to

Table 1 *Chronology of conferences, 1987–89*

Order in which 1987–89 conference held	Country	Date CC approved convention of conference	Months between date planned and date held	Date held	Date of preceding conference
1st	Albania	?	?	November 1987	1985
2nd	Romania	5 October 1987	2 ½	14–16 December 1987	1982
3rd	Bulgaria	July 1987	6	28 January 1988	1984
4th	Hungary	8 December 1987	5 ½	20–22 May 1988	1957
5th	Yugoslavia	7–8 December 1987	5 ½	29–31 May 1988	1973
6th	Soviet Union	June 1987	12	28 June–1 July 1988	1941
7th	Poland	31 March 1989	1	4–5 May 1989	1984

perestroika from within the party leadership and, if possible, to bring about personnel changes to the CC. What did leaderships of the fraternal parties of Central and East Europe hope to achieve at their respective conferences? It seems unlikely that other leaders had independently formulated precisely the same strategy as a reason for convening their conferences around the same time.

The second question which arises is: what did the usual procedure of a conference entail, and how did it differ from the congress? We can find this out simply by consulting the Party Rules that define the powers of the conference and congress.

Formal constraints of congresses and conferences

Comparison of different editions of the section in the Party Rules, 'higher party bodies,' which outlines the powers of the congress and extraordinary congress, indicates that the provisions regarding the congress have remained fairly static over time. Congress powers are essentially the same in all fraternal party rules, so we may look to the CPSU provisions as representative of them all, generically. The powers of the congress for all parties can be summarised as follows. The congress confirms decisions made by central party organisations; it reviews and changes the Party Programme and Party Rules; it determines party policy and it selects the CC and other central party organs. These rules changed very little between the Seventeenth CPSU Congress in 1934 and Twenty-seventh Congress in 1986.[31]

The congress:

1. hears and approves the reports of the CC of the central auditing commission and of the other central organisations;
2. reviews, amends and approves the Party Programme and Party Rules;
3. determines the line of the party in matters of home and foreign policy, and examines and decides the most important questions of party and state life, of the communist edifice;
4. elects the CC and central auditing commission.[32]

Unlike the five-yearly communist party congress, the NPC was not subject to formal rules of convention or 'formal constraints' in 1988. As has been mentioned, conference procedure was not specified, but simply defined in the Party Rules by the clause that the conference *could* be convened between five-yearly congresses and that the rules guiding delegate selection were to be determined by the CC. This wording implies that the conference might carry the powers of the congress between two congresses, should the CC decide such action was justified.

The Bulgarian, Hungarian and Soviet rules state only that a conference could be convened between congresses and that the CC would determine procedure:

> In the period between party congresses, the CC of the BCP [Bulgarian Communist Party] may convene the national party conference for the discussion of important questions of party policy. The procedure for convening the party conference is determined by the CC of the BCP.[33]

> The CC may convene a national party conference between two congresses. The rules for the representation of party organisations at national party conferences are laid down by the CC.[34]

> In the interim between party congresses the CPSU CC may convene, should the need arise, an All-Union party conference to discuss pressing party policy issues. The procedure for holding an All-Union party conference is determined by the CC CPSU.[35]

By contrast, the Romanian rules contained an additional provision for personnel changes to the CC:

> In between congresses, whenever it considers that certain important problems of the party and state policy should be discussed, the CC may call the national conference of the party. The delegates to the national conference are elected by the conferences of county party organisations according to the norms set by the party CC.

> Vacancies in the CC shall be filled by its alternate members. Party members other than alternate members of the CC of the Romanian Communist Party[36] may fill vacancies only with the approval of the party's national conference, according to the number of CC members approved by the congress.[37]

The LCY rules, although fuller, in essence empowered the LCY CC to determine the way in which conferences were convened much in the same way as the other parties' rules. Suggestions by other bodies could be made as to when a conference was convened, and delegate selection was to be 'in the main, in accordance' with the usual means of delegate selection. The CC, however, ultimately decided whether a conference would be convened, the number of delegates who would attend and the way in which these individuals would be selected, as is discussed in Chapter 6.

The exception to all of these was Poland, as the PUWP had removed any reference to the NPC from the Party Rules by the time the conference was held in 1989. Prior to that, the conference had been described similarly:

> Between congresses the national conference may be convened with the purpose of discussing current issues of party policy. The basis of delegate selection to the conference is determined by the Central Committee.[38]

The phrase in all of the rules that the conference 'could be convened between congresses' by association suggests that the conference was, like the congress, representative of the entire party membership at a national or federal level. However, a closer examination of these conferences in Chapters 2, 3, 5, 6 and 7 shows that in fact, unlike congresses, these forums were not nationally representative of the party, and instead were composed of a fraction of the congress. Those delegates selected were hand-picked. These chapters illustrate how this absence of 'formal constraints' enabled leaderships to use the conference in a discretionary way, as it seemed best to them at the time – to combat opposition within the party and consolidate power. As these informal procedures evolved, they essentially 'stuck' over time to form a set of informal rules guiding future conference convention. Thus, as will be illustrated, those procedures devised *ad hoc* soon came to constitute a set of informal institutional constraints.

This research does not claim that the NPC was the *only* forum where opposition could be purged or defeated; this was also accomplished elsewhere. Nor was the manipulation of delegate selection exclusive to party conferences; this practice has been historically documented in the cases of congresses and other party forums. What this research empirically shows is that the conference was clearly the preferred institution for this purpose because it was not subject to the same constraints as the congress or extraordinary congress in terms of delegate selection. Evidence suggests manipulation of delegates to the congress was not possible on the *same scale* as to the conference, as discussed in Chapters 2, 3, 5, 6 and 7. Furthermore, in the absence of formal rules, this manipulation came to be fixed as procedure as an informal institutional mechanism.

Historical survey of outcomes to trace the conference's informal constraints

In the absence of clear guidelines *de jure* defining and limiting the powers of the conference, we can build a profile of the conference as an institution by surveying what was achieved at each conference *de facto*. Thus we will be able to reconstruct what the conference as an institution represented to Gorbachev, the CPSU and the other regimes' leaders and parties respectively.

A historical survey of the conference as an institution precedes each of the case studies of the 1988 conferences in Chapters 2, 5, 6 and 7. Changes to the provisions in the Party Rules regarding conferences are also reviewed. This historical institutional analysis charts how each regime developed its own brand of 'national conference' so as to reconstruct the different traditions and constraining forces the variant types of conference may have rejected or internalised over the years. Therefore it is possible to gauge how political actors' strategies might have been shaped by the structure of the institution as it had evolved by the late 1980s. Furthermore, this analysis helps to identify the extent to which conference constraints may have served as a contributing factor in shaping conference outcome between 1987 and 1989.

Thus, for each of the regimes in turn there is a brief description of each party conference. The methodology of stripping down descriptions of these conferences to a bare minimum – about a paragraph on each one – is a means to an end; these outlines are a means to constructing an *ideal type* for the conference as an institution in each party. Such descriptions are a vehicle for illustrating a theoretical point, and would hardly 'pass a historian's muster'.[39] On the basis of these skeleton descriptions, an ideal type for the traditional powers and functions of each regime's conference will be constructed.

From evaluating, firstly, the nature of the conference as an *ideal type*, in terms of its powers and function and secondly, conference timing, we will be able to determine what sort of policy choice the conference represented to leaders in the late 1980s.

Last convened in 1941, 1957 and 1973 respectively, the Soviet, Hungarian and Yugoslav communist party conferences were, arguably, no longer salient institutions by 1988. This highlights the unprecedented timing of these meetings in 1988, when leaderships of each of these parties convened their conferences within the span of just over a month between May and July 1988, as Table 1 shows. As Chapter 2 demonstrates in the context of all preceding Soviet conferences, 1905–41, the CPSU General Secretary enjoyed wide powers in securing his desired outcome. Traditionally, conferences constituted a defeat of those in opposition to the General Secretary and then later, under Stalin, the rules were changed to allow the approval of CC personnel changes at conferences, as will be discussed in Chapter 2.

Hungary apparently never developed its own conference tradition *per se*. The pattern which emerges from previous meetings is that the conference had the powers of an emergency congress to approve personnel appointments that had been agreed *a priori* with the CPSU. So, we could say that historically the 'informal constraints' or operating procedure of the Hungarian conference was leadership change in accordance with Soviet policy. As Chapter 5 will show, the conference of 1988 does not deviate from this tradition in that, as is commonly agreed, the outcome was supported by and (according to some accounts) engineered by the centrist-Gorbachev wing of the CPSU. The conference saw an unprecedented change in personnel, the election of a new swathe of reform communists, including most notably the removal of the Party's First Secretary, János Kádár, from office and his replacement with the CPSU-backed Károly Grósz. The strong and polarised debate in 1987 and again in 1989 within the HSWP CC, over whether a conference or a congress be convened, provides evidence that to a large extent, actors equated their different policy preferences with their choice of institution as will be further detailed in Chapter 5.

Yugoslavia developed a very different brand of conference in the 1970s, designed as an experiment to replace the LCY CC as a trial solution for a future post-Titoist Yugoslavia. In the wake of growing nationalism and inter-republican tensions, the federal conference was designed as a forum to coerce errant republican parties to implement federal policies. Following its fourth convention in 1973, the conference was disbanded and removed from the Party Rules. The conference had failed to secure the implementation of federal laws and directives at the republican level and the new constitution of 1974, designed to protect the autonomy of Vojvodina and Kosovo, was largely ignored by Serbia. In 1982 new provisions regarding the conference were introduced into the LCY Party Rules in the same spirit as in the rest of Central, Eastern and South-eastern Europe, but the conference was only reconvened as such again in 1988. Communist parties across Central, Eastern and South-eastern Europe were facing crisis as the party's legitimacy declined, but this was experienced more poignantly by the federal party in Yugoslavia. Although federal party institutions maintained the power to legislate, republican governments did not always comply with federal law, and republican autonomy had considerably increased by 1988. The LCY conference in 1988, like those of the 1970s, was dedicated to strengthening the federal party's authority over the republican parties with the aim of maintaining the Federation. As Chapter 6 details, the conference constituted this traditional policy choice, although most unusually for the LCY, the event was organised in collaboration with the CPSU.

In the case of Romania and Bulgaria, both regimes had institutionalised the conference into a regularly occurring event. The Romanian conference had been institutionalised between the 1960s and 1980s by leader Nicolae Ceaușescu as a regular meeting convened every five years midway (usually in December) between the five-yearly congresses. As a kind of 'mid-term' between congresses, the conference ostensibly reiterated policies and the FYP approved at the preceding congress. At the same time, the conference was fashioned as a vehicle for approving controversial policies crucial to establishing Ceaușescu's extensive power base. Ceaușescu chose to endorse his most outrageous policies at the NPC, for example the appointment of his wife and son to the CC at the conferences of 1972 and 1982, which suggests that he considered the conference a more malleable forum than the congress. The 1987 Romanian conference was held according to the usual pattern midway between congresses in December, and the outcome followed the usual pattern.[40] Outcomes over these decades show that Ceauşescu used the conference to defuse opposition, which he often achieved by swelling the ranks of the Romanian Communist Party (RCP) with members of his family. This practice reached such proportions that the Romanian acronym for the party, 'PCR', was commonly described as referring to Nicolae Ceauşescu, his wife Elena Petrescu and their relations: '*Petrescu, Ceauşescu si Relatii*' instead of *Partidul Comunist România*..

Like the RCP, the BCP had a modern conference tradition, although it had not regularised convention to the same degree as the RCP. Therefore, although conferences had been convened every few years between the 1970s and 1984, there was no precisely regular pattern to such an extent that it would be possible to predict the next BCP conference for a certain month or year. From the 1970s, BCP conferences addressed and sought solutions to the inefficiencies in the command economy as evident in problems of supply, production and quality control. The conferences resulted in the dismissal of high-ranking ministers, held responsible for these shortcomings, which could be equated with the conference sanctioning personnel changes. The conference of 1988 breaks with this tradition, in that the main message of the conference was to espouse the need for *perestroika* of the political system as well as the usual demand for *perestroika* in production and quality control, which had been the focus of previous conferences. The First Secretary of the BCP, Todor Zhivkov, publicised at the conference his commitment to following the Soviet example of *perestroika*, and staging a show of strength for reform-communism. Whether this display was simply for the sake of window dressing or was a genuine attempt to pull the BCP into line with the CPSU, this suggests evidence that the BCP was in communication with the CPSU about the aims of the conference, or that the BCP was following the CPSU's lead in a new departure from existing policy. This will be assessed in greater detail in Chapter 4.

As will be discussed in Chapter 7, the PUWP conference was convened twice under Edward Gierek in 1973 and 1978 to discuss problems of inefficiency in the economy, and the increasing dependence of the Polish economy on Western imports. By the time the conference was next convened, under Wojciech Jaruzelski, in 1984, provisions regarding the conference had been removed from the Party Rules. The 1984 conference was the first all-party meeting convened after the period of martial law between December 1981 and the spring of 1983. At this meeting Jaruzelski reiterated that the unrest had threatened the survival of the socialist regime, that the measures taken had therefore been appropriate and that, moreover, this course of action had been successful. Convened as an organ of party publicity, the 1984 conference declared the results of an opinion poll that had been distributed to delegates, which expressed the view that the party's authority over society had risen significantly, and that party work had also improved. Unlike other fraternal parties, Poland was 'due' to convene another conference around 1988, and Gorbachev had been present at the 1986 PUWP congress when Jaruzelski informed the party of this forthcoming conference. The way in which the PUWP conference was deferred until 1989, and reasons for this, will be discussed in Chapter 7.

Conclusion

As has been noted, from details of the timing of these conferences between 1987 and 1989, circumstantial evidence suggests that these meetings might have been linked, and perhaps even arranged in consonance. Chapter 4 will examine whether there was CPSU influence and in particular how Gorbachev entreated leaders from the fraternal parties to convene their respective conferences, in the spirit of socialist international- ism, to rebrand their respective parties so as to salvage the socialist one-party regime model. As will be discussed, such action was also in keeping with the traditional Soviet policy of aligning the fraternal parties with the CPSU.

So far, we have identified the conference as an institution with fewer formal constraints than the congress. This chapter has outlined the historical institutional method applied in the case studies that follow to reconstruct, in the absence of formal rules, the 'informal constraints' that guided the conference and hence what 'policy choice' the conference represented to lead- erships in the late 1980s. Historically, this policy choice was a staged purge of the opposition and the consolidation of power by the General Secretary, as the next chapter will illustrate.

The application of such rational choice and historical institutional methods has been criticised as 'deterministic' and far too geared towards charting continuity rather than evolution,[41] much as the political culture explanation of continuity has been criticised for interpreting the present through a backward-looking lens, that simply magnifies those features rooted in the past.[42] Although this is very valid criticism, there is a particular logic to evaluating the NPCs of the late 1980s in this way for the following reasons. The time frame within which the party conference was developed, formalised and then discarded along with the rest of the one-party model in CEE, all within the space of a century, allows us the unusual luxury of examining the origins, development and demise of this particular institution within the context of the one-party model. Moreover, again unusually, this institution was one which was rarely or at least irregularly convened, so some examination of all cases is feasible. At the same time, the fact that the conference was subject to very few formal rules – that is, constraints – is a hurdle to understanding the nature of the conference, and a logical way to elicit this information is through historical analysis. With respect to interpreting the results of this historical analysis, there is a strong awareness underlying this research that the context within which conferences were convened over the twentieth century varied significantly between Leninist, Stalinist and Gorbachevian regimes. The historical and rational choice institutional analysis in the case study chapters that follow therefore provides background information to supplement modern material of the late 1980s from archives, interviews, memoirs and textual analysis of the conference stenographic reports.

Notes

1. V. Schmidt, 'Taking ideas and discourse seriously: explaining change through discursive institutionalism as the fourth new institutionalism', *European Political Science Review* 2:1 (2010), pp. 1–25.

2. See, for example, S. White, 'Gorbachev, Gorbachevism and the Party conference', *Journal of Communist Studies* 4:4 (1998), pp. 127–60; A. A. Solov'ev, 'Obshchepartiĭnye konferentsii v zhizni i deiatel´nosti KPSS', *Voprosy istorii KPSS* 6 (1988), pp. 79–92; S. S. Khizhniakov and O. V. Khlevniuk, *XVIII Partkonferentsiia: vremia, problemy, resheniia* (Moskva: s.n., 1990), p. 8.

3 Streeck and K. Thelen, *Beyond Continuity: Institutional Change in Advanced Political Economies* (Oxford: Oxford University Press, 2005), p. 9.

4 *Ibid.*, pp. 10–11.

5 J. Hough and M. Fainsod, *How the Soviet Union is Governed* (Cambridge MA: Harvard University Press, 1979), pp. 362–84.

6 M. Gorbachev, *Documents and Materials: Report and Concluding Speech by Mikhail Gorbachev [at the 12th Special Session of the Supreme Soviet of the USSR of the 11th Convocation]; Law of the USSR on Changes and Amendments to the Constitution of the USSR; Law of the USSR on the Election of People's Deputies of the USSR* (Moscow: Novosti, 1988).

7 P. Roeder, *Red Sunset: the Failure of Soviet Politics* (Princeton NJ: Princeton University Press, 1993), p. 88.

8 S. Whitefield, *Industrial power and the Soviet State* (Oxford: Oxford University Press, 1993), p. 163.

9 Hough and Fainsod, *How the Soviet Union is Governed*, p. 363.

10 Whitefield, Industrial Power and the Soviet State, pp. 178–205.

11 D. North, *Institutions, Institutional Change and Economic Performance* (Cambridge: Cambridge University Press, 1990), pp. 44–5; S. Steinmo, K. Thelen and F. Longstreth (eds), *Structuring Politics: Historical Institutionalism in Comparative Analysis* (Cambridge: Cambridge University Press, 1992), pp. 1–32.

12 M. Aoki, *Toward a Comparative Institutional Analysis* (Cambridge MA: MIT, 2001), p. 233.

13 G. B. Peters, *Institutional Theory in Political Science: the New Institutionalism* (London: Pinter, 1999), p. 25.

14 North, *Institutions, Institutional Change and Economic Performance*, p. 36.

15 *Ibid.*, p. 53.

16 G. Tsebelis, *Nested Games: Rational Choice in Comparative Politics* (Berkeley CA: University of California Press, 1990), p. 40.

17 J. Manza, 'Political Sociological Models of the US New Deal', *Annual Review of Sociology* 26 (2000), p. 305.

18 Tsebelis, *Nested Games*, p. 98.

19 K. Raustiala, 'Form and Substance in International Agreements', *American Journal of International Law* 99:3 (2005), pp. 581–614.

20 B. Hazan, *Gorbachev and his Enemies: the Struggle for Perestroika* (Boulder CO: Westview, 1990), p. 166.

21 *Ibid.*

22 S. Bialer, 'The changing Soviet political system: the Nineteenth Party Conference and after', in S. Bialer (ed.), *Politics, society and nationality inside Gorbachev's Russia* (Boulder CO: Westview Press, 1989), pp. 193–241; 199–211.

23 A. Brown, *The Gorbachev factor* (Oxford: Oxford University Press, 1996), pp. 176–77; B. Hazan, *Gorbachev's Gamble: the 19th All-Union Party Conference* (Boulder CO: Westview, 1990), pp. 5–13; G. Shakhnazarov, *Tsena svobody: reformatsiia Gorbacheva glazami ego pomoshchnika* (Moskva: Rossika; Zevs, 1993), pp. 45–6.

24 Interview with Anatoly Cherniaev, Moscow, 24 September 2002.

25   Hazan, *Gorbachev's Gamble*, p. 8.

26   The opening line of Gorbachev's speech and later reiterated. See, for example, CPSU (1988), *XIX Vsesoiuznaia konferentsiia KPSS, 28 iiunia–1 iiulia 1988: stenograficheskiĭ otchet v dvukh tomakh*, Moskva, vol. 1, p. 19.

27   Shakhnazarov, *Tsena svobody*, p. 46.

28   Interview with Anatoly Cherniaev, Moscow, 24 September 2002.

29   S. Whitefield, *Industrial power and the Soviet State* (Oxford: Oxford University Press, 1993), p. 218.

30   Albania's conference did not discuss economic or political but educational issues, as detailed in Chapter 4.

31   See A. G. Egorov and K. M. Bogoliubov, *Kommunisticheskaia partiia Sovetskogo Soiuza v rezoliutsiiakh i resheniiakh s"ezdov, konferentsii i plenumov TSK, 1898–1988* (Moskva: Izd-vo polit. lit-ry, 9-oe izd, 1983–1989), vol. 6, p. 139 for the rules approved at the Seventeenth Congress, 1934.

32   CPSU, *Rules of the Communist Party of the Soviet Union approved by the 27th Congress of the CPSU March 1st 1986* (Moskva: Novosti, 1986), p. 16.

33   Bulgarian Communist Party, *Ustav na Bŭlgarskata Komunisticheska Partiia, priet edinodushno ot VIII kongres na BKP* (Sofiia: Partizdat, 1971), p. 41, §35. These rules remained in operation until the 1988 conference.

34   Hungarian Socialist Workers' Party, *The 13th Congress of the Hungarian Socialist Workers' Party, March 25–28, 1985* (Budapest: Corvina, 1985), p. 280, §16.

35   Communist Party of the Soviet Union, *Rules of the Communist Party of the Soviet Union approved by the 27th Congress of the CPSU March 1 1986* (Moscow: Novosti, 1986), p. 17, §40.

36   Hereafter RCP.

37   Romanian Communist Party, *The Statute of the Romanian Communist Party* (Bucharest: Editura Politica, 1984), pp. 61–2, §21–2.

38   Polska Zjednoczona Partia Robotnicza (PZPR), *Statut Polskiej Zjednoczonej Partii Robotniczej uchwalony przez III zjazd PZPR* (Warszawa: s.n., 1959), p. 77, §31; PZPR, *Statut Polskiej Zjednoczonej Partii Robotniczej: ze zmianami i uzupełnieniami uchwalonymi przez VII Zjazd PZPR w grudniu 1975 r.* (Warszawa: Książka i Wiedza, 1978), p. 74, §31.

39   K. Shepsle and M. Bonchek, *Analyzing politics: Rationality, Behaviour and Institutions* (New York NY: Norton, 1997), p. 11.

40   D. Nelson, *Romanian Politics in the Ceauşescu Era* (New York NY: Gordon and Breach Science Publishers, 1988), pp. 331–4.

41   Schmidt, 'Taking ideas and discourse seriously', pp. 1–25.

42   F. J. Fleron, 'Post-Soviet political culture in Russia: an assessment of recent empirical investigations', *Europe-Asia Studies* 48:2 (1996), pp. 225–60.

2

The conference as a policy choice: the CPSU conference, 1905–41

Introduction

This chapter reviews the CPSU conference as an institution for the purpose of projecting what the conference represented in terms of a policy choice for Gorbachev in 1988. As discussed in Chapter 1, in the absence of formal rules constraining institutions, procedures naturally evolve that essentially 'stick' as informal rules, setting a precedent for future practice. These informal rules can prove at least as 'sticky' as formal ones. Patterns emerge from this survey of conference outcomes between 1905 and 1941, showing that as a policy choice, the conference was convened by the General Secretary as a forum at which he could consolidate his own power by more easily engineering his desired outcome and publicly defeating rivals and opposition. A historical review reveals this pattern for all eighteen conferences between 1905 and 1941.

Under Lenin, the conference provided the General Secretary with a forum where he was able to secure endorsement of his policies and defeat the opposition within a milieu of 'phoney' democratic debate. These institutional features became more pronounced under Stalin as he consistently used the conference to stage purges of the opposition. At the Eighteenth CPSU Congress in 1939, the Party Rules were changed, granting the conference direct powers to replace members of the CC between congresses. There is a brief discussion at the end of this chapter that illustrates how the conference constituted the same policy choice for Gorbachev in 1988. The corollary to this chapter – Chapter 3 – empirically shows how this applied to the Nineteenth CPSU Conference in 1988 and beyond.

Theoretical claim: the conference as a policy choice

Traditionally, Lenin and Stalin convened party conferences to stage a defeat of the left or right factions, and particularly chose conferences instead of congresses for this purpose because they were easier to control, providing more favourable conditions to achieve their desired outcomes. As Aleksandr Yakovlev has described:

> Of course, to a certain extent conferences were more pliable and Lenin always felt more self-assured at conferences than at congresses. At congresses, Lenin was sometimes defeated on certain issues... When an issue arose on which it was necessary to denounce somebody, or change someone in the leadership or purge someone, Lenin and especially Stalin used party conferences, as they were easier to manipulate than congresses... Or, if, let's say, some difficulties arose which were causing problems, then he would convene the conference to decide a position to adopt, and in the process it would serve to mobilise the masses on an issue... [the conference was] an organ of mobilisation.[1]

This statement supports the claim that, firstly, an actor's choice of institution is synonymous with a particular policy choice and secondly, the conference was a forum at which the General Secretary could wield greater power than at the congress, and thus stage a defeat or purge of opposition. The fact that conferences took place at critical junctures[2] suggests that the meeting was an emergency measure. At the same time, although the historical precedent of previous conference outcomes empowered the General Secretary, the extent to which he could achieve his desired goals at the meeting was still dependent on his capacity to control the event.[3]

How the conference evolved as an institution is reflected to some extent in changes made to the Party Rules. Before reviewing conference outcome as a way to reconstruct what informal institutional constraints had crystallised by 1988, the next section looks at how the conference was described in the Party Rules between 1905 and 1988.

'Formal constraints': provisions in the Party Rules

The origins of the institution have been traced to a provision in the Party Rules 'about periodic conferences of representatives from different party organisations'. This advocated that the party convene more meetings of members from different constituent organisations in order to solicit a broader range of opinions, which would better represent members' interests.[4] There was, however, no explicit reference to the conference in the Party Rules until 1939, which suggests that instead of being 'created' in 1905 the conference evolved over time, and was only later loosely described in the Party Rules. So, although the first Russian Social Democratic Workers' Party (RSDWP) conference was convened in 1905, and was followed in quick succession by another seventeen, there was no reference at all to this institution in the Party Rules until they were amended at the Eighteenth Party Congress, in March 1939. At that point, provisions concerning the conference were introduced, which specified that as much as twenty per cent of the CC could be replaced at a conference. The Rules specified that all decisions taken at a conference required the Central Committee's subsequent approval, at which point they became legally binding on all party organisations. The exception to this provision was personnel changes, which could be made at the conference without the CC's endorsement.[5]

Shortly after this change to the rules, the Eighteenth Party Conference was held in 1941, which, as might be expected, included personnel changes to the CC.[6] At the following (Nineteenth) Party Congress in 1952, provisions concerning the conference were removed from the Party Rules and were only reintroduced at the Twenty-third Congress in 1966. The new provision in the Rules regarding the conference was considerably different to that of the Stalinist era,[7] in that the powers to change CC personnel were removed:

> §8 The Party Rules provide that the CC, when necessary, can convene the All-Union party conference for the discussion of urgent issues of party policy, and the CC of the communist parties of the union republics can convene the republican party conferences.
>
> The procedure for convening the All-Union party conference is to be determined by the CC of the CPSU and [in the case of] the

republican party conferences [the procedure is to be determined] by the CC of the Union republics' communist parties.[8]

These provisions remained in essence the same, although they were slightly reworded in the 1986 rules, as discussed in Chapter 1.[9]

According to Soviet historiography, the reason why provision for a conference was included in the Party Rules from 1966 onwards was as a token tribute to the 'democratic Leninist tradition', which was retained as a commemorative keepsake of the party's historical development. As reported by this account, the conference as a dormant institution suddenly became salient to the party again after 1985 when Gorbachev revived Leninist principles, in which context convening the Nineteenth Party Conference more than forty years later was 'entirely natural'.[10] During the run-up to the conference in 1988, a long-lost democratic tradition was attributed to the conference, and the institution's fall into disuse in 1941 was explained as symptomatic of the leadership's departure from the democratic practice of consulting with the party membership, and a sign that the CC no longer sought party members' views.[11] This implied that in reviving the conference, Gorbachev was renewing the democratic tradition of wider consultation. However, as this chapter argues, this statement is based on false premises – that conferences between 1905 and 1941 genuinely served a consultative function, were representative of the party and operated according to democratic process.

Representation at conferences

To what extent were conferences representative of the party membership at large? A logical starting point, here, is to examine how delegates were chosen to attend conferences. The 1939 rules specify that delegates were selected by the regional and provincial party plenums and CC plenums of the Union Republics. However, the rules granted the CC the final say in determining procedure for selection and the norms of representation.[12] In 1966 this provision was amended to grant the CC control over regulating conference procedure. The provision in the 1939 rules may, therefore, seem more 'democratic' in that selection was performed in a more decentralised way, at local and regional level. In practice, however, this was not the case.

Although the conference was smaller, less broadly representative and authoritative than the congress, participants were recruited in the same way.[13] Delegates were chosen by provincial party conferences, which were in turn composed of delegates from district or county conferences. This procedure was essentially controlled by the CC, as provincial and local party secretaries were nominated by the CC, and the practice of 'secretarial hierarchy', whereby lower party organisations were subservient to higher ones[14] ensured that only personnel approved by the CC attended conferences. Delegate selection to conferences was carefully managed to ensure that these meetings were attended by those with strictly orthodox views, as noted by the Stalinist-era Politburo member, Leon Trotsky,[15] who was later outlawed for his controversial criticism of the party apparatus. Perhaps not surprisingly, therefore, under Stalin's leadership delegate selection to conferences was engineered to facilitate the desired outcome. However, as will be discussed, representation had always been cause for dispute, and Lenin was only magnanimous at conferences so long as his policies were approved. Scholars have identified how Soviet leaders' definitions of 'democracy' as applied to policymaking from 1917–91, were highly selective and changeable.[16] It therefore, perhaps, comes as little surprise that the long-lost 'democratic Leninist tradition' which Solov´ev and Khizhniakov attribute to the conference apparently never existed, as the following survey illustrates.

Conferences, 1905–41

Establishing Bolshevik supremacy: First–Seventh Conferences, 1905–17

Between 1905 and 1917, Lenin vested congressional powers in the conference, which enabled him to establish, unconstitutionally, Bolshevik supremacy within the party. Lenin achieved this by engineering Bolshevik majorities at conferences and then attributing to these meetings the powers of the congress. During this period the conference was the main decision-making organ: more than ten years elapsed between the Fifth Congress (1907) and the Sixth Congress (1917), during which time five party conferences were held.

The meeting claimed by Soviet historians as the 'first' party conference was that of the RSDWP in 1905,[17] which was initially planned as an extraordinary congress of the Bolshevik party to discuss the intended unification of the Bolshevik and Menshevik factions at the approaching Fourth 'Unification' Congress.[18] At the Third Congress in 1905, Lenin had stipulated that unification of the factions could only take place at a congress.[19] In preparation for this congress, both factions respectively convoked preliminary party meetings. The Mensheviks held their meeting in Petersburg at the end of November 1905,[20] while the Bolsheviks planned an extraordinary congress, which would be held in Finland where Lenin was residing. Ultimately, however, only forty-one members arrived at the meeting, and the small gathering was considered insufficiently representative of the party for a congress, so the Bolsheviks instead held a conference in December 1905 with the available delegation.[21]

The Second Conference, described as the first 'All-Russian' conference,[22] was convened by the RSDWP CC in 1906, in response to pressure from the local party organisations that action should be taken concerning Menshevik policies. Local organisations demanded that an emergency congress be held, but instead the party conference was convened. This is perhaps the earliest evidence that different contingents had different preferences over institutional choice, which they considered important to achieving their respective preferred outcome. The fact that Lenin advocated a conference suggests that he and his cohort considered that at a conference, he would be more able to engineer an outcome, which would benefit the Bolsheviks. The local organisations were possibly seeking the adoption of Menshevik policies, and considered that at a larger meeting (the congress), they would be more likely to achieve this.

Although the Mensheviks formed a slight majority at the conference, which enabled them to push through Menshevik resolutions on a number of issues, we might surmise that they would have had greater success in this respect at a congress. Moreover, Lenin overruled the Mensheviks' resolutions in some cases, a step which he justified by claiming that they had contrived a majority at the conference by sending representatives from fictitious organisations.[23] The Mensheviks were again in a majority at the Fourth Congress in 1907,[24] suggesting the Bolsheviks were not as predominant as Soviet historiography would have us believe. At this congress, changes were made to the election procedure, stipulating that only larger organisations, that exceeded 300 members, were authorised to send a representative to the congress.[25] We may infer that this threshold also applied to conference delegate selection. In May 1907, before the Third Conference, this threshold was raised to one representative for every organisation comprising at least 1,000 members.[26] We might conclude, therefore, that Mensheviks belonged to smaller organisations, and that this threshold was designed to reduce their representation at congresses and conferences. Certainly, after the Second Conference the Mensheviks never constituted a majority again. Their representation declined from thirty-eight per cent at the Third Conference to just fourteen per cent at the Sixth Conference.

The Third and Fourth Conferences focused on the same issues as the previous two. Resolutions passed, however, were treated as legally binding,[27] arguably perhaps because these were Lenin's preferred policies. Having constitutionally engineered a Bolshevik majority, Lenin was empowered to secure his preferred outcome at these conferences. The Fifth Conference in 1908 was used to discredit and crush opposition factions, and strengthen the central Bolshevik core of the party.[28] The Bolsheviks formed a majority at the conference, and led an attack on the remaining Mensheviks.[29]

The Sixth Conference, held in 1912, has understandably attracted more interest from scholars.[30] An entire article was devoted to this topic in *Voprosy Istorii KPSS*, May 1988, as part of a short series entitled 'In the run-up to the Nineteenth All-Union Party Conference' published by the journal before the Nineteenth Conference in June 1988.[31] At the Sixth Conference, the Party Rules were amended and personnel changes in the CC were made. At the time, divisions between the factions were particularly acute. Lenin hand-picked all conference delegates – only fourteen delegates with voting rights in total, twelve of whom were Bolsheviks.[32] This was the smallest conference of all eighteen in terms of delegation and in essence comprised little more than a Bolshevik conference. Interestingly, official Soviet sources do not specify the number of delegates that attended this conference, nor of which factions they were members. In contrast, however, delegate numbers for all other conferences are listed in these sources. We may surmise that the figures were omitted precisely because they clearly identify the unconstitutional nature of this very crucial conference, at which the Bolsheviks assumed power.[33] Soviet sources do agree with the historian Edward Carr, however, in that only two Menshevik 'party organisations' were represented. Egorov and Bogoliubov state that 'In total at the conference more than twenty party organisations were represented, that is almost all the active organisations in Russia; therefore in practice it had the significance of a party congress'.[34] This claim, that the conference was almost as representative of the party membership as a congress, is rather undermined by the fact that only fourteen delegates represented all these organisations.

The small gathering proclaimed itself a 'general party conference' and assumed the powers of the congress. Lenin stipulated in his conference report on 'the Constitution of the Conference' that in the absence of conditions necessary for the convention of a congress, the general party conference could act as a congress.[35] To ensure that resolutions approved at the conference carried the same weight as those of a congress, Lenin determined that 'the general party conference could act with the full weight of the "highest organ of the party"'– that is, the congress.[36] This conference thus acted *de facto* as a congress in that it made use of all four powers vested in the congress.[37] All members of the opposition were condemned as 'liquidators' and expelled from the party. A new CC was appointed and the Party Rules were changed to allow personnel changes to be made to the CC outside the congress. Through this provision, Stalin was co-opted to the CC shortly after the conference.[38]

The outcome of the Sixth Conference was a powerful declaration that the Bolsheviks were no longer simply a faction within the party but had assumed control of the entire party.[39] The very famous Seventh Conference, or April Conference, in 1917 was the occasion when Lenin declared his *April Theses*, which resolved that capitalism should be overthrown and urged further revolution to this effect. The adoption of the famous slogan from the *Theses* – 'all power to the Soviets' – gave concrete shape and constitutional mould to the Bolshevik scheme of revolution.[40] At this conference the Bolsheviks cut the last remaining links with the Mensheviks.[41] Like the Sixth, this conference assumed most of the powers of the congress, electing a new CC and amending the Party Programme, so that in terms of its political and organisational significance, the conference played the role of the party congress.[42] This was the first (Bolshevik) conference conducted legally on home territory in Petrograd and thus had a significantly larger delegation of 149. On Lenin's proposal, at the conference the RSDWP changed its name to the Russian Communist Party of Bolsheviks (RCP(B)).[43] At the Eighth Conference, two years later, the Party Rules were amended to effect the party's change in name.[44]

Purging the opposition: Eighth–Seventeenth Conferences, 1919–32

At the Eighth Conference in 1919, far-reaching changes were made to the Party Rules, which served to institutionalise the party's organisation. The conference formally endorsed the new structure of the CC[45] and the principle that the party should adopt a leading role through the mechanism of democratic centralism.[46] A semblance of democracy was maintained by the introduction of a new provision into the Party Rules that permitted free discussion on all issues until such time as a decision had been reached;[47] however, this was soon suspended at the Tenth Conference in 1921.[48]

At the Ninth Conference in 1920, the Party Rules were again amended, which served to strengthen party unity further.[49] Some reformist resolutions were also approved, however, which for a brief period promised to democratise the party machine by granting workers greater scope to participate in the decision-making process, and authorised debate between the two main factions within the party: the 'Oppositionists' and 'Democratic Centralists'.[50]

Nonetheless, by the Tenth Conference, the Democratic Centralists proved victorious, and subsequently all (other) factions within the party were outlawed. The Tenth Congress, held just two months earlier, had passed a resolution on party unity outlawing any factional activity. The relevant provision in the resolution, which outlawed factions – the famous 'Point Seven'[51] – was kept secret, to mask the growing power of the central party machine, until Stalin released it for general circulation at the Thirteenth Conference in January 1924.[52] The Tenth Conference, in May 1921, was called earlier than originally planned, just two months after the Tenth Congress,[53] ostensibly to discuss the logistics of implementing the New Economic Policy (NEP) approved at the congress. During the congress, a peasants' uprising had broken out in Kronstadt (the Kronstadt rebellion) because of impoverished living conditions.[54] The congress resolution concerning the NEP, geared towards improving socio-economic conditions, was further fleshed out at the Tenth Conference.[55] A more pressing reason for calling the conference, however, was to decide how to deal with the Mensheviks, now that the NEP – a policy that they had long advocated – had been adopted. Concerned that the new policy might offer legitimacy to the Menshevik faction, which could in turn mobilise support for the movement, a CC member, Karl Radek, advocated at the conference a crackdown on the Mensheviks, on the ground that they would claim power if they were left at liberty.[56]

The Eleventh Conference, held six months later in December 1921, continued work on developing the NEP and at the same time established how to consolidate the party's power in the event of a resurgence of the Mensheviks. The conference focused on developing a strategy to purge the party of any such factional elements.[57]

Amendments made to the Party Rules at the Twelfth Conference clarified this policy in Article 62, that 'factions, regardless of their size, are entirely subordinate to the corresponding party organisations'.[58] This provision defined a structure for maintaining the party's monolithic unity, which signalled a warning to any factions that threatened to undermine this cohesion.

Stalin convened the Thirteenth Conference as a counter-offensive against Trotsky's 'New Course', which had sharply criticised how the leadership engineered delegate selection for congresses and conferences, and suggested that the system of 'secretarial hierarchy' should be replaced with real party democracy. Appropriately, Stalin hand-picked the delegates to the Thirteenth Conference, to help secure his preferred outcome. To ensure this, the small number of delegates who were invited to represent the opposition were not granted voting rights at the conference. Although Trotsky had not demanded that groups or factions be legalised within the party,[59] Soviet sources summarising the conference proceedings stated that Trotsky's 'New Course' had signalled the beginning of an opposition bloc within the party that had necessitated Stalin's counter-attack in the form of his publication of 'Point Seven', which outlawed factions.[60]

The Thirteenth Conference marked the final stage in the party's institutionalisation of monolithic unity. Lenin died just three days after the conference and was succeeded by the triumvirate of Stalin, Grigory Zinoviev and Lev Kamenev. Unwilling to share power, Stalin engineered the Fourteenth and Fifteenth Conferences in 1925 and 1926 to alienate, discredit and then expel his two main rivals on the left, Zinoviev and Kamenev. Once he had achieved this, the way was clear for Stalin to become General Secretary, which happened shortly after the Fifteenth Conference in 1927.[61] Stalin's ties with the rightist Bukharin-Rykov-Tomsky[62] faction, which had been forged at the Fourteenth Conference,[63] were then cut when this faction became the subject of attack around the time of the Sixteenth Conference.

At the Fourteenth Conference, Stalin first marked his official split with the left and then secondly established a temporary alliance with the rightist bloc. In retaliation to Kamenev's, Zinoviev's and Trotsky's criticism of 'Socialism in one country' at a Politburo meeting a few months earlier, when they had argued that the relative Soviet technological and economic backwardness in comparison with surrounding capitalist countries made it impossible in practice to realise socialism in the Soviet Union unless surrounding countries followed suit,[64] Stalin had the Fourteenth Conference approve his own interpretation of the policy, which was then enshrined as official party doctrine.[65] Having weakened his opponents, he was then able to crush them publicly, and with the party's endorsement at the Fifteenth Conference. During the month leading up to the Fifteenth Conference, the opposition were coerced into signing confessions, which admitted that they were guilty of factional activity. Just three days before the conference, the CC expelled Kamenev and Trotsky from the Politburo, and Zinoviev from his Chairmanship of the Comintern Executive Committee.[66] These measures were endorsed by the party at the Fifteenth Conference, without granting the opposition an opportunity to respond.

At the Fourteenth Conference, a temporary alliance with the Rightist bloc was forged to justify the introduction of emergency measures supported by the Right, which would appease the discontented peasants. Stalin's offensive against the kulaks had targeted middle-class peasants as well as kulaks and they, too, had joined the uprising. In the summer of 1924, Stalin had been forced to make some concessions to the peasants, to put an end to the unrest.[67] At the conference, the party reduced taxes on the peasants' income,[68] and legalised their hiring labour and leasing land. Since these policies could have been interpreted as further endorsement of Menshevik policy, Stalin disassociated himself from them and invited Rykov and Bukharin to present them instead. The unfortunate way that Bukharin enthusiastically packaged the policy, with the slogan to the peasants of 'enrich yourselves', served as useful ammunition for Stalin when he engineered Bukharin's demise just a couple of months after the Sixteenth Conference.[69]

The main purpose of the Sixteenth Conference was to register party approval of the first Five Year Plan (FYP).[70] More importantly for Stalin, however, at the conference he established his primacy within the leadership, by staging the defeat of his rivals Bukharin and Tomsky to prevent their resurgence. The Sixteenth Conference endorsed Stalin's uncompromising position towards the rightist Bukharin-Rykov-Tomsky opposition, which subsequently enabled him to oust his main rivals.[71]

At the Seventeenth Conference, in 1932, having 'successfully' completed the first FYP ahead of schedule, the rightist faction was denounced and Bukharin was forced to publicly renounce his views.[72] The second FYP, which proposed more ambitious goals than the first, was endorsed by the conference.[73]

Purging the bureaucracy at the Eighteenth Conference, 1941

The next conference was held nearly ten years later. The long time lapse between these conferences and the factor of less frequent congresses and CC meetings have been explained as symptomatic of Stalin minimising the role of others in the decision-making process.[74] Another reason which could explain the sudden reduction in the frequency of conferences is that by 1932, Stalin no longer had rivals in the leadership that could be eliminated by means of a conference. Those that continued to pose a threat to him, either as perceived personal enemies or 'enemies of the state', required court trials instead, which Stalin staged in the thousands during the 1930s, resulting in masses of executions.

By 1938, party control over the state had been secured and the Soviet state ministries had been institutionalised. The ministries themselves by this time wielded very significant power over state resources, such that the Soviet Union has been described as a 'ministerial regime'.[75] It was precisely at this point that the conference's role was modified in two significant ways. Firstly, it was changed into a vehicle for purging the CC, should the need arise. As pointed out earlier on page 55, provisions in the Party Rules regarding the conference were first introduced at the Eighteenth Congress in 1939. The new rules provided that 'those particular members of the CC that fail to fulfil their duties' could be replaced,[76] which suggests that Stalin may already have had some targets in mind. The conference had not made CC personnel changes since the Seventh Conference, under Lenin's leadership, in 1917. This could be explained by the fact that Lenin had only vested such congressional powers in the conference under those conditions when a congress could not be convened. Whatever his reason for formalising this power, Stalin made use of it at the Eighteenth Conference of 1941.[77]

Secondly, 'Ministerial socialism'[78] had created an entirely new balance of power. Timothy Dunmore has argued that by 1939 even Stalin's decisions had to be in line with the industrial ministries' interests to ensure that they would be implemented.[79] In part, the aim of the Eighteenth Conference in 1941 was to address this non-implementation, and to pressure representatives from the ministries to comply with existing laws and policies..Thus Stalin used the conference to combat ministerial power that challenged his authority. As an emergency measure to improve productivity, a new code of work discipline had been enacted in June 1940, which increased daily hours of work from seven, as enshrined in the constitution, to eight hours. At the conference, the party organisation representatives were instructed to play their part in ensuring that this law be enforced.[80]

Discussions at the conference focused on inefficiencies arising from the duplication of administration in both state and party, which had resulted from poor communication between the two. The local party organisations had been leaving supervision of the industrial enterprises to the industrial commissariats, mistakenly believing it to be their responsibility.[81] At the conference, both state and party organisations were thus criticised for mismanaging the economy and provisions were made to convert industry to war production.[82]

The policy choice of the Nineteenth Conference, 1988

As will be explained in the next chapter, Gorbachev made use of the conference much as Lenin and Stalin had, to confirm his authority, to stage a defeat of the left and right, as well as to gain control of the state bureaucracy. Gorbachev had justified his decision to convene the Nineteenth Party Conference on the ground that he was reviving the 'democratic Leninist tradition' of the early conferences between 1905 and 1912. At these meetings Lenin had ostensibly engaged the Menshevik opposition in debate with the Bolsheviks. However, as this chapter has shown, whenever there was a danger that this opposition might gain the advantage, Lenin disabled them, and the number of delegates representing this opposition systematically declined at conferences. Thus the conference was never a 'democratic forum for debate' and was configured in such a way as to rubber-stamp Lenin's policies.

Gorbachev's decision, therefore, to revive the institution may be better understood with reference to the institutionalist literature, which claims that at 'critical junctures' dormant institutions once again become salient, 'with implications for political outcomes'.[83] New political actors make use of latent institutions to further their own (new) goals. It would appear, given the time lapse of some forty years between the Eighteenth and Nineteenth Party Conferences, that it was in this spirit Gorbachev hoped to further *perestroika*. Claiming the old 'democratic Leninist tradition' of debate with the opposition, allying himself and his supporters with the Bukharinist tradition (which, ironically, had been publicly crushed at the conferences of the 1920s), Gorbachev used the conference to mobilise support for *perestroika*, and by association tar the CC hardline opposition with the same brush as the Stalinists of the 1920s and 1930s. With a time lapse of more than forty years, very few, if any, delegates would have been present at both conferences. However, it is interesting to note that in preparation for the Nineteenth Conference in 1988, the minutes of the Eighteenth Conference were often consulted as a guide, especially in the decision-making with regard to organisational and procedural questions.[84] We can conclude, therefore, that the Stalinist Eighteenth Conference would have shaped expectations of outcome in the run-up to the conference.

Conclusion

As has been described, Stalin further developed the conference as a forum to discredit opposition, strengthen his own power base and push through policies that would have been less likely to receive endorsement at a congress. The conference was vested with the powers of an emergency congress under both Lenin and Stalin at the Sixth, Seventh and Eighteenth Conferences, at which an unrepresentative delegation acted on behalf of the entire party. The brief discussion in this chapter has shown that the conference was a very powerful tool for the General Secretary. No doubt the party was aware that at a conference the General Secretary could pursue his own agenda unimpeded by the wider party membership. For this reason, perhaps, the provision to convene a conference was removed from the Party Rules at the next (Nineteenth) congress in 1952. When these provisions were reintroduced more than a decade later (as noted in Chapter 1) the conference's powers were significantly curtailed. Yet, at the Nineteenth Party Conference in 1988, once again, the Party Rules were amended to increase the powers of the conference, making provision for personnel changes in CPSU bodies at all levels. As Chapter 3 will discuss, Gorbachev tried to convene a second conference two years later, during his 'turn to the Right', but was unable to mobilise the necessary support for this within the CC.

Like Stalin, Gorbachev made use of the conference in 1988 to rein in powerful state institutions and in the earlier tradition of the conference to defeat his opponents publicly. There is certainly some irony to Gorbachev's choice of a Stalinist-era institution (and one which Stalin had shaped a good deal more than Lenin had) to pursue the radical agenda of destalinisation and party modernisation, to 'make *perestroika* irreversible'. Gorbachev sought to endorse reforms at the conference that would weaken the existing party apparatus to allow the growth of an alternative institutional base, which would allow him to pursue his agenda and safeguard against his own removal.

Gorbachev's position within the party and his power over the state was particularly unassailable around the time of the Nineteenth Party Conference and the months that followed it.[85] As the next chapter will illustrate, Gorbachev's strong performance at the Nineteenth Party Conference was in large part thanks to his choice of institution. The conference provided him with the necessary levers to stage a defeat of his opponents on left and right, which served as a warning to other potential rivals. As has been emphasised, it would be ridiculous to impute to Gorbachev a Stalinist agenda whereby political purges were often followed up with executions. Instead, this research identifies an instance where Gorbachev borrowed an old institution with a set of 'informal constraints' that afforded him the greatest advantage in achieving his desired goals.

Notes

1   Interview with Aleksandr Yakovlev, Moscow, 31 October 2002.

2   A. A. Solov´ev, 'Obshchepartiïnye konferentsii v zhizni i deiatel´nosti KPSS', *Voprosy Istorii KPSS* 6 (1988), p. 79.

3   D. Mann, *Paradoxes of Soviet Reform: the Nineteenth Communist Party Conference* (Washington DC: Center for Strategic and International Studies, 1988), p. 13.

4   A. G. Egorov and K. M. Bogoliubov, *Kommunisticheskaia partiia Sovetskogo Soiuza v rezoliutsiiakh i resheniiakh s˝ezdov, konferentsii i plenumov TSK, 1898–1988* (Moskva: Izd-vo polit. lit-ry, 9-oe izd, 1983–89), vol. 1, p. 134.

5   From the party rules approved at the Eighteenth Congress, 1939, see Egorov and Bogoliubov, *KPSS v rezoliutsiiakh i resheniiakh*, vol. 7, p. 100–1, §37–§39.

6   See current chapter, p. 79; Chapter 3, p. 98.

7   S. S. Khizhniakov and O. V. Khlevniuk, *XVIII Partkonferentsiia: vremia, problemy, resheniia* (Moskva: Izd-vo polit. lit-ry, 1990), p. 100.

8   From the party rules approved at the Twenty-third Congress, 1966; see Egorov and Bogoliubov, *KPSS v rezoliutsiiakh i resheniiakh*, vol. 11, p. 29.

9   See Chapter 1, p. 43.

10   Khizhniakov and Khlevniuk, *XVIII Partkonferentsiia*, p. 100.

11   Solov´ev, 'Obshchepartiïnye konferentsii v zhizni i deiatel´nosti KPSS'.

12   Egorov and Bogoliubov, *KPSS v rezoliutsiiakh i resheniiakh*, vol. 7, p. 100, §37.

13   E. H. Carr, *The Interregnum, 1923–1924* (London: Macmillan, 1954), pp. 332–3.

14 Carr, *The Interregnum*, p. 298.

15 L. Trotsky, *Novyĭ kurs* (Moskva: Izd-vo Krasnaia Nov', 1924), pp. 48–9.

16 D. Priestland, 'Soviet Democracy, 1917–1991', *European History Quarterly*, 32:1 (2002) pp. 111–30.

17 A. Prokhorov (ed.), *Bol'shaia sovetskaia ėntsiklopediia* (Moskva: Sovetskaia ėntsiklopediia, 3-oe izd., 1969–81), vol. 19, p. 340.

18 L. Trotsky, *Stalin: an Appraisal of the Man and his Influence* (London: Hollis and Carter, 1947), p. 69.

19 L. Schapiro, *The Communist Party of the Soviet Union* (London: Methuen, 1970), p. 73.

20 Trotsky, *Stalin*, p. 69.

21 Egorov and Bogoliubov, *KPSS v rezoliutsiiakh i resheniiakh*, vol. 1, p. 162.

22 *Ibid.*, p. 231.

23 *Ibid.*

24 Trotsky, *Stalin*, p. 72.

25 Egorov and Bogoliubov, *KPSS v rezoliutsiiakh i resheniiakh*, vol. 1, pp. 206–7. Fourth Congress § 8.

26 *Ibid.*, pp. 263–4.

27 *Ibid.*, pp. 290, 299.

28 E. H. Carr, *The Bolshevik Revolution, 1917–1923* (London: Macmillan, 1950–53), vol. 1, p. 50.

29 Egorov and Bogoliubov, *KPSS v rezoliutsiiakh i resheniiakh*, vol. 1, p. 311.

30 IU. A. Amiantovyĭ and Z. N. Tikhonova, 'Protokoly VI (prazhskoĭ) konferentsii RSDWP', *Voprosy Istorii KPSS* 5 (1988), p. 39.

31 *Ibid.*, pp. 39–56.

32 Carr, *The Bolshevik Revolution*, vol. 1, pp. 63–4.

33 Egorov and Bogoliubov, *KPSS v rezoliutsiiakh i resheniiakh*, vol. 1, pp. 382–3; Solov´ev, 'Obshchepartiĭnye konferentsii v zhizni i deiatel´nosti KPSS', p. 82.

34 Egorov and Bogoliubov, *KPSS v rezoliutsiiakh i resheniiakh*, vol. 1, pp. 382–3.

35 *Ibid.*, p. 386.

36 *Ibid.*

37 See Chapter 1, p. 42.

38 Schapiro, *The Communist Party of the Soviet Union*, p. 128.

39 Carr, *The Bolshevik Revolution*, vol. 1, pp. 63–4.

40 *Ibid.*, pp. 83–4.

41 R. Service, *A History of Twentieth-Century Russia* (London: Penguin, 1997), p. 48.

42 Egorov and Bogoliubov, *KPSS v rezoliutsiiakh i resheniiakh*, vol. 1, p. 492.

43 B. Souvarine, *Stalin: A Critical Survey of Bolshevism* (New York NY: Arno Press, 1972), p. 154.

44 M. Pavlov, *Izmeneniia v Ustave VKP(B): istoricheskoe razvitie ustava partii* (Leningrad: Lenizdat, 1940), p. 41.

45 Prokhorov (ed.), *Bol'shaia sovetskaia ėntsiklopediia*, vol. 27, pp. 124–6.

46   Egorov and Bogoliubov, *KPSS v rezoliutsiiakh i resheniiakh*, vol. 2, p. 196.

47   Schapiro, *The Communist Party of the Soviet Union*, p. 195.

48   *Ibid.*, p. 219.

49   Egorov and Bogoliubov, *KPSS v rezoliutsiiakh i resheniiakh*, vol. 2, p. 296;
      Prokhorov (ed.), *Bol'shaia sovetskaia ėntsiklopediia*, vol. 27, pp. 124–6.

50   R. Sakwa, *Gorbachev and his Reforms, 1985–1990* (New York NY: Philip
      Allan, 1990), pp. 30–1.

51   J. Hough and M. Fainsod, *How the Soviet Union is Governed*, p. 102.

52   *Ibid.*, p. 101.

53   Egorov and Bogoliubov, *KPSS v rezoliutsiiakh i resheniiakh*, vol. 2, p. 419.

54   Schapiro, *The Communist Party of the Soviet Union*, pp. 207–9.

55   *Ibid.*, pp. 219–20.

56   Schapiro, *The Communist Party of the Soviet Union*, pp. 219–20.

57   Egorov and Bogoliubov, *KPSS v rezoliutsiiakh i resheniiakh*, vol. 2, p. 456.

58   *Ibid.*, p. 583.

59   Schapiro, *The Communist Party of the Soviet Union*, p. 285.

60   Egorov and Bogoliubov, *KPSS v rezoliutsiiakh i resheniiakh*, vol. 3, p. 145.

61   A. Brown (ed.), *The Soviet Union: A Biographical Dictionary* (London:
      Weidenfeld and Nicolson, 1990), p. 366.

62   Nikolai Bukharin, Aleksei Rykov and Mikhai Tomsky were all members
      of the Politburo and Presidium by 1924. Rykov and Tomsky had been
      elected in 1922, Bukharin in 1924.

63   Trotsky, *Stalin*, p. 470.

64   D. Volkogonov, *Stalin: Triumph and Tragedy* (London: Phoenix Press,
      2000), pp. 109–10.

65   G. Hosking, *A History of the Soviet Union* (London: Fontana, 1990), pp.
      136–7.

66   Trotsky, *Stalin*, p. 471.

67   A. Ulam, *Stalin: the Man and his Era* (London: Tauris, 1989), p. 249.

68   E. H. Carr, *Foundations of a planned economy, 1926–1929* (London:
      Macmillan, 1969–78), p. 752.

69   Ulam, *Stalin*, p. 250.

70   Carr, *Foundations of a planned economy*, p. 517.

71   Schapiro, *The Communist Party of the Soviet Union*, p. 379.

72   *Ibid.*, p. 395.

73   Ulam, *Stalin*, p. 323.

74   Volkogonov, *Stalin*, p. 217.

75   S. Whitefield, *Industrial Power and the Soviet State* (Oxford: Oxford
      University Press, 1993), p. 21 citing Dunmore.

76   Egorov and Bogoliubov, *KPSS v Rezoliutsiiakh i Resheniiakh*, vol. 7, p.
      101.

77   Khizhniakov and Khlevniuk, *XVIII Partkonferentsiia*, pp. 34–6.

78   Whitefield, *Industrial Power and the Soviet State*, p. 20.

79   *Ibid.*, pp. 24–5.

80   Schapiro, *The Communist Party of the Soviet Union*, pp. 494–5.

81   *Ibid.*, p. 495.

82   Volkogonov, *Stalin*, p. 374.

83   S. Steinmo, K. Thelen and F. Longstreth (eds), *Structuring Politics: Historical Institutionalism in Comparative Analysis* (Cambridge: Cambridge University Press, 1992), pp. 16–18.

84   Khizhniakov and Khlevniuk, *XVIII Partkonferentsiia*, pp. 104–5.

85   A. Brown, *The Gorbachev factor* (Oxford: Oxford University Press, 1996), p. 177.

3

The rhetoric of reform or a consolidation of power? Gorbachev's defeat of left and right at the Nineteenth CPSU Conference, June 1988

Introduction

Aware of increasing factionalism in the party and the CPSU's growing estrangement from society, Gorbachev sought to stage a victory for *perestroika* at the Nineteenth CPSU Conference. This chapter analyses how he used the conference to stage a defeat of opponents to *perestroika*, on both left and right, and illustrates how the constitutional reforms adopted at the conference were directed towards breaking the hardliners' grip on the party and the bureaucracy's power over both party and state. In conclusion, Gorbachev's unsuccessful attempt to reconvene the CPSU conference in 1991 further demonstrates how his choice of institution signalled a particular policy choice, aimed at purging opponents and consolidating the General Secretary's position. Opposition to this proposal indicated Gorbachev's dwindling support, but moreover suggests others' awareness that, as an institution, the conference favoured the General Secretary's preferred outcome.

CSPU modernisation to maintain the existing regime

During the months preceding the conference, Gorbachev purged the party leadership of those who opposed *perestroika*. The purpose of his reforms was to secure the survival of the existing regime and maintain the *status quo* by modernising the CPSU. Gorbachev had adopted the agenda of the Hungarian and Czechoslovak reform communists of the 1950s and

1960s, which sought to democratise inner party life and re-engage society in the political sphere.[1] As subsequent chapters will show, Gorbachev's new policy had significant implications for the fraternal regimes of Central and Eastern Europe that had replaced the reformist leaderships and normalised politics after liberalisation threatened the party's leading role in these states. Gorbachev's liberalisation strategy did not, however, entail relinquishing the leading role of the party, nor did he encourage this of the fraternal regimes. Gorbachev took a much stronger line, however, with respect to the constituent republics of the Soviet Union, as apparent from the case of 1989 when he strongly advised the Lithuanian Communist Party leader, Algirdas Brazauskas, against relinquishing this leading role. Inevitably, though, Gorbachev's new approach challenged preceding doctrine to some extent, and therefore mobilised critics, in particular, among the old-timers in the leadership. At the same time, Gorbachev needed to demonstrate to the party, society and the West that his liberalisation policy was genuine. The ouster of high-profile old-timers in the party was proof of this wholesale rejection of previous regimes, and in terms of Gorbachev's domestic policy was intended to attract new party members, as by this time party membership (particularly among the young) had decreased very sharply.[2] This was particularly reflected in Komsomol membership enrolment numbers, which fell by half between 1984 and 1987.[3]

Gorbachev therefore solicited individuals outside the party to mobilise support for his centrist-reformist group within the Politburo.[4] This was to engage society in CPSU politics, with the aim of nurturing, developing and above all preserving the existing regime rather than promoting the emergence of a multiparty system. Through this liberalisation process, however, Gorbachev equipped intellectuals and more reformist party personnel with the necessary resources to achieve regime change.[5] So although Gorbachev intended the CPSU to retain its monopoly of political control, the party simply very soon lost its capacity to do so.[6] The ensuing 'democratisation' of the Soviet Union has therefore been viewed as the unforeseen consequence of this newly enfranchised contingent mobilising in popular support for Gorbachev's opponent, Boris Yeltsin.[7]

This liberalisation strategy, which Gorbachev himself termed *demokratizatsiia*, has been interpreted in various ways by commentators. Although the empirical research in this work indicates that Gorbachev was not inclined towards 'democratisation' *per se*, a brief discussion of how this issue has been contested in the existing literature is helpful at this juncture to gain deeper insight into the boundaries of this liberalisation and why defining it has given rise to some confusion.

Gorbachev's policy of demokratizatsiia

The problem of unravelling Gorbachev's long-term policies for the CPSU, and whether full-scale democratisation really was on his agenda, is complicated by the fact that the system collapsed so quickly and without precedent. Such speed, the relative peaceful nature of collapse, and the fact that reform was initiated from within the leadership, could support the view that this had been intended all along, or there was at least resignation on Gorbachev's part to the possibility that such a situation would evolve. Those that hold to this line of argument generally believe that liberalisers embark on their path in full knowledge of the probable outcome to this liberalisation, and so are reconciled to introducing 'democratisation on the instalment plan'.[8] Gorbachev's policies have accordingly been interpreted, *post facto*, as motivated by a hidden agenda of democratisation which he disguised from his more orthodox colleagues by ostensibly adhering to the party's ideology in his officially stated policies. On these grounds, some claim that Gorbachev was a 'closet democratiser', and that he often modified his speech to avoid upsetting the conservative hardline contingent, but ultimately intended the full-scale democratisation of the Soviet Union. The phenomenon of political actors saying one thing – their 'stated' policy position – to placate opponents or supporters and yet holding fast to a different principle that they maintain as their 'ideal' policy is, of course, commonplace.[9] Scholars attest that during his time as General Secretary, Gorbachev often hid his 'ideal' policy position, especially during the early years 1985–87, when he began introducing radical policies intended to undermine the power of hardliners. The corollary to this argument, however, goes much further in claiming that as a 'democratiser and would-be democrat', Gorbachev 'had to conceal his intentions', and so used epithets commonly associated with traditional CPSU policy as a smokescreen for his hidden agenda of democrati-sation. Although there is logic to this line of reasoning, we cannot equate Gorbachev's hidden agenda to unseat his oppo-nents with a hidden agenda to democratise, as a number of counterfactuals discount this.

There is little evidence to support the claim that Gorbachev intended full-scale democratisation, even after the CPSU had constitutionally relinquished the party's leading role in 1990. As late as February 1989, Gorbachev maintained that the CPSU should keep its leading role. He publicly dismissed the notion of introducing a multiparty system as 'rubbish', and insisted that those advocating such a course of action were 'demagogues and irresponsible elements'.[10] In other words, more reformist members of his administration had other ideas. Such individuals include, for example, Aleksandr Yakovlev. Moreover, the fact that some individuals in the party may have been more inclined towards this democratising trajectory made it perhaps easier for Gorbachev to align himself with these individuals *post facto* and claim that this had also been his intention, at least from the late 1980s.

After 1990, when Article Six (regarding the leading role of the party) was removed from the Constitution, which served to legalise other political parties, the CPSU continued to persecute independent parties and favoured those groups that retained close ties with the authorities, such as Vladimir Zhirinovsky's ultra-nationalist Liberal Democratic Party of Russia.[11] We could conclude from this that Gorbachev intended the CPSU to retain its supremacy or 'leading role' by patronising only those parties that remained tied in with the existing regime, perhaps in the mould of the pre-1989 'multiparty' regimes of, for example, Bulgaria, the GDR or Poland.

This is further borne out by the fact that once these different parties began to call for full-scale regime change or a return to the *status quo ante* in April 1991, Gorbachev tried to mobilise the party leadership (the CPSU Central Committee and Central Control Commission (CCC)) against the forces on left and right, which threatened to dissolve the existing constitutional order. As material on page 99 suggests, his use of language suggests he wanted the party to introduce emergency measures, which would secure law and order. Although he made few explicit proposals, he appears to have been testing the waters with his colleagues to find out what support he could muster, and how far they would go, in retaining the *status quo* of the regime and pursuing *perestroika*. This makes sense in the context of what some of Gorbachev's closest advisers stated at interview: that Gorbachev was committed to reforming and liberalising the one-party system but that he never intended to relinquish the party's leading role.[12] Therefore, Gorbachev's motivation to liberalise party structures is perhaps best explained by his short-term strategy, which was to consolidate his own power, and defeat his opponents,[13] thereby firmly and publicly positioning the party on his centrist-reformist path of *perestroika*.

This interpretation is corroborated by the Hungarian case study in Chapter 5. As well as members of the CPSU, high-ranking members of the HSWP concurred that Gorbachev had no plans to relinquish the leading role of the CPSU[14] and, as is detailed in Chapter 5, HSWP archival resources also suggest that Gorbachev intended at the conference to consolidate the party's power and organise a show of loyalty for the socialist fraternity's cause. Similarly, textual analysis of the conference minutes suggests that Gorbachev aimed to consolidate the party's power by publicly denouncing opponents of *perestroika* on left and right. The perceived 'opposition', including those that tainted the new administration simply from having been in post during a more repressive era, was neutralised at the conference by resolutions which endorsed the transfer of power to state institutions from those areas of the party where the greatest 'opposition' to *perestroika* was concentrated.[15] Thus, via his reforms, Gorbachev sought to consolidate the power of the party at the Nineteenth CPSU Conference.[16]

The vital need to attract new blood into the party is further reflected in delegates' speeches at the CPSU, HSWP and LCY conferences, which in the main express concern at the decline in party membership and growing discontent in society as a result of economic conditions. These issues also dominated discussions at CC and Politburo meetings in the months preceding these conferences, as is apparent in CPSU, HSWP and PUWP archival documents and in the LCY press, as detailed in the current chapter and in Chapters 5, 6 and 7. In the case of Poland, similar concerns were expressed, and in March 1988 the PUWP convened a seminar of senior party academics to discuss how to modernise the system to re-engage society. At this meeting speakers explained the need to reform the socialist model as a whole, and referred to similar problems experienced in other socialist states,[17] in particular Yugoslavia, where the party no longer exerted any influence over society.[18] In all cases, as subsequent chapters will illustrate, there was an overriding message that the party consolidate its power in the wake of disillusionment among party and non-party members alike.

Policies were therefore shaped to provide broad appeal to society, in order to regenerate interest and faith in the party. The most powerful of these was *'glasnost'*, which required all officials to own up publicly to wrongs they had committed, and was employed by the press to expose corruption by naming and shaming 'anti-*perestroishchiki'*. To some extent the term was used ambiguously to denote transparency, and to encourage more open and frank exchange and deeper discussion of issues. In terms of reappraising history, *glasnost* was a vehicle for the destalinisation process in the regime, and sought to portray history truthfully, or at least further reconcile official accounts of the past with the public's common perception of these events. Initially, this reappraisal met with some resistance from hardliners, and in March 1988 a little-known scientist, Nina Andreeva, sent a letter to the newspaper *Sovetskaia Rossiia*, which was published. The letter received a good deal of attention, as it refuted recent press publications that had criticised Stalin's policies, interpreted the purges of the 1930s and 1940s as 'repression', and claimed that all those serving in the government at that time should be accountable for these crimes. Although Andreeva herself became prominent as the founder of the Bolshevik platform of the CPSU in 1991, the letter she published which became a cause célèbre was interpreted by Gorbachev and his aides as engineered by hardliners in the central administration, led by Yegor Ligachev.[19]

Gorbachev used this event to help mobilise support for *perestroika* in the run-up to the conference, and construed it as an onslaught against his policy of freedom of speech and truthful reportage, whereas the main thrust of the letter appears rather to have been directed towards protecting old-timers in the party who had served under Stalin. The fact that those who had served under previous more repressive regimes should be removed from office was an issue raised a few times at the conference, and although interpreted as evidence of spontaneous *glasnost*, certain evidence suggests otherwise, as will be touched on later.

Glasnost at the conference

As the first televised and broadly publicised CPSU meeting, the Nineteenth CPSU Conference was designed to reflect the transparency of *glasnost*. Gorbachev himself encouraged delegates at the meeting 'to speak freely', which may have created a more open atmosphere. Delegates interviewed, however, did not consider themselves in a position to speak out freely and critically about the party, were not permitted to do so, or did not feel that delegates' views were taken into account during the working sessions.[20] One said that the participation of delegates was a 'formality' and that the meeting was held according to the usual protocol whereby the rank and file were generally expected to approve all motions proposed.[21]

This begs the question whether delegates would, in any event, have chosen to express strong alternative views. Officially, of course, there were no factions in the party in 1988, as all factions had been outlawed at the Tenth Congress in March 1921. In theory, therefore, the party was a monolithic entity and to a large extent was still perceived to operate as such by delegates that attended the conference.[22] However, Gorbachev himself was concerned at the existence of alternative 'left' and 'right' views among the leadership in opposition to his centrist position.[23] Despite Gorbachev's concern, however, there was little evidence of these 'factions' at the Nineteenth CPSU Conference. The vast majority of those 'elected' to the conference as delegates were 'regulars', as the *nomenklatura* system of selection prevailed, such that almost two-thirds of delegates were party officials.[24] This suggests that these individuals could have been relied upon to act supportively of the leadership at the event, and certainly, speakers' views rarely diverged from the centrist policies expressed in Gorbachev's speech and summarised in conference resolutions. The pattern which emerges from the data recorded in the conference minutes shows unanimous and passionate commitment to *perestroika*, and that the small incidence of other views expressed had been debated and resoundingly defeated at the conference. Although some exchanges may have been spontaneous, the current chapter identifies evidence of scripting and organisation, which appears to have been directed to maximise dramatic effect of the endorsement of *perestroika* by the conference delegates.

At those points when divergent views were expressed, other delegates reacted strongly to condemn these opinions which, as the next sections demonstrate, created the effect of a resounding defeat of the left and right.

Defeating the 'left': Abalkin and Yeltsin

Practically the only two delegates[25] who voiced opinions at the conference, as published in the conference minutes, which could be perceived as 'left' of the policies of *perestroika* were Leonid Abalkin, the Director of the Institute of Economics of the USSR Academy of Sciences, and Boris Yeltsin, a minister of state for Construction. At interview, Abalkin stated that he had not allied himself with Yeltsin in particular and so they did not formally constitute a united front against Gorbachev. Because, however, these speakers voiced opinions which could be interpreted as 'left' of Gorbachev, they have been categorised as such for the purpose of this discussion. Yeltsin had been suspended from his high-ranking post as Chairman of the Moscow Party Organisation in 1987 following his confrontation with Yegor Ligachev at the October 1987 plenary session of the CC. Abalkin and Yeltsin both questioned whether democratisation could be achieved within the one-party system, and stated that the economic reforms of *perestroika* had made little impact, and were insufficient to bring about the needed transformation of the economy. Moreover, they disagreed with Gorbachev's proposal to combine party and state posts. They were systematically singled out by other delegates for criticism on these issues.

Abalkin's defeat

Abalkin, who spoke during the second session of the conference, first raised the issue of whether democratisation was possible within the bounds of the one-party system. He stated that there was a crisis of confidence in the CPSU and queried whether the proposed quasi-market reforms could be effectively implemented within the constraints of the existing system. He questioned whether the *status quo* could be maintained through the modernisation of the party (as a means to winning back the masses). Abalkin suggested that this was the issue people were expecting the conference to resolve, as he said in his speech:

> Are we in a position to provide a democratic organisation of social life if we retain the soviet [way of] organising life and the one-party system? Yes or no? And if yes, then how?[26]

In response to Abalkin's remark, five delegates, including Gorbachev, responded that democratisation was certainly possible within the one-party system. Most of these were Gorbachev loyalists, and were promoted in the months following the conference. The first of these was Absamat Masaliev, member of the CPSU CC, and First Secretary of the Kirghiz Communist Party, in the second session shortly after Abalkin. Masaliev was promoted to the Politburo in 1990, which suggests that he was perceived as 'pro-*perestroika*'. In his speech he did not say in what way he disagreed with Abalkin's argument, which could suggest that the priority was first and foremost to register disapproval of Abalkin rather than provide a counter-argument to his views. By discrediting Abalkin as an individual, the need to actually engage with his argument was conveniently dispensed with:

> First of all about the role of the party in society; I cannot, there is no time to argue with comrade Abalkin. He just spoke and put the question whether it is possible to provide democracy within a one-party system. Yes or no? I think, and this is my own personal opinion, that experience shows that if we realise those ideas and tasks, which were put forward by comrade Gorbachev... then we shall achieve this. [Applause][27]

In the third session, Boris Kachura, the First Secretary of the Ukrainian CC and CPSU CC member, stated that the leading role of the party should be retained by persuasion,[28] but that the CPSU would never relinquish this leading role:

> The party has no intention, nor ever will, of relinquishing to anyone else the role of political vanguard – that is axiomatic. At the same time it is clear that we cannot manage [things] by old methods. Therefore we support the novel and deeply creative approach of the CPSU Politburo directed towards solving this and other burning issues. Today as at all other great turning points in history, monolithic unity in the ranks of the party is essential. The delegates of the Ukrainian party organisation fully support the political line of the CPSU CC, its Politburo, and the position

and tasks laid down in comrade Gorbachev's report, which are aimed at deepening *perestroika*.[29]

The Director of the Institute of World Economics and International Relations of the USSR Academy of Sciences, Evgenii Primakov, who was promoted to the Politburo in 1989 and to a post in Gorbachev's Presidential Council, also defended *perestroika*. He again firmly stated that political pluralism in the form of a multiparty system would be detrimental because this would result in undesirable political views being legalised and given a platform:

> The crux of the matter is not just the fact that the one-party system is a historic feature of our state. The important thing... is the obvious fact that any alternative [to the one-party system] under the current historic conditions would result in irreversible harm to *perestroika* within the framework of socialism. And for us today this is the most important criterion. ... a multiparty system could be abused by nationalistic and dogmatic elements of all persuasions. And this would be a terrible blow to *perestroika*.[30]

Two speakers explained that the role of opposition would be assumed by the press, within the existing one-party state. During his speech in the third session, Mikhail Ul'ianov, Chairman of the RSFSR board of theatrical actors of the USSR, who was elected to the newly established CoPD in 1989, raised the issue of the role of the press. The exchange between Ul'ianov and Gorbachev concerning this, and the role of the press, appears somewhat rehearsed, and certainly puts Gorbachev in a good light. They reminisced over the Nina Andreeva letter, and then Ul'ianov asked whether he might pose a question to Gorbachev, and when invited to, said, 'Mikhail Sergeevich, are you in favour of silencing the press, or on the contrary, as I have understood, in favour of supporting the press even when they make a mistake? In this struggle, mistakes could be made.'[31] Gorbachev responded in the affirmative and said that the role of political opposition was to be assumed by the press, which even within the bounds of a one-party system would create a better model of democracy than that of any existing 'bourgeois democracy':

> Here there must be complete clarity. If someone is subjected to criticism in the press, but this expression is the truth, then digest it, and go to people, explain to them how they've gone wrong, and think about how to resolve the situation. Then our party will begin

to thrive. Then under a one-party system we will have secured a democracy never even dreamt of in any bourgeois democracy, which wishes to present itself as a model of democracy.[32]

Similarly in the eighth session, during the speech of Viktor Afanas'ev, member of the CC and the chief editor of *Pravda*, Gorbachev interceded about the new-found role of the press in publishing criticism from any recalcitrant elements in the CPSU about *perestroika*, and how this had made the press itself unpopular. When asked by Gorbachev whether this critique of the press had been published, Afanas'ev said it had, to which Gorbachev responded: 'Now there is no area left that is shielded from criticism.'[33] Gorbachev's quip may have been intended to remind Afanas'ev that he needed to support *perestroika* more actively, which his newspaper, *Pravda*, had been slow to do. Afanas'ev then registered his agreement with Gorbachev's position that there was no need for a political opposition to the party, as no class or social bases for such opposition parties existed. He confirmed, instead, that the press would provide the necessary criticism to introduce an element of competition into the party.[34]

Aside from querying the one-party system, Abalkin was the only one to claim that the economic situation was in reality worse than had been publicised, suggesting the country was in economic crisis, and he stated that CPSU economic policy would not bring the country out of stagnation in three years, as officially forecast. When asked at interview whether he had been requested to submit his speech in advance for approval, he said that he had not, and that he had not shown his speech to anyone before he delivered it, as he expected his comments would not be welcomed at the conference. He did concede, however, that his colleagues were familiar with his views and that he had consulted with them in preparing his account of the economic situation, so we may infer that some would have known what he was likely to say in his conference speech, and that this would be critical of *perestroika*.[35] Afterwards, measures were taken to ensure that Abalkin's unorthodox economic appraisal was edited before publication in the conference minutes. Abalkin claimed that he was called into the secretariat at the end of the conference to edit the economic indicators in his speech under the supervision of other specialists,[36] a step which could be interpreted as censorship of Abalkin's expert appraisal.

Other economists, apart from Abalkin, were also criticised by fellow delegates. This would, arguably, have deflected responsibility for the failures of *perestroika* from the Politburo to the economists. An enterprise director attacked the President of the USSR Academy of Sciences, Gurii Marchuk, for failing to suggest how *perestroika* could be implemented:

> Comrades! We need to apply science to the notion of self-financing. I attentively listened here to Gurii Ivanovich [Marchuk]. He is a man for whom I have a great respect. I expected bold suggestions from him. I heard none. That is a shame, Gurii Ivanovich. [Applause][37]

Similarly, Valentin Mesiats, a long-standing member of the CC and First Secretary of the Moscow regional committee of the CPSU, berated the academician economists present at the conference for their failure to suggest how *perestroika* could be better implemented in practice:

> Our academician economists could have said a few weighty words which would equip the practical workers with a scientifically based way of solving [their] new economic and social tasks, which would, as they say, harness them together with the whole country in their practical implementation. It is precisely this that we, as delegates, expected from the speeches here of the country's leading scientists: our esteemed comrades Arbatov, Abalkin and yes, from you, Gurii Ivanovich Marchuk.[38]

Throughout the rest of the conference, after Abalkin's speech, other speakers consistently expressed disagreement with Abalkin's economic forecast and his criticism of *perestroika*. Speakers registered little, if any, approval of Abalkin's comments. The following explanation for this may be advanced. Abalkin's appraisal of the economic situation was at odds with how Gorbachev himself had construed the situation in his own speech. Therefore, as well as challenging Gorbachev's policies, this could have been perceived as a personal challenge to Gorbachev's authority. Georgii Arbatov, the Director of the USA and Canada Institute in Moscow, stated that although he had a high regard for Abalkin, he had nonetheless criticised Abalkin at the conference as a mark of respect for Gorbachev.[39]

Denunciation of Abalkin occurred systematically in each but the last of the conference sessions.[40] Evgenii Chazov, who had been promoted to the post of Minister for Health the previous year in 1987 and who was a cardiologist by profession, was quick to dismiss Abalkin's economic appraisal for being too theoretical. Chazov claimed that economic policy had been correctly pursued in accordance with reality ('real opportunities') as opposed to conducting economic policy according to 'theory' as proposed by Abalkin. Chazov also challenged Abalkin's suggestion of decentralising the economy to local authorities.[41]

During the third session, Vladimir Kalashnikov, CC member and first secretary of the Volgograd Party Committee and later elected to the CoPD in 1989 (until he retired in 1990), registered his disapproval of Abalkin's criticism: 'We should not just talk about difficulties and shortcomings, as was expressed in comrade Abalkin's speech; we need positive changes, a persistent, active approach.'[42] After two subsequent speeches, Georgii Arbatov also distanced himself from Abalkin's views by disagreeing with Abalkin's gloomy forecast of the economy on the basis of growth figures.[43] Kachura then described Abalkin's criticism as unconstructive and divisive:

> Yesterday... Leonid Ivanovich Abalkin spoke. I doubt it is possible to agree with all the views he expressed. I would just like to emphasise that for the lack of faith expressed by the workers in *perestroika* full and equal responsibility should be borne also by the academician economists. We need to fight for *perestroika*'s success; we all need to fight together, especially the academician economists.[44]

During the fourth session, Efrem Sokolov, CC CPSU member and First Secretary of the Belarusian Communist Party, and briefly promoted to member of the Politburo in 1990, claimed on behalf of the Belarusian delegation that, contrary to Abalkin's views, democratisation within the one-party state was indeed possible:

> The delegation of the Communist Party of Belarus... does not share the doubt expressed in Abalkin's... speech concerning the capacity of securing democratisation under conditions of the one-party system and the soviet organisation of society.[45]

The Rector of the Moscow State University and CC member, Anatolii Logunov, was less damning in his appraisal of Abalkin's comments, proposing during the fifth session that an approach of trial and error was needed in the absence of economic theory.[46] During the sixth session the director of a scientific research institute in Moscow upbraided Abalkin for his failure to suggest an alternative plan of action:

> Here I have the right to reproach comrade Abalkin. In his speech there was criticism of actions that have been taken, but we had a right to hear from him a detailed, constructive plan of action, as he is the Director of the Institute of Economics.[47]

The regular occurrence of criticism against Abalkin gives the impression that the majority of delegates were convinced that Gorbachev's economic policy could, as he promised, pull the country out of economic stagnation within three years.

Those who denounced Abalkin were individuals of high standing, whose opinions on the matter would be perceived as expert (although not necessarily in the sphere of economics), and had either risen to prominence during the Gorbachev era and remained prominent or were promoted while Gorbachev remained relatively popular – that is, until 1990. Abalkin recalled that following his speech he was thoroughly isolated at the conference and during the recess following his speech he was shunned by friends and associates.[48] Whether critique of Abalkin was sequenced as such for effect was not definitively proved; however, an analogous case, in the sequencing of Yegor Ligachev's and Boris Yeltsin's speeches, supports this, as the next section discusses.

Yeltsin's defeat

The organisation of Yeltsin's speech and the sequencing of subsequent speakers contributed to how events developed at the conference. Yeltsin was the last to speak in the seventh session and then the final session, the eighth, was dominated by criticism of Yeltsin. Yegor Ligachev has been seen as one of Gorbachev's most significant opponents on the 'right', although he was promoted to the Politburo in 1985 just after Gorbachev became General Secretary. He might, therefore, be better viewed, in a sense, as a 'welcome' conservative force in the Politburo, and one whom Gorbachev was able to stand symbolically at odds with to portray himself as a reformist. Invited to speak during the eighth session, soon after Yeltsin, Ligachev was naturally provoked into denouncing Yeltsin, following their quarrel the previous October, and rounded off his speech with the retort, 'Boris – you are wrong!', concerning his criticism of *perestroika* as insufficiently radical. This dispute between Ligachev and Yeltsin quickly became the focal point of the conference, in a sense drawing fire from Gorbachev, and is how the conference is perhaps best remembered.[49] Two respondents agreed that it was likely Yeltsin's and Ligachev's slots at the conference had been organised purposely in close succession so that they might 'waste' their speeches arguing with one another. Professor Arbatov responded that it was possible Gorbachev and his advisers had an idea what these individuals would say, and so organised their speeches purposely in this order.[50] This view was similarly endorsed by Valerii Vorotnikov, who was a rank-and-file delegate member at the conference, and later served as an independent deputy of the Duma until 2003. Vorotnikov stated that there was clearly forethought about the specific characters of those giving speeches and whose speech should follow whose at the conference, but to participants at the conference at the time, this was not very clear.[51]

The issue concerning Yeltsin related to a CPSU CC session in October 1987, when Yeltsin had publicly attacked Yegor Ligachev and implicitly criticised Gorbachev over the slow pace of reform. Yeltsin dramatically resigned and was consequently removed from the Politburo and from his position as head of the Moscow Party Organisation. During his conference speech, Yeltsin made a plea for the issue of his political rehabilitation to be discussed.[52] Prior to this, two delegates had advocated that the conference discuss the issue of Yeltsin. During the sixth session, a rank-and-file delegate, German Zagaĭnov, asked for clarification on Yeltsin's position, and questioned why details of the matter had not been disclosed and the precise nature of Yeltsin's 'leftist' crazy ideas, so that the conference could determine whether or not they might provide an alternative solution.[53]

During the seventh session, another rank-and-file delegate who was a worker from a car factory, Anatolii Mel'nikov (not to be confused with Vladimir Mel'nikov, later discussed in this chapter) advocated that the issue of Yeltsin be discussed, and although he did not explicitly ask for the conference to consider the matter of Yeltsin's rehabilitation, he suggested that transparency would inform the party to make the right choices at the forthcoming elections. We may infer that both Zagaĭnov and Mel'nikov were supporters of Yeltsin, and that Yeltsin was more likely to receive support from the broader party member-ship at the conference than from within the leadership:

> Ignorance of the essence of an issue engenders absurd conjec-tures... as has happened with comrade Yeltsin. We want to know what's going on with this, not out of simple curiosity, but so that come election time of the CC and Politburo, preference may be given to those comrades whose opinions reflect the views of the majority of communists and all workers.[54]

During this session, five delegates voiced criticism of Yeltsin at some length. One speaker, the Chairman of the CC of the USSR Trade Unions, Stepan Shalaev, who was the second speaker in this session, announced, 'I am not allowed to stop here [to comment] on comrade Yeltsin's speech,'[55] which Gorbachev confirmed with his response: 'That is the rule.'[56] We may wonder whether Shalaev was a known supporter of Yeltsin and was prevented from voicing his opinions for that reason. In any event, although not documented in the minutes of the conference, Gorbachev, perhaps concerned that public opinion at the conference could form a majority in favour of rehabilitating Yeltsin, must have indicated to delegates in the interim that the conference would not be deciding the matter. Although Yeltsin was later reinstated, it is unlikely that Gorbachev would have wished the rehabilitation of one of *perestroika's* vocal critics to occur by popular demand at the conference, as this would inevitably have undermined Gorbachev's authority. Viktor Afanas'ev, perhaps eager to regain some favour with Gorbachev, explained that the matter should not be decided at the conference, because it was simply impractical given the sheer number of delegates present, and the fact that less than ten per cent of delegates present had witnessed Yeltsin's offending speech at the October 1987 CC Plenum. The ensuing 'noise in the hall' following Afanas'ev's statement could suggest that a significant proportion of the delegates disagreed with this decision.[57]

Following Afanas'ev's speech, Vladimir Volkov, the secre-tary of a factory party committee from the town of Sverdlovsk where Yeltsin had been head of the regional party organisa-tion until 1985, came to Yeltsin's defence. Although Volkov refrained from advocating Yeltsin's rehabilitation, he strongly asserted that the failure to publish materials from the October

1987 Plenum, which would have publicised Yeltsin's views, had shown a lack of transparency on the part of the leadership, which had served to weaken its authority.[58] In the context of the new era of *glasnost* in the party, such a claim must have been embarrassing to Gorbachev.

In conclusion, however, the final damning words against Yeltsin were made in the last speech of the conference's last session. Igor Lukin, First Secretary of the Moscow regional workers' committee, recently appointed and relatively young, claimed to have seen through the 'hypnotic quality of Yeltsin's words', and stated that the Moscow regional committee had clashed with Yeltsin's style and methods. Lukin claimed that Yeltsin was driven by pure ambition and that his strategy of securing rehabilitation at the conference by pitting conference delegates against the Presidium would not succeed. Although he had not been present at the October 1987 CC Plenum in question, Lukin vehemently criticised Yeltsin, and authoritatively asserted that it was too soon for his rehabilitation, on the basis of how he had behaved at the conference.[59]

In the same way that Abalkin's views had been widely condemned, Yeltsin's proposal to create a second party was dismissed as 'personal ambition'. Despite the resounding condemnation of Yeltsin among delegate speakers, there is evidence to suggest that this was not necessarily the view of quite a number of delegates at the conference. Moreover, Yeltsin's subsequent popularity, which resulted in his serving two terms as President following the collapse of the CPSU, suggests that a large proportion of the party membership is likely to have supported him. One respondent said that Yeltsin had a great deal of support, but that it was 'in the corridors' rather than at the podium.[60] This suggests that, whether by design or not, delegates who supported Yeltsin were not invited to speak. Gorbachev and his closest advisers were certainly worried that Yeltsin challenged Gorbachev's authority, as evident from a private letter sent by one of Gorbachev's close aides, Anatoly Cherniaev, to Gorbachev. Cherniaev expressed his concern that had Yeltsin been 'pensioned off', this would inevitably have been misconstrued by the West as the 'sunset of *perestroika*'.[61] This suggests that Gorbachev was at least partly motivated to reinstate Yeltsin to maintain his reputation as a reformer in Western circles.

Defeating the 'right': bureaucracy, anti-perestroishchiki and Ligachev

Defeating the bureaucracy by combining party and state posts

Existing scholarship has identified that at the Nineteenth CPSU Conference, Gorbachev sought to curtail the power of the ministries and bureaucracy, as 'the industrial ministries had become the dominant players in the game of Soviet politics'.[62] Ministries had ultimate control over the distribution of state resources, the power to duplicate party legislation and could prevent the implementation of any party initiative which threatened the ministries' livelihood.[63] This misplaced ministerial power constituted one of the main reasons for reform initiatives, which attempted to break the ministerial grip on the state. The mood of 'anti-ministerialism' in the party was particularly 'virulent' at the time of the Nineteenth CPSU Conference and perestroika represented the CPSU's last and unsuccessful attempt to regain its power from the industrial ministries.[64]

Gorbachev attested this concern in a Politburo meeting on 8 September 1988, when he ironically said that in the past the Politburo and CC had unquestioningly approved any proposal made by the ministries for fear of otherwise ending up in a prison camp.[65] Accounts of the Nineteenth CPSU Conference have thus identified the state bureaucracy as a powerful opponent, which Gorbachev symbolically defeated at the conference,[66] and that this was the central goal of the conference.[67]

In this light, certain reforms introduced at the conference, which were packaged by Gorbachev as liberalising or democratising by design, could be construed rather as geared towards breaking ministerial power. The combination of the posts of First Party Chairman and Head of the Soviets has been interpreted in both ways. Essentially, the new legislation empowered party secretaries to chair also their corresponding local soviet, but that this would only occur in the event that they were successfully elected to the local soviet. If they failed to be elected to the soviet, they would have to resign their party post as well. The 'democratising' argument is that first secretaries needed 'electing' to their party posts, as failure to be elected to the soviet also resulted in a first secretary's loss of position in the party. This has therefore been interpreted by some as introducing greater accountability within the party, in that first secretaries needed to win the support of their electorates to remain in post. An alternative interpretation of this policy is that Gorbachev promoted the merging of the two secretarial posts of party and soviet as a means of removing unwanted personnel and primarily to replace ministerial staff with CPSU members in a bid to loosen the ministerial hold over state power. Ultimately, the combining of party and soviet posts would ensure that some soviet posts would be filled by party members, essentially filling some ministerial positions with CPSU members.

According to Leonid Abalkin, this policy was not included in the original *Theses* (resolutions for approval at the conference) published before the conference, and delegates only first heard it proposed by Gorbachev in his conference speech.[68] If this was the case, then it is interesting that as many as ten delegate speakers at the conference voiced their approval of the proposal to combine soviet and party posts, and few spoke out against it. Among the opponents were Abalkin, who thought it would simply serve to consolidate party power, and Yeltsin, who suggested conducting an all-national referendum on the issue. A worker from the Orenburg regional party, who also opposed the proposal, stated, 'It seems to me that we should not combine the two posts. This is an emotional reaction'.[69] Abalkin pointed out that the proposed changes simply constituted a vote of confidence rather than radical change to the existing apparatus and that more candidates were required to ensure that the party was being led by society. He moreover questioned how this contributed to the separation of powers between party and state.[70] At interview, Valerii Vorotnikov confirmed that he also had evaluated the proposal negatively at the conference, viewing it as the concentration of power in the hands of one official and at odds with the concept of the separation of powers between party and state.[71]

Yeltsin's objection, however, could appear to have been motivated by some self-interest. 'As a minister', he found the policy incomprehensible, which could suggest he was aware of the implications of the policy. Yeltsin proposed that a referendum be called on the subject and conference delegates applauded his suggestion.[72]

As with the systematic criticism of Abalkin, agreement with the proposal of combining the secretarial posts recurred at evenly spaced intervals throughout the conference, after Gorbachev's speech, in sessions two,[73] three,[74] four,[75] five,[76] seven[77] and eight.[78] This consistent endorsement throughout the conference could have appeared, to conference delegates in the hall, that of a majority consensus. In spite of this apparent unity, it is interesting to note that by 1991, as will be discussed later in this chapter, the decision to combine posts had still not been fully implemented, which again demonstrates a significant element of recalcitrance among the party to *perestroika*, which was not manifested at the conference.

Defeating 'anti-perestroishchiki' and Ligachev

High-ranking hardliners such as Ligachev, who had evidently shown Gorbachev resistance in the past, according to his close aides at interview,[79] certainly did not speak out against *perestroika* at the conference. This could be explained by the fact that Ligachev was far more consumed with the pressing issue of Yeltsin and his even more unorthodox ideas, which drew fire away from Gorbachev, as discussed earlier. Or alternatively it could be explained by the theory that Ligachev was not as inimical to Gorbachev as has been conveyed, but rather that it suited Gorbachev to portray Ligachev as such when it suited him, for the sake of dramatic relief to emphasise Gorbachev as a reformer.

Although there was little evidence of hardline opposition at the conference, one of the reasons Gorbachev decided to hold a conference was to remove this hardline opposition from the leadership. Gorbachev convened the conference to obtain further ratification of the decisions made at the January and June 1987 plenary sessions, which would oblige those members of the leadership on the right who opposed Gorbachev's policies and advocated a return to the *status quo ante* to proceed with the implementation of *perestroika*.[80] He had originally planned to use the conference to enact personnel changes, although, as mentioned in Chapter 1, a significant proportion of the 'right' – that is, hardliners who stood in the way of *perestroika* – had already been pensioned off before the conference in June 1988.[81] Gorbachev's final blow to the rightist opposition was the conference's endorsement of the proposal to limit party officials to serving just two terms of office, which provided the means to oust the remainder of the long-standing old guard. Delegates voiced their approval of this proposal in practically every session, which would have conveyed unanimity on the issue, and there was apparently very little, if any, dissent. Endorsement of this proposal occurred twice in session two,[82] three times in session three,[83] twice in session five,[84] five times in session six,[85] three times in session seven[86] and once in session eight.[87]

Gorbachev introduced other reforms at the conference, which have been equally interpreted as finally ousting the 'dead souls' that posed the most likely opposition to his reforms.[88] As stated earlier, however, the research in this book suggests that the ouster of the old guard was more symbolic, and was performed in order to distance the new Gorbachev leadership from previous regimes, and from crimes committed before 1985, to make the party more palatable to Soviet society. Decisions that facilitated the massive ouster of the old guard included: the replacement of the Supreme Soviet by the CoPD; the restructuring of the CC and the reduction in its personnel; and the downgrading of the Secretariat of the CC and its 'replacement' with six commissions. Gorbachev-era personnel were appointed to head up the six new commissions, and were given a remit which essentially duplicated the work of the Secretariat. Meanwhile the Secretariat soon ceased to function, as it was deprived of the supporting workforce required to maintain its operation.[89] Gorbachev's skilful handling of these proposals, and most significantly his last resolution for approval at the end of the conference that would amend the constitution to put these proposals into effect within a few months,[90] marked the final stage in his adroit victory over the right. Such victory, however, could only be guaranteed by the right mix of delegates. As mentioned in Chapter 2, in order to ensure a successful outcome at the conference for the General Secretary, some preparation was needed to ensure the requisite support would be present at the conference. Many were aware of this, as shown by the ensuing struggle between the different factions in the lead-up to the conference, over which party members would attend as delegates.

The staging of the conference

Representation

Delegate selection for the conference became a highly publicised issue during the spring of 1988, as fears grew that the number of conservatives selected might outweigh possible Gorbachev supporters at the conference. In April 1988 liberals outside the party, including the dissident scientist Andrei Sakharov, who was rehabilitated in 1986 by Gorbachev and elected to the CoPD in 1989, signed a petition to urge the postponement of the conference until such time that a more democratic means of delegate selection might be introduced.[91] Such protests were mirrored in the Soviet republics, as intellectuals in Lithuania objected to the appointment, by the Communist Party of Lithuania on 28 May, of hardliners as conference delegates. A new association, called the 'Movement for *Perestroika*', better known thereafter as 'Sajūdis' was hurriedly formed and by 3 June had mobilised around the issue of delegate selection. Whether or not encouraged directly by Gorbachev, the activities of Sajūdis were certainly welcomed by Gorbachev.[92] Indeed, in the case of the RSFSR, Gorbachev tried to ensure that as many supporters as possible attended the conference by encouraging his newly formed pro-*perestroika* organisations to demand that local organisations elect liberal delegates.[93]

As the conference approached, public concern over the way in which delegates were being selected for the conference grew, resulting in demonstrations in Moscow and Leningrad on 28 May 1988 to protest against the way in which delegates were being selected.[94] All across the RSFSR thousands of demonstrators took to the streets to oppose the election of conservatives to the conference.[95] This battle over electing '*perestroishchiki*' was alluded to at the conference by Gorbachev loyalists, Mikhail Ul'ianov,[96] and the First Secretary of the Georgian Communist Party, Dzhumber (Jumber) Patiashvili,[97] who has been considered more conservative than Gorbachev loyalist and Soviet Foreign Minister Eduard Shevardnadze, yet took part in the opposition movement, which led to Shevardnadze's ouster in the Rose Revolution in Georgia in 2003 and was subsequently elected to Parliament. Filipp Popov, the first secretary of the Altai party committee, also elected to the CoPD in 1989, in

his conference speech, however, concluded that since sufficient *'perestroishchiki'* had been selected, 'in the end worthy
people were chosen': 'What a high degree of interest there was
in the selection of delegates to this really historic forum, which
has not taken place for nearly fifty years. But in the end worthy
people were chosen,'[98] and the majority at the conference were
supporters of *perestroika*.[99]

Despite the large number of conference delegates who
supported Gorbachev, complaints were made at the conference
regarding the issue of representation and the disproportionate number of party officials and intellectuals who had been
invited to speak. One speaker stated that only three per cent of
the delegates at the conference were under the age of thirty,[100]
which could suggest that younger party members were not
sufficiently supportive of *perestroika* to recruit for the conference. Ironically, following one such complaint, Gorbachev read
out at the conference a question posed by one of the regional
CPSU party committees: '... The Yaroslavl' delegation asks the
question: "How has the list of speakers been compiled? Why
are there no workers, collective farm workers, office workers?
Of twenty speakers there is only one worker."'[101] To rectify this
perceived imbalance, more workers were invited to speak in later
sessions. By the time of the sixth session, one worker invited to
speak, Vadim Nizhel'skii, noted ironically in his speech that he
was the fourth worker who had been invited to speak that day.
He implied that those invited to the podium were those who
were likely to 'speak out in favour of *perestroika*':

> Comrade communists, delegates of the party conference, I will
> not keep you for long. I am already the fourth metallurgist and
> worker who has been allowed to speak today. This could serve to
> illustrate either the extent to which the situation has become very
> problematic, and raises a lot of issues, in metallurgy, or that we are
> speaking out more heatedly in favour of *perestroika*.[102]

In the run-up to the conference, an article about the alleged
bribery of delegates was published in the magazine *Ogonëk*;
the article claimed that delegates were being bribed in advance
to speak out in favour of *perestroika* at the conference. An
announcement was made at the conference that the issue had
been 'investigated' and refuted as unfounded. Nonetheless,
there is some evidence to suggest that speakers were primed
in advance.

Vladimir Mel'nikov's 'doctored' speech

A delegate representing the Writers' Union claimed that Gorbachev 'directed and managed it all like a puppeteer, and pulled the strings'.[103] Yurii Chernichenko recounted how a friend of his, Georgii Baklanov, who was in the same conference working group as Gorbachev, had told Chernichenko about a 'note' addressed to Gorbachev that had been read out the previous day during the working group. The note had said: 'Mikhail Sergeevich, how is it possible to coexist with anyone who has thrived under such a regime? How can we stand being with them?'[104]

The note implied that there should be a purge of all high-ranking officials who had thrived during the pre-*perestroika* era. The contents of this note were repeated, supposedly *ad hoc*, by Vladimir Mel'nikov, the First Secretary of the Komi Regional Party, in his speech the next day, as rehearsed during the previous day's working group:

> In the course of discussion of the *Theses* we received from many communists and non-party members a more categorical order: he who in former times actively pursued a policy of stagnation should now in the period of *perestroika* no longer be allowed to work in the central party and soviet organs. They should be accountable for everything personally. [Applause][105]

Chernichenko considered that Gorbachev's response was equally rehearsed: 'And perhaps you have some concrete suggestions? [Animation.] Otherwise we might sit here and wonder to whom this refers: to me or to him?'[106] Similarly, Mel'nikov's reply, in the context of the session, appeared prepared: 'I would say this refers to M.S. Solomentsev in the first instance, to Comrade A.A. Gromyko, V.G. Afanas'ev, G.A. Arbatov and to others.' [Applause][107] Chernichenko stated that if he had not heard this himself the day before the speech, then he would have believed the exchange was genuinely *ad hoc*. 'If Georgii Baklanov had not told me the day before about this, then I would have believed that pathetic scene.'[108]

According to Chernichenko, Gorbachev was very much in control at the conference, and the climate was such that people spoke with care to protect their own posts. In the context of Chernichenko's claim, Vladimir Mel'nikov's entire speech could appear scripted. He spoke about ecological problems, demanded solutions to the nationalities question and endorsed Gorbachev's policies of enterprise, self-management and the consolidation of party power. He bemoaned the failure of the anti-alcohol campaign and advocated personnel changes and a crackdown on corruption. These comprised the central tenets of Gorbachev's *perestroika*. Mel'nikov spoke with authority on where the economy was failing, was able to name precisely who had been slacking and in particular listed the 'enemies' in the leadership that had prevented the proper implementation of *perestroika*. In this context, he criticised Nikolai Ryzhkov, the chairman of the USSR Council of Ministers, who was also chairing the session. He also defended the delegate composition of the conference, claiming that it was indeed representative of the party at large. Whether Mel'nikov's speech was entirely staged by Gorbachev or just in part, this does suggest at least one instance of an exchange arranged in advance for effect. Mel'nikov artfully criticised Gorbachev's opponents on both left and right. Those on the right who stood in the way of *perestroika* were castigated.[109]

In Gorbachev's own memoirs, this exchange was cited as evidence of *glasnost* and spontaneous debate among delegates at the conference,[110] and others have also interpreted this as one of the conference's most significant displays of spontaneous *glasnost*.[111] If, however, this exchange was indeed staged, as it appears to have been, then for those at the conference 'in the know', the remarks may have been directed as a warning that individuals could be ousted by 'popular demand' should the need arise. It is difficult to estimate how many, either present at the conference or simply following the proceedings, would have been aware of the provenance and intended effect of Mel'nikov's comments.

Gorbachev's proposal to reconvene the conference

Returning to the paradigm from Chapters 1 and 2, which suggested that general secretaries considered the conference more flexible than the congress for achieving their desired outcome, there is other supporting evidence beyond the Nineteenth CPSU Conference of 1988. Gorbachev proposed in February 1990 that an RSFSR conference be convened and then again in April 1991, that the CPSU conference be called.

The RSFSR conference, June 1990

By the early spring of 1990, the CPSU was becoming more polarised into different factions over how the reform trajectory should proceed. Issues of republican sovereignty and how to maintain the political integrity of the CPSU were hotly disputed, and at the plenary session of the CPSU CC in February 1990, Gorbachev proposed in his report that these issues be decided at an RSFSR conference.[112] A Gorbachev loyalist, Georgiĭ Razumovskiĭ, elected to the Politburo in 1988 but ousted just a few months later in July 1990, made the proposal that the RSFSR conference take place before the forthcoming Twenty-eighth CPSU Congress.[113] The decline in Gorbachev's close allies, such as Razumovskiĭ, in the top leadership after 1989 indicates Gorbachev's declining authority in the CPSU leadership.

This proposal sparked heated debate at the session concerning who should attend the conference. Ivan Polozkov (the First Secretary of the Krasnodar Regional Party, and later elected in June 1990 to the newly created post of First Secretary of the RSFSR Party) and Boris Yeltsin both advocated that delegates should be selected more widely from the party.[114] Gorbachev defended his position regarding delegate selection from the pool of delegates to the Twenty-eighth Congress, but Veniamin Afonin, from Bashkir, then supported Polozkov's and Yeltsin's proposal.[115] Some argued that the creation of Russian republican party organs that would essentially duplicate those of the CPSU would inevitably result in weakening the Soviet Union.[116] During the spring after this Plenum, the Baltic States declared their sovereignty, and before the conference was convened on 19 June, Yeltsin, in his capacity as Chairman of the RSFSR Supreme Soviet, followed suit and declared RSFSR sovereignty on 12 June 1990. The ensuing 'war of laws' over the summer and autumn of 1990 thoroughly undermined Gorbachev's authority, as Yeltsin duplicated Gorbachev's CPSU legislation with his own parallel RSFSR legislation.[117] Over the following months, other republics followed the Russian example and declared their sovereignty.[118] In an attempt to reassert his authority, Gorbachev made what has been described as his 'turn to the Right' in the autumn of 1990.[119] This created the political milieu which led to a series of violent crackdowns on nationalist insurgents by the Soviet military in Lithuania in January 1991.[120] Whether this use of force was actively endorsed by Gorbachev has never been established.[121] In any event, public opinion blamed Gorbachev for this aggression and demonstrators in Moscow expressed their sympathy with the Lithuanian cause.[122] In response, Gorbachev was forced to organise a referendum in March 1991 to determine the fate of the Soviet Union.[123]

Gorbachev's proposal to reconvene the CPSU conference (1991)

Under increasing pressure within the party to convene an emergency congress, in April 1991, Gorbachev suggested that the CPSU instead convene the conference. Gorbachev proposed that at this conference, personnel changes and further amendments to the Party Rules could be made. As mentioned in Chapter 2, at the Nineteenth CPSU Conference in 1988, a new provision had been added to the Party Rules which empowered any future conferences to replace up to twenty per cent of all party committees, including the CC.[124] These changes to the conference rules as endorsed at the Nineteenth Conference have been interpreted by some commentators as Gorbachev making provision for personnel changes at a future conference.[125]

At a joint plenum in April 1991, the CPSU CC and CCC discussed economic, political and social problems, which had reached crisis proportions. The resolution from this meeting endorsed the introduction of immediate measures to restore law and order in the RSFSR and the remaining republics which had not declared their independence from the Soviet Union. As the next and subsequent sections indicate, Gorbachev was trying to mobilise support against Yeltsin's 'Democratic Russia' group, and the increasing autonomy of the RSFSR that had ensued from the 'war of laws' between Gorbachev and Yeltsin. This essentially posed the most imminent threat to the future of the Union.

> The joint plenary session of the CC and the CCC of the CPSU notes that events which have unfolded in the country are becoming extremely dangerous and are fundamental to the future of the Soviet people, the Union and Socialism. As a consequence of the unprecedented 'war of laws' long-standing administrative structures, in particular the financial system, are being destroyed.

Standards of living have fallen sharply. People are unsure of tomorrow and are distraught. People's trust in the political centre as well as [their trust in] the local organs is declining. The situation is socially explosive. .... The characteristic feature of the present... is an increasingly active bloc of anti-socialist powers in favour of non-parliamentary methods of confrontation. ... The army, state security services and law enforcement agencies are being entirely discredited. We cannot fail to take into consideration that there also exists a conservative mood in society that strives for the restoration of the command-administrative system. The CPSU CC and CCC plenum supports the joint Declaration by the President of the USSR and the leaders of nine Union Republics for immediate measures to be taken to stabilise the situation in the country and resolve the crisis.[126]

In his speech at this Plenum, on 24 April, Gorbachev conveyed a sense of emergency and the need for action rather than wider consultation: 'Right now, what's most important is that we don't give way to the temptation of emotional decisions. But, of course, the current moment does not lend itself to calm academic deliberations.' He described the conflicting opposition forces, which both threatened regime change. What Gorbachev identified as the greatest danger was that these two wings of the opposition had apparently joined forces:

Not only in words, but also in deeds attempts are being made to knock the country off the path of reform, either by throwing it into an ultra-revolutionary state, threatening to destroy our system of government, or by plunging it back into the past, to a thinly veiled totalitarian regime. I do not think I need to explain what these 'left' and 'right' radicals have in mind. Both these trajectories are harmful. And the greatest danger that faces us at the moment is that they have come together in spite of the fact that [they] apparently have an irreconcilable mutual hatred.[127]

Apparently the two sides had come together in their demands that the leadership organs of the CPSU should be dissolved and that Gorbachev, among others, be removed from post:

Look at the unanimity with which they offer the same slogans! For a few months now the extremist leaders of the 'Democratic Russia' movement have been using in their political platforms a good deal of the workers' justified dissatisfaction with difficult economic conditions, and are inciting the workers' collectives to demand that the Congress of People's Deputies and the USSR Supreme Soviet be disbanded, and that the President and Office of Ministers all retire. Now, some party committees in the RSFSR along with some other republics, and even some of the deputies from the group 'Union', are making the same demands, almost word for word.[128]

Gorbachev stated that preserving the current constitutional order was of paramount importance and that under no circumstances should it be allowed to disintegrate: 'Any sensible person can draw, from their analysis of the situation, only one conclusion: under no circumstances should the current constitutional order be allowed to collapse.'[129] Moreover, he dismissed increasing demands for an extraordinary congress, on the ground that he would not change the policy, which others disputed, of combining state and party posts:

> Increasingly frequently, I hear demands that an extraordinary congress be convened to solve the so-called organisational problem. We have many times discussed just how appropriate the combining of party and state posts is under current circumstances. I have not changed my position on this issue. For those who have not done so already then they simply must combine [posts]...[130]

It is of interest that this policy had originated at the Nineteenth CPSU Conference, and had been apparently very well supported and endorsed. At this point Gorbachev then suggested another All-Union (CPSU) party conference be convened to deal with the proposals contested by left and right, to change the Party Rules, and possibly to make personnel changes. In essence therefore, Gorbachev was advocating a conference that would enjoy the powers of a congress:

> Just a brief word about the Party Programme, of which many are demanding speedy endorsement. In my opinion the party's project and the work in progress on it could be reviewed at an All-Union party conference in accordance with the CPSU Party Rules, held towards the end of this year. Also, at a conference we would be able to resolve more rapidly certain pressing organisational issues in connection, for example, with amendments to the Party Rules, and if necessary also personnel issues.[131]

In July 1991, following Yeltsin's victory in the RSFSR presidential elections on 12 June, the resolution approved by the Plenum of the CPSU CC declared that an extraordinary CPSU congress, the Twenty-ninth, would be convened instead by the end of 1991.[132] This suggests that Gorbachev was outnumbered by opposition forces in the party and so had to concede to convening a congress instead of a conference. This in turn bears out that the conference was perceived within the party as a forum where the General Secretary had the advantage over his opponents and was better able to influence events and shape outcome. Indeed, the fact that the conference of 1988 had apparently almost unanimously endorsed the policy of combining party and state posts,[133] and yet the policy remained unimplemented, does suggest that the conference, or at least delegate speakers, were not a representative cross-section of the party. The agenda, which Gorbachev intended to pursue at the next conference, must have sounded rather retrograde in the context of 1991, and appears, at this point, to have been geared towards maintaining the *status quo*, and retaining the integrity of the Soviet Union, within a closer federation than other republican leaders wished.

In the end, neither a CPSU conference nor congress was convened,[134] as the August Coup occurred a few days after the August summit of negotiations between the republican leaders, approving the Union Treaty, which strengthened republican autonomy to such an extent that it *de facto* made the Soviet Union and all its institutions redundant. Gorbachev's insistent request in April 1991 that constitutional order be maintained at all costs supports those accounts, which suggest that Gorbachev may have been involved in or incited the August Coup.[135] Certainly this would explain his magnanimous treatment of all those involved in the Coup immediately following the event. Having failed to reconvene a conference, at which he could maximise his control, and where he would have been more likely to secure some formal endorsement for preserving the future of the Soviet Union (albeit perhaps in any event short-lived), the putsch may be explained as a desperate and bungled last attempt to stage his own comeback. Aleksandr Yakovlev, in his own memoirs, stated that between 1989 and 1991 Gorbachev increasingly lost touch with reality, and that he was particularly surprised by the way in which Gorbachev behaved strangely after the Coup. Instead of taking decisive measures, he continued to pine after his lost Union Treaty.[136] These events marked the beginning of the end of Gorbachev's role as President of the CPSU, and the Soviet Union was dissolved in December 1991.

Conclusion

This chapter has illustrated how the Nineteenth CPSU Conference was convened as a show of strength for Gorbachev's *perestroika* and the choice of institution itself constituted the particular policy choice by Gorbachev of an orchestrated defeat of his opponents to both left and right. Gorbachev skilfully used the conference to stage public approval of *perestroika*, to denounce publicly the views of the 'left', and to pass resolutions that would further weaken the power of the right.

As an institution, the conference provided the General Secretary with an ostensibly 'all-party' forum where he had greater control (than at the congress) over the outcome and could reassert his authority over the party. Gorbachev's unsuccessful attempt to reconvene the CPSU conference in 1991 and the subsequent decision to convene the congress suggests that Gorbachev's opponents in the party were more numerous and would not afford him the protection, which a conference would have granted. As Chapters 5 and 7 will show, debate over convening a conference or congress became polarised between different factions in the party in the Hungarian and Polish cases. Those who advocated a congress sought the broader participation of the party membership, anticipating that this would be more likely to secure their desired outcome in opposition to what the General Secretary proposed.

The next chapter examines the function of the conference in terms of Gorbachev's policy towards the fraternal states of Central and Eastern Europe, which was planned as a wave of conferences convened in support of *perestroika*, which sought to maintain the one-party model across the socialist fraternity.

Notes

1   R. Sakwa, *Gorbachev and his Reforms, 1985–1990* (New York NY: Philip Allan, 1990), pp. 33–6.

2   G. Gill, 'Liberalisation and Democratisation in the Soviet Union and Russia', *Democratization* 2:3 (1995), pp. 313–36.

3   S. Solnick, *Stealing the State: Control and Collapse in Soviet Institutions* (Cambridge MA: Harvard University Press, 1998), p. 114.

4   R. D. Anderson, *The Russian Anomaly and the Theory of Democracy*, Studies in Public Policy, 309 (Glasgow: University of Strathclyde, 1998), p. 14.

5   P. Roeder, *Red Sunset: the Failure of Soviet Politics* (Princeton NJ: Princeton University Press, 1993), p. 212.

6   R. Karklins, 'Explaining Regime Change in the Soviet Union', *Europe-Asia Studies* 46:1 (1994), pp. 37–8.

7   Anderson, *The Russian Anomaly and the Theory of Democracy*, p. 15.

8   O'Donnell and Schmitter cited in Brown, *The Gorbachev Factor*, pp. 182–84.

9   M. Laver (ed.), *Estimating the Policy Position of Political Actors*, (London: Routledge, 2001), pp. 66–7.

10 R. Sakwa, *Gorbachev and his Reforms, 1985–1990*, p. 184.

11 T. Remington, *The Russian Parliament: Institutional Evolution in a Transitional Regime, 1989–1999* (New Haven CT: Yale University Press, 2001), p. 24.

12 Interview with Anatoly Cherniaev, Moscow, 24 September 2002; interview with Aleksandr Yakovlev, Moscow, 31 October 2002; telephone interview with Yurii Chernichenko, 3 October 2002.

13 C. Young, 'The Strategy of Political Liberalisation: a Comparative View of Gorbachev's Reforms', *World Politics* 45:1 (1992), pp. 48; 60.

14 Interview with Rezső Nyers, Budapest, 5 June 2003; interview with Zoltán Szabó, Budapest, 2 June 2003.

15 E. Huskey, *Presidential Power in Russia* (New York NY: M.E. Sharpe, 1999), p. 14.

16 Interview with Valerii Vorotnikov, Moscow, 30 October 2002.

17 Archiwum Akt Nowych, PZPR II/51 *Stenogram z obrad zespołu do opracowania propozycji reform modelu socjalistycnego państwa polskiego w dniu 11 marca 1988 r.*, Prof. Adam Łopatka's speech.

18 *Ibid.*, Prof. Jerzy Musziński's speech.

19 Interview with Anatoly Cherniaev, Moscow, 24 September 2002; interview with Aleksandr Yakovlev, Moscow, 31 October 2002.

20 Telephone interview with Yurii Chernichenko, 3 October 2002; interview with Valerii Vorotnikov, Moscow, 30 October 2002.

21 Interview with Valerii Vorotnikov, Moscow, 30 October 2002.

22 Telephone interview with Anatoly Lukyanov, 31 October 2002; interview with Valerii Vorotnikov, Moscow, 30 October 2002; telephone interview with Yurii Chernichenko, 3 October 2002.

23 Gorbachev's fond, 87.Apr.28b.doc, as quoted in Chapter 4, p. 124.

24 P. Palazchenko, *My Years with Gorbachev and Shevardnadze: the Memoir of a Soviet Interpreter* (University Park PA: Pennsylvania State University Press, 1997), pp. 96–97; G. M. Hahn, *Russia's Revolution from above, 1985–1999: Reform, Transition and Revolution in the Fall of the Soviet Communist Regime* (New Brunswick NJ: Transaction, 2002), pp. 68–9.

25 G. Zagaïnov in session six and A. Mel'nikov in session seven also proposed that candidates should compete on the basis of the different factions within the CPSU; they made this proposal before Yeltsin at the end of session seven.

26 Communist Party of the Soviet Union, *XIX Vsesoiuznaia konferentsiia KPSS, 28 iiunia – 1 iiulia 1988: stenograficheskiĭ otchet v dvukh tomakh* (Moskva: Izd-vo politicheskoĭ literatury, 1988). Abalkin, vol. 1, p. 119.

27   *Ibid.*, Masaliev, vol. 1, p. 125.
28   *Ibid.*, Kachura, vol. 1, p. 200.
29   *Ibid.*, Kachura, vol. 1, p. 204.
30   *Ibid.*, Primakov, vol. 2, p. 33.
31   *Ibid.*, vol. 1, p. 198.
32   *Ibid.*, Gorbachev, vol. 1, p. 198.
33   *Ibid.*, Gorbachev, vol. 2, p. 100.
34   *Ibid.*, Afanas'ev, vol. 2, p. 100.
35   Interview with Leonid Abalkin, Moscow, 30 October 2002.
36   *Ibid.*
37   CPSU, *XIX Vsesoiuznaia konferentsiia KPSS*, Vladimir Kabaidze, vol. 1, p. 241.
38   *Ibid.*, Mesiats, vol. 2, p. 4.
39   Interview with Georgii Arbatov, Moscow, 29 October 2002, p. 6.
40   That is, in sessions two to seven. Abalkin spoke in the first session after Gorbachev's opening report on the first day, which constituted the entire first session of the conference.
41   CPSU, *XIX Vsesoiuznaia konferentsiia KPSS*, Chazov, vol. 1, p. 122.
42   *Ibid.*, Kalashnikov, vol. 1, p. 136.
43   *Ibid.*, Arbatov, vol. 1, p. 156.
44   *Ibid.*, Kachura, vol. 1, p. 203.
45   *Ibid.*, Sokolov, vol. 1, p. 222.
46   *Ibid.*, Logunov, vol. 1, p. 261.
47   *Ibid.*, German Zagaïnov, vol. 1, p. 334.
48   Interview with Leonid Abalkin, Moscow, 30 October 2002.
49   'Boris, ty ne prav!' came to be a popular slogan, as depicted on one of the many designs of commemorative matchboxes *Russia of the Twentieth Century*, no. 130, XIX CPSU Conference: Boris – you are wrong!' http://phillumeny.onego.ru/labels/russian/history/page5/page5_r.html (last accessed 1 December 2010).
50   Interview with Georgii Arbatov, Moscow, 29 October 2002.
51   Interview with Valerii Vorotnikov, Moscow, 30 October 2002.
52   CPSU, *XIX Vsesoiuznaia konferentsiia KPSS*, Zagaïnov, vol. 2, p. 61.
53   *Ibid.*, German Zagaïnov, vol. 1, p. 336.
54   *Ibid.*, A. Mel'nikov, vol. 2, p. 10.
55   *Ibid.*, Shalaev, vol. 2, p. 70.
56   *Ibid.*, Gorbachev, vol. 2, p. 70.
57   *Ibid.*, Afanas'ev, vol. 2, p. 99.
58   *Ibid.*, Volkov, vol. 2, p. 102.
59   *Ibid.*, Lukin, vol. 2, pp. 104–5.
60   Interview with Valerii Vorotnikov, Moscow, 30 October 2002.
61   Anatoly Cherniaev's fond, Ch.87.Nov.01.
62   S. Whitefield (1991), *Soviet Industrial Ministries as Political Institutions, 1965–1990*, MS D.Phil. Thesis, Oxford, p. 17.

63 *Ibid.*, pp. 10–16.

64 S. Whitefield, *Industrial Power and the Soviet State* (Oxford: Oxford University Press, 1993), p. 207.

65 RGANI fond 89.Perechen'.42.dokument.22, p. 181.

66 B. Hazan, *Gorbachev and his Enemies: the Struggle for Perestroika* (Boulder CO: Westview, 1990), pp. 212–58.

67 P. Roeder, *Red Sunset: the Failure of Soviet Politics* (Princeton NJ: Princeton University Press, 1993), p. 219.

68 Interview with Leonid Abalkin, Moscow, 30 October 2002.

69 CPSU, *XIX Vsesoiuznaia konferentsiia KPSS*, Nizhel'skii, vol. 1, p. 339.

70 *Ibid.*, Abalkin, vol. 1, pp. 118–19.

71 Interview with Valerii Vorotnikov, Moscow, 30 October 2002.

72 CPSU, *XIX Vsesoiuznaia konferentsiia KPSS*, Yeltsin, vol. 2, p. 57.

73 *Ibid.*, Bakatin, vol. 1, p. 96.

74 *Ibid.*, Arbatov, vol. 1, p. 159; Kachura, vol. 1, p. 200.

75 *Ibid.*, Sokolov, vol. 1, pp. 222–3; Mironenko, vol. 1, p. 238.

76 *Ibid.*, Saranskikh, vol. 1, p. 298; Laptev, vol. 1, pp. 306–7.

77 *Ibid.*, Mesiats, vol. 2, p. 6; Grossu, vol. 2, p. 40.

78 *Ibid.*, Niiazov, vol. 2, p. 97.

79 For example, Ligachev is considered to be responsible for the Nina Andreeva letter; interview with Anatoly Cherniaev, Moscow, 24 September 2002; interview with Aleksandr Yakovlev, Moscow, 31 October 2002.

80 Interview with Valerii Vorotnikov, Moscow, 30 October 2002.

81 See Chapter 1, p. 39.

82 CPSU, *XIX Vsesoiuznaia konferentsiia KPSS*, Bakatin, vol. 1, p. 99; Masaliev, vol. 1, p. 127.

83 *Ibid.*, Arbatov, vol. 1, p. 159; Ul'ianov, vol. 1, p. 195; Fedotova, vol. 1, p. 205.

84 *Ibid.*, Logunov, vol. 1, p. 266; Saranskikh, vol. 1, p. 295.

85 *Ibid.*, Fedorov, vol. 1, p. 315; Zakharova, vol. 1, p. 325; Zagainov, vol. 1, p. 335; Songaila, vol. 1, p. 343; Aidak, vol. 1, p. 349.

86 *Ibid.*, Oleinik, vol. 2, p. 32; Volodin, vol. 2, p. 54; Yeltsin, vol. 2, p. 57.

87 *Ibid.*, Ligachev, vol. 2, p. 87.

88 Brown, *The Gorbachev Factor*, pp. 184–5; Sakwa, *Gorbachev and his Reforms*, p. 17; Young, 'The Strategy of Political Liberalisation', pp. 61–2.

89 Brown, *The Gorbachev Factor*, pp. 184–5.

90 R. G. Suny, *The Soviet Experiment: Russia, the USSR and the Successor States*, (Oxford: Oxford University Press, 1998), p. 461.

91 D. Mann, *Paradoxes of Soviet Reform: the Nineteenth Communist Party Conference* (Washington DC: Center for Strategic and International Studies, 1988), p. 27.

92 A. E. Senn, *Gorbachev's Failure in Lithuania* (London: St Martin's Press, 1995), pp. 18–19.

93 M. McFaul, *Russia's Unfinished Revolution: Political Change from Gorbachev to Putin* (Ithaca NY: Cornell University Press, 2001), p. 67.

94   Mann, *Paradoxes of Soviet Reform*, p. 31.

95   V. Brovkin, 'Revolution from Below: Informal Political Associations in Russia 1988–1989', *Soviet Studies* 42:2 (1990), p. 236.

96   CPSU, *XIX Vsesoiuznaia konferentsiia KPSS*, Ul'ianov, vol. 1, p. 195.

97   *Ibid.*, Patiashvili, vol. 1, p. 272.

98   *Ibid.*, Popov, vol. 1, p. 149.

99   *Ibid.*, Afanas'ev, vol. 2, p. 101.

100   *Ibid.*, Mironenko, vol. 1, p. 235.

101   *Ibid.*, Gorbachev, vol. 1, p. 249.

102   *Ibid.*, Nizhel'skii, vol. 1, p. 337.

103   Telephone interview with Yurii Chernichenko, 3 October 2002.

104   *Ibid.*

105   CPSU, *XIX Vsesoiuznaia konferentsiia KPSS*, Mel'nikov, vol. 1, p. 269.

106   *Ibid.*, Gorbachev, vol. 1, pp. 269–70.

107   *Ibid.*, Mel'nikov, vol. 1, p. 270.

108   Telephone interview with Yurii Chernichenko, 3 October 2002.

109   Those on the left named in Mel'nikov's speech included Georgii Arbatov. Arbatov, who had been a loyal supporter of Gorbachev, stated *after* the interview (interview with Arbatov, Moscow, 29 October 2002) that he was upset with Gorbachev when Mel'nikov named him in his speech. This admission could imply that Arbatov considered Gorbachev responsible for the content of Vladimir Mel'nikov's speech, confirming Chernichenko's statement that the speech was scripted. Since this statement is not in the interview transcript itself, it does, however, remain unconfirmed.

110   M. Gorbachev, *Memoirs* (London: Bantam, 1995), pp. 331–2.

111   See, for example, D. Tosić, *Snaga i nemoč: naš komunizam 1945–1990* (Beograd: Akademija Nova, 1998), p. 324.

112   'Plenum TSK KPSS 5–7 fevralia 1990 goda: stenograficheskiĭ otchet 7 fevralia 1990 goda, utrennee zasedanie' *Izvestiia CC CPSU* 3 (1990), pp. 41–89.

113   *Ibid.*, pp. 60–1.

114   *Ibid.*, p. 61.

115   *Ibid.*, pp. 61–2.

116   *Ibid.*, pp. 66–7 (S. F. Akhromeev).

117   E. Primakov, *Gody bol'shoi politike* (Moskva: Izd-vo Sovershenno sekretno, 1999), pp. 76–7; M. Beissinger, *Nationalist Mobilization and the Collapse of the Soviet State* (Cambridge: Cambridge University Press, 2002), pp. 385–442.

118   Brown, *The Gorbachev Factor*, pp. 286–7.

119   *Ibid.*, pp. 269–72; 285–93; Breslauer, *Gorbachev and Yeltsin as Leaders*, pp. 104–7.

120   Breslauer, *Gorbachev and Yeltsin as leaders*, p. 105.

121   *Ibid.*

122   Brown, *The Gorbachev Factor*, pp. 280–3.

123   *Ibid.*, pp. 260–7.

124 McFaul, *Russia's Unfinished Revolution*, p. 45; Mann, *Paradoxes of Soviet Reform*, p. 46.

125 Mann, *Paradoxes of Soviet Reform*, p. 46.

126 Communist Party of the Soviet Union, 'Postanovleniia ob'edinennogo plenuma TSK i TSKK KPSS o polozhenii v strane i putiakh vyvoda ėkonomiki iz krizisa', *Partiĭnaia zhizn'* 10:maĭ (1991), p. 4.

127 *Ibid.*

128 Communist Party of the Soviet Union, *Materialy ob'edinennogo plenuma Tsentral'nogo Komiteta i Tsentral'noi Kontrol'noi Komissii KPSS, 24–25 aprelia, 1991 g.* (Moskva: Izd-vo polit. lit-ry, 1991), p. 7.

129 *Ibid.*, p. 8.

130 *Ibid.*, p. 13.

131 *Ibid.*, p. 14.

132 Communist Party of the Soviet Union, 'Informatsionnoe soobshchenie o plenume Tsentral'nogo Komiteta Kommunisticheskoĭ Partii Sovetskogo Soiuza', *Partiĭnaia zhizn'* 16:avgust (1991), p. 4.

133 As discussed in the present chapter, pp. 89–90.

134 In fact the CPSU continued in a different format for another two years under the auspices of a very right-wing faction under Sergeĭ Borisovich Skvortsov, which did indeed hold what they claimed to be the 'Twentieth All-Union party conference of the CPSU' held in two stages in February and May 1992. The Twenty-ninth Congress of the CPSU was held in July 1992 at which it was voted that Gorbachev should be formally expelled from the party, perceived as having been too liberal. Although a Thirtieth CPSU congress was planned for 1993, this never took place.

135 R. Sakwa, 'A cleansing storm: The August coup and the triumph of perestroika', *Journal of Communist Studies and Transition Politics*, 9:1 (1993), pp. 131–49; M. Sixsmith, *Moscow Coup: the death of the Soviet system* (London: Simon and Schuster, 1991), pp. 149–58.

136 A. Yakovlev, *Omut pamiati* (Moskva: Vagrius, 2000), pp. 507–9.

4

Keeping the 'outer empire' in step with the CPSU: Gorbachev's policy of fraternal party alignment via the NPC 1987–88

Introduction

As explained in Chapter 1, the conference was an institution rarely convened in the communist parties, except in Poland and South-eastern Europe where conferences were more regularly convened, and a series of conferences had not been called in synchronism within the same time frame since the 1920s, when the Communist International (Comintern) had commanded all communist parties to purge their respective personnel of the leftist faction via a party conference. As an institution, the conference was traditionally a forum where the party leadership sought to consolidate its power and defeat opposition, as illustrated in Chapter 2.

This chapter outlines how Gorbachev encouraged these regimes to convene their respective NPCs for the purpose of securing the alignment of these parties with *perestroika*, the consolidation of party unity and the modernisation of the party. By shedding new light on the role of the NPC in Gorbachev's controlled liberalisation strategy, the chapter demonstrates that Gorbachev expected the fraternal parties to adopt this policy in the spirit of 'socialist internationalism' as a way to maintain the Soviet Union's 'outer empire' under proposed quasi-market conditions rather than with the intention of democratisation and the severing of Soviet ties with these states. One interviewee, Zoltán Szabó,[1] stated that:

> It's quite possible that Gorbachev encouraged these party confer-
> ences to change their leaders and to put his allies in the most

important posts in each party. Perhaps he thought that restricted... reforms could be made in all of the socialist countries and then socialism and the socialist bloc would be more effective, perhaps a bit more democratic, but I don't think it was his intention... perhaps only [if] he thought 'well, if it's the price of the efficiency, then never mind' but he thought that economically and socially these states would be more efficient and more effective having implemented these reforms, but this reform caused the collapse of socialism within one year and a half from the Elbe to Vladivostok.[2] I don't think Gorbachev imagined that the regimes in the Soviet bloc would collapse. He thought that with the changes [brought about] by reformists as the leaders of the communist parties this would stabilise the system, but of course once the change began there wasn't any stopping it.[3]

Conferences for the purpose of policy alignment with the CPSU

This chapter examines evidence of CPSU influence brought to bear on these regimes' leaders to convene their conferences. From this, inferences are made about Gorbachev's reasons for convening a conference, *how* he encouraged fraternal parties to follow suit, party leaders' responses to this and how this CPSU influence was apparent in conference outcomes. Material supports the argument in Chapter 3 that Gorbachev's policy of *demokratizatsiia* constituted 'liberalised enlightened control by the communist party'[4] rather than democratisation *per se*. His policy of convening conferences across these fraternal states had a dual purpose. At the domestic level the fraternal conferences were designed as a show of solidarity for *perestroika*, which had come under attack, and the aim of replacing leaderships was to cement *perestroika* in the fraternal states. This process of modernisation was intended to make the one-party state more efficient and improve its image, both at home and abroad, which would in turn increase its appeal with the aim of preserving the socialist model.

Archival documents, as cited in this chapter, testify Gorbachev's demand that party unity be strengthened and that *perestroika*, including personnel changes, be endorsed by all the regimes of Central, Eastern and South-eastern Europe at an NPC. These exchanges indicate that what underpinned this policy was a plan to salvage the existing system through party modernisation. In the face of increasingly strong Western leverage and influence over these regimes' economies and societies, the NPC was called to strengthen party unity and legitimise the one-party state. Shortly after the Warsaw Pact Treaty had been renewed in 1985,[5] Gorbachev began convening closed meetings with the fraternal leaders of the Warsaw Pact countries in October 1985, 'in the spirit of the International',[6] at which he urged they pool their strategies for dealing with the problems they shared in their respective states, to preserve the future of socialism.[7] Gorbachev stated at the first of these meetings that he expected support from the fraternal parties in helping to protect the socialist movement from the effects of divisive Western policy:

> We take on the problems of socialist states as if they were our own and we count on you to adopt the same approach. The West wants to pit our states against one another: it's applying a particular economic policy, setting up credit... and using other methods.[8]

From the context, Gorbachev was thus appealing to his Warsaw Pact counterparts, in the spirit of the Treaty, for a collaborative effort to protect the socialist fraternity. Subsequent agreements signed in June 1986 by all member states, with the exception of Romania, emphasised fraternal party commitment to Gorbachev's new-thinking policy with respect to continued negotiations with the West over disarmament, and the readiness of socialist states to work more closely together in developing and exploiting their common economic potential.[9]

Gorbachev's strategy of protecting the 'empire' from the West

Gorbachev's policy towards the fraternal states therefore did not in essence diverge from that of previous CPSU General Secretaries when Western democratising influences were prevalent. Policy towards the fraternal parties had always been to discourage neutralism and strengthen the electoral appeal of centrist parties against any possible challenge by the far left, which could facilitate democratisation.[10]

Similarly, between 1987 and 1988 Gorbachev encouraged the fraternal parties to combat democratising Western influence, and consolidate a centrist line in the party by defeating opponents on the left and right. Gorbachev urged fraternal parties to discourage any nascent opposition groups and to mobilise greater support for the communist party. Archival records confirm the commonly held view that Gorbachev advocated some liberalisation across the fraternal parties of Central, Eastern and South-eastern Europe, but these documents offer a new account as to why Gorbachev urged this. The existing literature documents how reformists in the CPSU encouraged the fraternal parties to reform but argues that there is little evidence to support official Soviet 'control' over events at this time.[11] Contrary to this account, transcripts of meetings between actors in the various leaderships indicate significant Soviet influence over policy and implicit in these conversations, as is apparent in the extracts that follow, is that this relationship was acknowledged as such by both sides. We can perceive from these texts Gorbachev's tone of polite but firm superiority and in turn the fraternal party leaders express a sense of dependence and accountability. The language suggests the relationship between the CSPU and fraternal parties was mutually understood as such.

As early as 1986, Gorbachev informed the fraternal party leaders of the economic crisis that threatened their states. At a meeting of these leaders, on 10–11 November 1986, according to Vadim Zagladin's archival fond,[12] Gorbachev updated leaders on policies of planned disarmament, and 'new thinking' in foreign policy. He claimed the Soviet Union had provided the fraternal economies with considerable financial support, through the CMEA, and that during the period 1971–75 indicators suggested economic growth in the fraternal socialist countries had far outstripped that of the West, but that in 1984 this performance had suddenly declined. Gorbachev plainly stated at this meeting that the Soviet Union could not sustain financial contributions to the socialist economies on this scale and that these were, in any event, unjustifiable.[13] Interestingly, one Hungarian interviewee, Rezső Nyers, remarked that the idea of convening the Hungarian conference had first been suggested in 1986, although he did not specify where and when this was first raised.[14]

From the context of Gorbachev's speech, we might surmise that Gorbachev first suggested at this November meeting that all parties convene their respective party conferences to modernise the party and declare a new stage in relations among the parties. Gorbachev had already by this time attended the Tenth PUWP Congress in July 1986, at which he delivered a speech to delegates that effectively renounced the Brezhnev Doctrine of military intervention with respect to Poland. As will be discussed in Chapter 7, some evidence suggests that Gorbachev formulated his plan to convene the CPSU conference from the Polish example. It seems, therefore, that by November 1986 Gorbachev had already decided on this course of action and at the meeting urged the fraternal party leaders to act in concert and convene their respective conferences for the purpose of modernising their parties and to announce publicly the new relationship between the Soviet Union and the fraternal parties with respect to the CMEA and Brezhnev Doctrine. Simultaneously, Gorbachev sought support from these fraternal leaderships against hardliners in the party that opposed *perestroika*, and he required of them a show of solidarity in the form of mirror-image conferences.

The CPSU persistently publicised its forthcoming conference to the fraternal states. At a meeting with the Central and East European ambassadors to Moscow in February 1987, before the decision to convene a conference had been approved by the CPSU CC, Vadim Medvedev[15] outlined the strategic importance of the CPSU conference. He summarised the proceedings of the January Plenum at which the CPSU leadership had accused the party of inertia in the face of a growing economic crisis, and that the decline in the party's membership, particularly among the youth and women, necessitated further democratisation within the party, state structures and electoral system. He stressed at this meeting that the main aim of these proposed reforms – *perestroika* – was geared towards re-engaging society in the party and consolidating the party's leading role. As Medvedev said: 'the slogan of *perestroika* is: more socialism, more justice, and more democracy. We are above all concerned with strengthening the role of the party, increasing its authority, increasing its connection with the masses.'[16]

A few months later, in November 1987, Medvedev met with representatives from the fraternal parties to urge reform. Referring to the matter discussed at the 10–11 November 1986 meeting between Gorbachev and these parties' leaders, Medvedev reiterated the pressing need to restructure economic relations and emphasised how the CPSU could no longer afford to subsidise CMEA economies. Medvedev explained that profitable economic trade between the Soviet Union and fraternal parties in terms of trading raw materials for finished goods had become exhausted at the end of the 1970s. He encouraged the fraternal states to find new opportunities for technology transfer elsewhere and initiate greater cooperation with academics and scientists abroad.[17]

The new relationship between the Soviet Union and the fraternal states was secured in bilateral agreements between Gorbachev and the respective fraternal party leaders, and was publicised in the press. As Wojciech Jaruzelski, First Secretary of the PUWP,[18] stated in an interview with the party newspaper, *Życie Partii*:

> [Gorbachev's] visit comes at a time of qualitatively new collaboration between the states of the socialist fraternity. As of today [the collaboration] is no longer just a matter of pooling of our potential, as we usually do, the agreements that have been made are instead characterised by our engagement in a common effort to accelerate our progress in science and technology, with determination and initiative, to bring concrete changes to our standard of living. We fervently hope that [Gorbachev's] visit, our discussions and the agreement have played a significant role especially in strengthening the Warsaw Pact and its security activities in Europe as well as [helping in] the modernisation of the organisation and function of the CMEA.[19]

These agreements were made in synchronism with discussions about the NPC, which promised the political revitalisation of the party through its modernisation. Between the spring of 1987 and the spring of 1988, Gorbachev held meetings with fraternal party leaders to encourage party reform via their prospective NPCs. The transcripts of these conversations show that these conferences were referred to as meetings where modernisation of the party should be enacted, personnel changes and a show of strength for *perestroika* were to be made, but that the regime's *status quo* be maintained.[20]

Conversations between Gorbachev and the fraternal leaders exemplify Gorbachev's motive for controlled liberalisation. He firstly claimed that Western governments had established political opposition cells in Central and East European societies, turning people away from the party. Secondly he attributed to Western influence a sudden widespread pacifist tendency among conscripts in the army. In these discussions Gorbachev argued that these factors posed an immediate threat to the fraternal parties, necessitating the consolidation of the party's leading role in society.

Whether alleged Western infiltration was the main reason party membership had declined, as Gorbachev suggested in these discussions, is difficult to assess. In any event, poor economic performance in these states had resulted in a palpable decline in living standards and the system's difficulty in maintaining the costly 'social contract' of full employment, especially in Yugoslavia,[21] had made these regimes increasingly unpopular. The policy of import-led growth since the 1960s had led to these states' growing economic reliance on the West for technology transfer and the import of goods, which had resulted in sizeable foreign debts. The oil shocks of the 1970s and subsequent world inflation led to the escalation of the Central and East European regimes' foreign debts,[22] but it is questionable whether party leaders were fully aware of the extent of the financial crisis. A number of respondents claimed that Kádár was not informed and that his sources had not provided him with a full picture of the gravity of the situation.[23] A likely contributory factor to this is that these command economies had devised accounting practices at every level that doctored figures to provide an account of economic performance that would be politically acceptable and financially lucrative. This account distorted economic indicators to such an extent that some members of the leadership may have been genuinely unaware of the real situation.

In Hungary, those who were best informed were high-ranking economists or those with links to the intelligence services. These individuals were evidently the first to know about the crisis, but it is not clear whether this information always reached the top leadership.[24] In the case of the Soviet Union, one delegate present at the CPSU conference suggested that delegates were sufficiently aware of the gravity of the economic situation to consider this a threat to the party's legitimacy, and to Gorbachev's own position:

> The country needed redirecting in terms of economic and political policy and as it happened we all welcomed the conference, as economic conditions were very serious, and you know that in a situation where the economy is bad, then the leader also loses his post.[25]

Although it may have been common knowledge that disillusionment in society with the CPSU was the result of economic crisis, Gorbachev identified other more pressing sources of threat for fraternal parties. During conversations with fraternal party leaders, Gorbachev labelled 'Western infiltration of society' as the main cause for society's growing disillusionment with the party. Whether Gorbachev really believed at this point in time that Western influence was indeed the central reason for society's disillusionment, or whether he flagged this to deflect attention from the alternative explanation that crisis was systemic and had come from within, is not clear. Whether or not Western cells existed in Central and Eastern Europe, they had not brought the growth of a coherent opposition movement in the Soviet Union. Research has identified that there were no nascent opposition groups in Soviet society beyond those that Gorbachev himself had created: his own *neformaly*. Hence it would appear that in the Soviet Union, Gorbachev was trying to re-engage a society that had simply lost interest in the party.[26]

In the case of other states where underground political opposition groups had formed, it is possible that Western support for or foundation of such fledgling opposition groups in countries such as Poland, Czechoslovakia, Hungary and Yugoslavia could have been considered an imminent threat to regime stability. Gorbachev's perception of the seriousness of the Western threat of infiltration at the time is not clear and since cold-war ideology pervades the language in these transcripts, the threat may be exaggerated. So, whether Gorbachev put such great store by Western political infiltration as Western economic leverage is not clear. In any event, acknowledging Western economic supremacy could have been perceived as spreading fear and a defeatist attitude. Therefore, suggesting Western political interference as a significant factor could have helped create the image of a common enemy to these countries. The language of the transcripts does suggest that meetings were held with the aim of rousing leaders to rally round a common 'socialist' cause.[27]

Gorbachev's own motivation to achieve political alignment in the 'outer empire' could be interpreted as traditional Soviet foreign policy towards these states, but additionally, and more crucially for Gorbachev, the mirroring of his policy outside the Soviet Union was a show of strength for his own centrist position at a time when his policies were subject to opposition from both left and right. Whatever Gorbachev's perception of the real cause of the crisis, he clearly identified a crisis of legitimacy in all these regimes and offered the solution of raising the party's profile via personnel change and modernisation. This policy was underpinned by a demand that the parties of Central, Eastern and South-eastern Europe present a united front on this.

Explanatory factors for fraternal leaderships' compliance with the CPSU

If we look at the Warsaw Pact as an international agreement, then compliance by signatory states with the terms of the Treaty is more likely to have been motivated by a coincidence of interests between fraternal leaderships and Gorbachev, rather than the threat of 'enforcement' in the event of non-compliance.[28] In any event, possibilities for 'enforcement' were limited, as Gorbachev had already publicly renounced the use of military intervention in these states as early as 1986[29] (under the terms of the Stockholm Agreement); therefore the threat of force must be discounted as a potential means of pressure brought to bear by Gorbachev in motivating these fraternal parties to follow this policy. As this chapter bears out, the fraternal parties traditionally perceived as most 'faithful' to the CPSU failed to follow the liberalising model set by the CPSU in 1988, some did not convene their conference, and others postponed it.

To some extent the outcome at these conferences depended on the balance of power between hardliners and reformists in these parties' leaderships, because institutional 'constraints' (or the lack thereof) helped ensure that these meetings could be controlled by leaderships, while this was not guaranteed in the case of congresses. This factor significantly insulated leaderships at conferences from possible dissent within the party. The leadership could bring in those rank-and-file members of the party who they anticipated would prove supportive and exclude those who they thought might jeopardise the desired outcome. Regardless of this 'insulation', we might logically assume anyway that those regimes among the socialist fraternity that were more reformist would have been those most willing to convene conferences to align their parties with Gorbachev's *perestroika*, as depicted in Table 2.

Table 2 Regime type and conference outcome

State	Regime type (1 = least reformist and 5 = most reformist*)	Conference held	Outcome	Convened in response to Gorbachev?
Romania	1	✓	Maintain *status quo*	Probably not
Albania			N/A	Probably not
Bulgaria	2	✓	Espouse *perestroika*, but maintain *status quo*	Yes
Czechoslovakia		✗		
GDR	3	Regional conferences held instead	N/A	Probably
Hungary			Gorbachevian: effect leadership change /modernise party	
Soviet Union	4	✓		Yes
Yugoslavia				
Poland	5	✓	Gorbachevian, but in context of Poland, May 1989 conference advocated a return to the *status quo ante*	Yes

* According to Stepan and Linz's typology, they distinguish these nine regimes in five different categories, including: 'Sultanist' (Romania); Early Post-Totalitarian (Albania and Bulgaria); Frozen Post-Totalitarian (Czechoslovakia and the GDR); Mature Post-Totalitarian (Hungary, the Soviet Union and Yugoslavia); and Authoritarian (Poland). See Linz and Stepan, *Problems of democratic consolidation*, pp. 38–54.

This could explain why Hungary and Yugoslavia both achieved Gorbachevian outcomes at their respective conferences, as will be described in Chapters 5 and 6. The exception to this rule, however, is Poland, which is commonly understood as the most advanced of all the fraternal regimes of Central and Eastern Europe, as it had the most developed opposition movement. Since Poland convened its conference a year after the other three, and the outcome did not entail personnel change, nor the liberalisation of party structures, we might conclude that other more important causal factors must have been at work, which explain why some regimes complied and others did not. As detailed in subsequent sections in this chapter, this may be better explained as the result of the balance of power within those parties, which was in favour of ousting the First Secretary. Another factor which explains some fraternal parties' compliance with Gorbachev's request (regardless, however, of conference outcome) would be these states' varying economic dependence on the Soviet Union. All the fraternal states' economies were very vulnerable by 1987, as they had been adversely affected by global and domestic[30] economic shocks during the 1970s and 1980s.

Fraternal economic dependence on the Soviet Union

By the late 1980s, these states were burdened with increasingly large foreign debts as a result of pursuing policies throughout the 1970s of 'import-led growth', which entailed the large-scale importation of goods and technology from the West,[31] as already mentioned. In 1987 Bulgarian, Czechoslovakian and Romanian gross foreign debts had grown to between $5,400 and $5,800 million,[32] the GDR $15,900 million, Hungary $17,800 million, Yugoslavia $20,000 million, the USSR $29,900 million and Poland $39,200 million.[33] Central, Eastern and South-eastern Europe's economic dependence on the Soviet Union, administered mainly via the CMEA, evolved and became unsustainable. The Soviet Union supplied these states with subsidised energy and raw materials, which were wastefully used to produce virtually unsaleable goods. Moreover the level of trade between the fraternal states was low, because the system offered few incentives for this.[34]

What compounded the problem was that energy consumption rose in the CMEA countries during the 1970s by nearly fifty per cent (with the exception of the Soviet Union, where consumption remained the same), whereas the West halved its consumption in the wake of the world oil price rises.[35] Meanwhile the Soviet Union continued to subsidise these CMEA exports heavily, curtailing possible alternative hard currency revenue from exporting this oil to the West. A couple of years after the second world oil shock, in 1982, the Soviet Union changed its oil allocation policy, reducing export to the CMEA by nine per cent and increasing shipment to the West.[36] The impact of this upon each state varied, as the Soviet Union had different bilateral agreements with each and the fraternal states' reliance on these subsidised imports also varied according to the nature of their energy profiles. During the 1970s, excessive Soviet energy supply to the CMEA states had been flagged as a growing problem and by 1981, restrictions had been imposed to penalise wasteful use of these heavily subsidised supplies. At the Twenty-sixth CPSU Congress of 1981, the CC alluded to Soviet expectations that there should be greater returns from CMEA countries for this energy supply and insisted that these states introduce energy-saving technology to reduce consumption.[37]

Energy consumption by CMEA states continued to preoccupy the CPSU. In October 1985, Gorbachev expressed his concern at an American document that had been leaked, which described Western hopes of the socialist countries' economic collapse through the entire consumption of Soviet oil and energy resources by the socialist fraternity.[38] Gorbachev recounted this to Bulgarian Communist Party leader Todor Zhivkov[39] at his palace near Sofiia. Just a few months later, the sudden collapse of world oil prices in mid-1986 affected the Soviet economy particularly adversely, as the value of its exports fell by more than half, forcing the Soviet Union to reduce Western imports and increase foreign borrowing to cover trade deficits. Under such conditions the continued subsidised Soviet export of oil to the CMEA countries became increasingly untenable and the Soviet Union demanded more in return from its CMEA partners at the Forty-second CMEA Conference held in Bucharest, on 8–9 November 1986.[40] A summit of CMEA party leaders was consequently held in Moscow immediately following this, on 10–11 November, where Soviet ministers berated CMEA member states for not fulfilling their part of the bargain in exchange for the promised

Soviet energy supplies. To cut waste, the Soviet government demanded that direct links be set up between Soviet and CMEA enterprises to gain better control over supplies in a bid to reduce the unnecessary waste. This was understandably unpopular with the other CMEA states as this promised to curtail their freedom to export any superfluous Soviet oil to the West in exchange for hard currency.[41] The CMEA states continued to flout these directives, so that by July 1988, after the Forty-fourth CMEA Meeting, the Deputy Foreign Minister of the USSR, Ivan Aboimov, declared that the desired progress in the 'Comprehensive Programme for Scientific and Technical Progress', which agreed CMEA cooperation in scientific research on the part of the other CMEA countries, had not been achieved.[42] Notably, the endorsed plan of action, although never realised in practice, was to create a 'unified socialist market', which would embrace certain quasi-market features, including currency convertibility. This was intended to encourage the CMEA states to trade among themselves instead of exporting goods to the West in exchange for hard currency. The Soviet Union hoped to reduce its own increasing dependence on expensive Western imports which had resulted from the dearth of cheap East European alternatives.[43]

There was a tacit agreement among the socialist fraternity that a certain degree of political compliance was expected in return for subsidised Soviet energy supplies. In part, the impetus for these leaderships to 'liberalise' in keeping with Gorbachev's policies, or at least to appear to be doing so, may have been motivated by a need to maintain the necessary subsidised Soviet oil supplies that bolstered their failing economies. Indeed, purchasing oil from the Organisation of the Petroleum Exporting Countries (OPEC) or Western states in hard currency was not financially viable for these states[44] and was undesirable for the Soviet Union, which viewed the increasing economic dependence of the outer empire on the West as politically destabilising because it brought with it possible Western political influence. There is no evidence that the Soviet Union used the necessary reduction in oil supplies as political leverage over the fraternal states;[45] however, aware of the diminishing and limited Soviet resources, these states were probably vying to maintain levels of Soviet allocation. Since dependence varied among these states, we could conclude that the extent of political compliance may have been shaped by the different levels of economic dependence; if this is true, then we would expect those states more dependent on Soviet oil imports to have been more ready to align themselves politically with Moscow. The converse of this is that the Soviet Union was equally unwilling to sever these economic ties. Oil supply to the 'outer empire' from Western sources on credit would have been the only way that these economies could have financed such imports given the low quality of their exports, which rendered them largely unsaleable in the West. The consequent economic dependence on the West, however, carried with it the Western political agenda of democratisation.

Evidence of policy alignment with the CPSU from conference outcomes

Albania

There is no apparent evidence that the Albanian leadership was sympathetic to any form of regime liberalisation in the late 1980s. Until 1990, Albania maintained its own particular Stalinist brand of Communism. Following Khrushchev's departure from Stalinism, Albania broke away from the Soviet Union in the 1960s, and chose instead to align with China. Although Albania had later broken also with China by the 1970s, the regime never realigned with Moscow, remaining outside the Warsaw Pact and the CMEA. When Enver Hoxha died in 1985, his 'heir', Ramiz Alia, maintained the Stalinist Hoxha tradition under the guidance of Hoxha's widow. Alia convened an Albanian NPC in 1985 as a tribute to Hoxha.[46] The mass of personnel changes made by Alia in 1988 has been interpreted more as a consolidation of his power, replacing many appointed by Hoxha with his own supporters.[47] As late as 1989, at the Eighth Plenum of the CC in September, Alia publicly denounced Gorbachev, the 'revisionist betrayal' of *perestroika* and the reformist wing of the CPSU as counter-revolutionary forces.[48] This suggests that the top Albanian leadership was still hostile to liberalisation during the period of convention of NPCs across Central, Eastern and South-eastern Europe between 1987 and 1989.

Although Albania held a party conference around the time under examination, in late November 1987, the conference was more symbolic – held in honour of the seventy-fifth anniversary of Albania's national independence. Two papers were presented: one on the subject of the use of 'rote-learning' in education, and a second criticising the standard of statistical reporting.[49] Hence this national conference was not of the same nature as those that took place in Bulgaria, Hungary, Poland, Romania, the Soviet Union and Yugoslavia. It was not, like the other six, scheduled between party congresses to discuss the projected non-fulfilment of the Five Year Plan or, as in the case of Romania, the projected fulfilment of the Plan. Instead, the Albanian People's Assembly met just a month later, on 28 December 1987, to confirm projected plan fulfilment and forecast a thirteen per cent rise in the national income for 1988.

Romania

Perhaps not surprisingly, there is similarly no evidence of CPSU influence over the Romanian conference outcome. Although by 1980 Ceauşescu's regime had become financially more dependent on the Soviet Union than it had been for years,[50] Romania had been a net exporter of oil until 1975, and had since then been importing oil from the Soviet Union only in small quantities. However, the dependence on this oil import was negligible vis-à-vis the change in Soviet allocation policy of the late 1980s.[51] A spate of fires in Romanian oil fields in 1987 caused further supply problems but Ceauşescu enforced a stringent domestic policy of reduced energy consumption to deal with this and the growing foreign debt. Such measures were feasible for the Romanian leadership precisely because of the extent of Romanian party control over society. Romanian economic independence from the Soviet Union, in spite of Romanian membership of the Warsaw Pact and CMEA, gave Ceauşescu the leeway to risk alienating Moscow, as had his predecessor Gheorghe Gheorghiu-Dej, who had secured the withdrawal of Soviet troops from Romanian territory in 1958.[52]

Ceauşescu disapproved of Gorbachev's changes to the Warsaw Pact Treaty, and had refused to sign the Protocol in 1986.[53] During an official visit to Romania in May 1987, Gorbachev publicly denounced Ceauşescu's regime and advocated liberalisation.[54] Nonetheless, Ceauşescu stated at the RCP conference, a few months later in December 1987, that

Romania was not in economic crisis, and he proposed more stringent reductions in domestic economic consumption, thus publicly flouting Gorbachev's reform initiative. Prior to the conference, Gorbachev had attempted and failed to cultivate reformist elements within the Romanian CC. Aware of this initiative, Ceauşescu sent Ion Iliescu, a reformist member of the RCP, abroad to prevent any possible contact with reformist CPSU envoys during Gorbachev's visit to Bucharest in 1987.[55]

If leaders in Albania and Romania were aware of the CPSU's explicit demand that they convene their respective NPCs, then their conferences could be interpreted as particularly defiant displays of non-alignment with Gorbachev's policy of liberalisation in that neither Alia nor Ceauşescu espoused any aspect of *perestroika*, nor admitted any acknowledgment of systemic, political or economic crisis at these meetings.

Bulgaria

During the 1980s, Bulgaria had the highest dependence of all the fraternal countries on the Soviet Union for its energy needs, making the Bulgarian economy particularly vulnerable to adverse changes in Soviet oil export policy. Since Bulgaria re-exported surplus Soviet oil to the West in exchange for hard currency, the Soviet reduction in oil exports to Bulgaria resulted in both energy shortages and balance of payments problems.[56] Whether the Bulgarian economy's dependence on the Soviet Union directly influenced Zhivkov's political policy-making is not known. The BCP conference of January 1988, however, does display strong adherence to Gorbachev's *perestroika*, and while direct alignment with the CPSU was promised, Zhivkov stipulated that these policies were not to be enacted until 1991.[57]

The transcript of a meeting between Gorbachev and Georgi Atanasov,[58] in Moscow on 28 April 1987, does not directly mention the planned CPSU conference but instead refers to the forthcoming June 1987 Plenum. However, there is a common thrust to all these discussions: Gorbachev strongly advised Atanasov to keep a tight rein over society and maintain the leading role of the party, reiterating what he had said to the other leaders – that modernisation of the party was required to make the party more inclusive of non-members but that these people should not be allowed to take control of the party. As Gorbachev stated at this meeting, 'Everything must be initiated by the party or the party will find itself at the tail end of events and that is impermissible.'[59] Gorbachev voiced concern to Atanasov over the opposition he was experiencing within the party to his planned directives (including the proposition that the party conference be convened) for the forthcoming June 1987 Plenum: 'From the left there is criticism that action is too slow and from the other side they are asking for a volte-face back to previous methods. Abroad they are trying to discredit everything about us.'[60] This neatly sums up the divisions in the CPSU at the time, and the centrist line Gorbachev sought to steer between the left and right factions within the party. The following exchange indicates that both sides expected that certain fraternal party policies required approval from the CPSU. There is evidence here of expected CPSU influence over Bulgarian affairs and compliance on the part of Atanasov, who restated in a formulaic manner the relationship between the two states: 'I agree with Zhivkov that the success of our joint movement depends to a large extent on the success of the movement in the Soviet Union. Acknowledging our dependence we act correspondingly in our country.'[61]

The sense of Bulgarian inferiority to the Soviet Union was stressed during this exchange by Gorbachev's criticism of the low quality of exported goods from Bulgaria to the Soviet Union, and how it had become customary for CMEA countries to export low-quality goods, which they could not sell to the West, to the Soviet Union. As Gorbachev said, 'You must not turn our country into a dumping ground for un-saleable goods.'[62]

The BCP held its national conference in January 1988, six months before the CPSU conference. Zhivkov's conference speech articulates many of the main tenets espoused six months later by Gorbachev in his own speech, at the CPSU conference, including ecological concerns, the plan to introduce competitive elections for party posts, *glasnost* and transparency in party procedures, as well as the acknowledgment that changes in the world economy had brought about a new era 'launching socialist countries into a new stage of dynamic development' and consequently the need for 'a new model for socialism'. To encourage higher productivity and reduce waste, wage incentives were to be introduced as well as other market mechanisms to better regulate the economy.[63]

Significantly, Zhivkov did not refer to economic or political 'crisis', but demanded instead that the party and society adapt to changing world circumstances. Ostensibly, Zhivkov embraced Gorbachev's policies fully, stating clearly his support for these:

> Our party values highly and accentuates the historical significance of the CPSU's course of complete *perestroika* of Soviet society. And although it is hardly necessary to say so here, I can confirm that there is complete correspondence between the Soviet Union and Bulgaria over all tasks and measures of *perestroika*, a conclusion which was confirmed to me by my meeting with comrade Mikhail Gorbachev.[64]

Personnel changes were also effected following the conference, although Zhivkov remained in post, essentially serving to freeze policy in the *status quo*. He used the empty rhetoric of reform but prevented its implementation by negating the real need for it. This is most apparent from the fact that all measures proposed at the conference were postponed until the forthcoming Fourteenth BCP Congress 1991.[65] The 1988 Bulgarian conference paid lip service to Gorbachev, and was clearly convened with reference to the Nineteenth CPSU Conference, although radical changes in the leadership (including Zhivkov's removal from office) were not achieved. In terms of the Bulgarian conference *outcome*, it is unlikely that Gorbachev would have been satisfied with the result.

In 1988 the CPSU had little faith in Zhivkov as a proponent of *perestroika* and reform of the BCP in step with Gorbachev's domestic policies. Zhivkov had been First Secretary of the BCP since 1954 and President since 1971. By 1988, reformists in the Soviet Union already favoured Petŭr Mladenov (at the time foreign minister and later Zhivkov's successor in November 1989). At the Warsaw Pact meeting of July 1989, Mladenov secretly conveyed to Gorbachev that, unlike Zhivkov, he would reform the BCP.[66] As the most loyal of the Soviet Union's East European allies,[67] Zhivkov sought to satisfy Gorbachev with the promise of introducing Gorbachevian *perestroika*, and in publicly doing so, he hoped to avoid the wholesale modernisation of the BCP (including his own removal from office) that the reforms demanded.[68]

An article published in October 1988 in the *World Marxist Review*, comprising interviews with Bulgarian, Hungarian,

Soviet and Yugoslav officials, compared their respective conferences. These four conferences occurred in sequence beginning
with the BCP in January 1988, the HSWP and the LCY in
May, followed by the CPSU conference in June. What is most
apparent from the article is that with the exception of the
Bulgarian interviewee, all stated a common purpose to their
conferences: that the prospective meetings were to deal with
political, economic or social crisis.[69] The Bulgarian respondent
instead said that 'the special thing about the BCP conference is
that it did not mark a sharp turn in the development of socialism in Bulgaria'. In response to the question, 'Can one identify
common elements in the approach of the fraternal parties to
the essence of the modern concepts of socialist development?',
the Hungarian representative answered, 'Apparently, the thrust
of our reforms is the same: they are to make continued and
successful development of socialism possible.'[70] In contrast,
the Bulgarian replied that the Bulgarian model of socialism was
'yet to be worked out'.[71] The *World Marxist Review* certainly
emphasised that these conferences were viewed as comparable and part of a common fraternal initiative. The fact that
the Bulgarian delegate's response differed significantly from
the others does suggest that reforms in tune with Gorbachev's
perestroika were indeed not planned for the BCP.[72]

Therefore, although analysis of the Bulgarian conference
indicates some evidence of Soviet influence over conference
convention, the modernisation required to breathe new life
into the party via top-level personnel changes was clearly not
on the agenda. This suggests that there was no (or insufficient) collaboration between CPSU and BCP actors to effect
the desired Gorbachevian conference outcome at this time. By
analogy with other conferences, as will be explored later, we
can assume that Gorbachev expected, or hoped, that at the
BCP conference a reformist such as Mladenov would replace
Zhivkov. But, as will be discussed later, a reformist fraternal
party conference outcome does not necessarily mean that the
reformist wing of the CPSU had more 'control' over a particular regime and hence over conference outcome. Instead this
could be explained by reformists in these regimes managing
to gain the advantage in achieving their desired outcome and
being successfully supported in this by the reformist wing of
the CPSU.

Czechoslovakia and the GDR

Reductions in Soviet oil exports to Czechoslovakia and the GDR in the 1980s, although very sizeable, affected these economies much less than the other CMEA members, because of their energy profiles. Domestic coal production in Czechoslovakia and the GDR insulated them from this adverse shock.[73] The economic reforms of the 'kombinat', introduced years earlier, and the subsidies from West Germany enabled the GDR economy to function better than other centrally planned economies.[74] Because the Czechoslovak and GDR economies were less dependent on the Soviet Union, this may have given these leaderships greater political freedom from Moscow, which is reflected in the fact that the Communist Party of Czechoslovakia (CPCZ) leadership felt strong enough to flout Gorbachev's request for personnel change in the party. Although in 1987 and early 1988, Czechoslovakia was at the forefront in implementing Soviet CMEA policy for developing trade relations with the West (in particular with Western Europe and West Germany) and was the first to embrace currency convertibility with the rouble in early 1988, the Jakeš leadership rejected wholesale Gorbachev's political *perestroika* and *glasnost* policies. The CPCZ leadership was still largely peopled with those who had assumed power in 1969 after Soviet intervention and 'normalisation' of Czechoslovakia in 1968, and the principles of *perestroika* approved at the Nineteenth CPSU Conference very much resembled the CPCZ 'Action Programme' of 1968 that had led to the events of the Prague Spring. Since those that replaced Aleksandr Dubček's liberal government[75] had founded their regime's ideology on the rejection of this reformist programme of 1968, adoption of Gorbachev's political *perestroika* in 1988 would naturally have undermined their legitimacy. The fear of adopting *glasnost* lest it should result in the growth of civil rights movements as had burgeoned in 1968 acted as another strong check on the CPCZ's approval of such policies.[76]

Miloš Jakeš replaced Gustav Husák[77] as First Secretary of the CPCZ in December 1987. Although still an opponent of Gorbachev's reforms, Jakeš had been appointed with Soviet approval as a more liberal leader, and more in tune with Gorbachev's centrist policy. Since all reform communists from the pre-1969 era had been removed from the party, there was little pressure from the membership to adopt Gorbachev's political *perestroika*. Indeed, civil rights groups such as Charter 77 were more favourably disposed towards Gorbachev's political reforms, as were the disenfranchised remnants of the victims of the normalisation of 1968, including Alexander Dubček. Hence the convocation of a party conference even to pay lip service to Gorbachev's political reforms could have provoked a serious reaction from these civil rights groups. Alternatively, it might have necessitated the enfranchisement of the pre-1969 reformists and perhaps their reinstatement in the top leadership.[78]

In January 1988, Gorbachev asked Jakeš whether the CPCZ intended similar measures as at the planned CPSU conference in June 1988. Questioning what might be expected of the Czechoslovak leadership, Jakeš inquired of Gorbachev whether personnel changes to the CPSU CC were intended at the conference. When Gorbachev agreed that there would be personnel changes, Jakeš explained that the CPCZ planned instead to deal with such matters at the local party conferences between April and May. He clarified that the primary party organisations and the regional and *oblast* party organisations would be holding elections at the end of January 1988. Gorbachev, however, urged personnel changes in the Czechoslovak party leadership, insisting that personnel issues could not be put off, as the following exchange illustrates.

> **Gorbachev:** At the forthcoming All-Union party conference we want to review the progress of *perestroika* and questions of future democratisation. The important thing is to find new ways to democratise the party and all of society. We are currently conducting plenums of the party committees and meetings of communists at which they are discussing 'the results of the electoral organs on the work of the leadership of *perestroika*'. The debates are more heated and interesting than we've had in years. We are thinking of increasing the role of the Soviets [councils]. Regarding the party, the party alone can act as the vanguard. The party will take the principal decisions in the area of politics, nationalities' relations, defence, ideology, cadres etc. As far as concrete implementation of these decisions is concerned, an active role should be played by the Soviets [councils] and economic organs.

> **Jakeš:** You said that you are preparing for the conference. Do you have any intentions of making changes to the composition of the CC?

Gorbachev: Of course there will certainly be some; these all concern people being asked to retire. I'd again like to stress that the conference is to deepen the concept of the understanding of *perestroika.*

Jakeš: Well, we are holding local party conferences to review such conditions between April and May. At the end of January 1988, there will be elections in the primary party organisations and in the regional, and *oblast*, party organisations. At the end of March at the CC CPCZ plenum we will discuss the results of the elections and we will set tasks for the party to develop in the way of *perestroika.* These experiences will then be enacted between April and May by the party conferences at the regional level and then the county level. We want to engage the party and strengthen its involvement with *perestroika.*

Gorbachev: *Perestroika* in our country began at the party's initiative. But that means above all, that it is the party which needs to be the subject of *perestroika.* The party needs to set an example in all things.

Jakeš: Between May and June we are thinking of holding a special plenum and discussing the question of the party's ideological work under conditions of *perestroika.*

...

Gorbachev: We know from our own experiences how important the rotation of cadres and the influx of new forces is. ... I understand that there are certain personnel changes that need to be made as first priority and must not be delayed.

Jakeš: We will solve our personnel problems sensibly. After all that A. Kapek[79] has said, he should clearly be asked to retire. That would be the best solution in the given situation. L. Štrougal's[80] behaviour in the leadership is ambiguous. On the one hand he is capable of working [cooperatively] and on the other he often demonstrates his capricious character. Recently I spoke with him about my ideas on the personnel changes I just outlined to you. He at once said he disagreed with them, although he did not present a very convincing counter-argument. Regarding F. Hanus,[81] he said 'that one has ambition' and he said that J. Janík[82] is poorly educated. He also said that he was not sure whether Hoffmann[83] should be sent on party work. Finally, Štrougal threatened that, in the event of the proposed line of personnel changes, he would resign [lit. retire]. I said to him that of course he could retire but in any event he should not constantly threaten this as a way of pressuring the leadership.[84]

The tone of the text suggests that Jakeš assumed the CPCZ should act in accordance with CPSU policy. This attitude is evident from Jakeš' question whether Czechoslovakia should follow Poland's example and promote the idea of a demilitarised corridor between the North Atlantic Treaty Organisation (NATO) and Warsaw Pact countries. Gorbachev responded that the Czechoslovak leadership should discuss this with the Soviet Ministry of Defence and work this out in a way 'that is generally within the sphere of our overall policy':

> Gorbachev: I think that your colleagues should work that out with our Ministry of Defence and Ministry of Foreign Affairs. In principle we welcome the initiatives on policy from the fraternal parties that conduct themselves in a way that is generally within the sphere of our overall policy.[85]

The final exchange as to whether Czechoslovakia should follow the example of Poland clearly indicates an understanding that fraternal parties were expected firstly to consult on these issues, and secondly to follow CPSU directives, although with respect to convening a party conference, this did not take place in either the CPCZ or the GDR's Socialist Unity Party of Germany (SED).

Although the SED did not hold a national party conference, in February 1988, an event on a similar scale[86] as the conference was convened by Erich Honecker (First Secretary since 1971) in the form of a meeting of the Secretariat of the SED CC and First Secretaries of all the Districts. At the meeting, delegates discussed the progress of the 1986–90 FYP ratified at the Eleventh Party Congress and future implications of the dismantling of Soviet missiles on GDR territory.[87] As he had done on other occasions since 1987,[88] Honecker stressed at the meeting that in the GDR's struggle to perfect its own brand of socialism, it was beneficial to follow the example of other socialist states but that purely 'copying them' would prove detrimental. Throughout 1987 and 1988 Honecker reiterated that *perestroika* was unnecessary for the GDR, as the SED had already introduced economic reforms during the 1970s, and he expressed his disapproval of *glasnost*. Consequently, of all the Central, Eastern and South-eastern European parties, the SED remained least in step with CPSU domestic policy.[89]

Thus Honecker's regime made it quite plain that it had no intention of following the reformist leaderships in pursuing radical reform. An SED conference had only ever been held three times,[90] the first being in January 1949, the second in 1952 and the third in 1956.[91] Since Honecker had been a member of the SED CC since 1946,[92] it is quite possible that he was present at all three conferences. However, most likely fearful that he would be replaced at a conference, Honecker did not follow the Soviet example and convene the NPC. Indeed, given Honecker's public rejection of *perestroika* and *glasnost*, a conference would have been impossible without a complete reversal of policy. Instead, by convening a meeting of just the top party officials, Honecker was able to ensure a compliant gathering of delegates that would allow him to maintain the *status quo*. By excluding rank-and-file members from the meeting, he minimised the risk of being forced to make radical changes in keeping with *perestroika* by popular demand. Such changes would have inevitably led to his resignation.

By December 1988, Honecker had evidently capitulated. At the Seventh Plenum of the SED CC in December 1988, he abruptly announced that the forthcoming Twelfth Party Congress was to be brought forward a year. This rescheduling was a signal to many at the time that Honecker was planning to step down from his long-standing post as party leader and that the rearranged congress would be the event at which power would change hands.[93] Moreover, it was a step commensurate with holding an extraordinary congress or NPC, in that these were all-party meetings where leadership change could be made.

Czechoslovakia held parliamentary elections and thus made personnel changes. Following the instatement of Miloš Jakeš in March 1988, regional party conferences were held instead of an NPC in Czechoslovakia during May 1988. These regional conferences dealt mainly with the evaluation of progress towards plan fulfilment since the Seventeenth Party Congress, how to implement *perestroika* and the re-election of local-level party organisation CCs.[94]

Although elections took place at these local conferences in May 1988 and personnel change occurred, significantly an NPC was not convened for this purpose. Similarly, the GDR held local conferences in early spring 1988. Holding a conference would have implicitly demanded a declaration of the new course of the party, which would have entailed the public renunciation of the Brezhnev Doctrine, in accordance with the new dynamic of the Warsaw Pact, and *glasnost* regarding previous party history, which was also encouraged by Gorbachev. Since both Honecker and his CPCZ counterpart, Gustáv Husák, were old-timers whose legitimacy as leaders had been primarily founded through the dynamic of the Warsaw Pact, it was highly likely that such an event would have been embarrassing to them, and resulted in their public replacement. Instead both leaders chose to 'bow out' in different ways, and did so more or less within Gorbachev's desired time frame.

Hungary

Following the change in Soviet oil allocation to the CMEA states, the reduction in oil exports to Hungary in particular affected the Hungarian economy very adversely because of the country's relatively high consumption of oil.[95] Hungary's economy was, therefore, more dependent on the Soviet Union, and this factor may have influenced the HSWP to do Moscow's bidding and convene a conference. Following the CMEA meeting on 10–11 November 1986, bilateral talks between János Kádár and Gorbachev were held on 12 November.[96] During these talks Gorbachev offered Kádár increased economic assistance to Hungary, which Kádár accepted.[97] Whether this assistance was offered as a *quid pro quo* for political compliance with CPSU policy is not documented. On 4 November 1987, Kádár attended a meeting of the international communist movement in Moscow,[98] at which Gorbachev confirmed his redefinition of the Brezhnev Doctrine.[99] Kádár was, however, opposed to Gorbachevian *perestroika* for the same reasons as the GDR and Czechoslovak leaderships and, similarly, for some months, refused to hold a conference.[100] Kádár had come to power and his regime had been legitimised around the ideology that the events of 1956 constituted a 'counter-revolution'. The most likely outcome of a conference was therefore his own removal from office, along with the rest of his generation that had swept to power between 1956 and 1957. This was indeed the result of the conference.[101]

This was feasible because the HSWP leadership included a growing number of reform-communists, some of whom had been dismissed (by Soviet sanction)[102] from the Politburo for their pursuit of radical economic reforms during the 1970s, including Rezső Nyers and Jenő Fock. These two remained in the CC and advocated the appointment of other reform-ists, including Imre Pozsgay.[103] Additionally a new generation of reform-communists peopled the Politburo, notably Károly Grósz, János Berecz,[104] and in the CC Péter Medgyessy[105] and Mátyás Szűrös.[106] Thus the balance of power in the party was becoming favourable for a leadership change in the direction of a centrist Gorbachevian government. As Gabriel Partos has described: '1987–8 were characterized by a convergence of views between reformist Hungary and Gorbachev's more vigorous application of *perestroika.*'[107]

Commentators document that in Hungarian political circles, it had become very clear by 1987 that Gorbachev was cultivat-ing Károly Grósz to replace János Kádár, who had been First Secretary since the Soviet invasion of 1956.[108] In 1986 during Gorbachev's visit to Budapest, Kádár had publicly proclaimed his non-alignment with new Soviet policy by openly criticis-ing Gorbachev's policies. The preferred heir apparent, Grósz, engineered the timing of the conference, and according to many different sources, collaborated with Moscow in success-fully bringing about Kádár's resignation, evidently on 3 May 1988 (a couple of weeks before the conference). The confer-ence itself resulted in the dismissal of a significant number of the old guard from the CC and the first public display of open opposition to government, in the form of an ultra-reformist branch of the HSWP. There is significant evidence to suggest Soviet intervention in the conference's outcome.[109]

At an HSWP CC meeting in December 1987, Gyúla Horn,[110] a staunch supporter of Grósz and the ouster of Kádár, detailed a plan of action for the consolidation of party power at a proposed NPC the following year. Significantly, what Horn proposed was very similar indeed to what had been outlined by LCY President Boško Krunić for their forthcoming LCY conference. Each favoured the plan of consolidating the party's power at a restricted meeting where controlled change could be proposed and where discussion of the crisis could be contained:

> In my opinion the party conference can adopt a role extremely quickly in the matter of foreign affairs. I think that here there is not a lot to debate with the public or with the party membership. Then it could also spread to ideological questions because those are also real issues. We should also occupy ourselves with the [issue of the] leading role of the party as we have already said many times before how society relates to it. Then there is the question

of the development programme and the topic of the stabilisation programme.[111]

Horn stated that criticism of the regime from within the party and among non-party members in society was undermining the HSWP, and that other fraternal states were experiencing similar problems. Horn proposed reform of the political system and personnel changes, but made it clear that the conference should 'in no way be an advertisement for the introduction of a multiparty system' and that the leading role of the party within the existing one-party system should be emphasised at the conference.[112]

Yugoslavia

Although Yugoslavia had followed a policy of non-alignment with Moscow since 1948 and consequently had not qualified for membership of the CMEA when it was founded in 1949, from 1964 Yugoslavia was granted associate member status of the CMEA and by the 1980s was heavily dependent on Soviet oil imports. The Soviet Union was Yugoslavia's greatest trading partner during the 1980s, exchanging oil in return for Yugoslav exports. The Yugoslav economy was already in crisis by this time, burdened with a very sizeable foreign debt, high unemployment and inflation, and so the reduction in Soviet oil exports badly affected Yugoslavia. Such dependence on the Soviet Union seems rather counter-intuitive given that Yugoslavia was not a member of the Warsaw Pact, nor a member of the CMEA, and had cultivated strong links with the West. Nor was this substantial aid widely acknowledged.[113] Nonetheless, this economic dependence may have made the Yugoslav leadership more willing to meet Moscow's political needs. Relations between the two parties were significantly revitalised after Gorbachev's visit to Yugoslavia in March 1988, and promised an era of greater collaboration.[114] At this time, Yugoslavia was subject to pressure from the International Monetary Fund (IMF) for the repayment of a large hard currency debt, and as in the case of Poland, this economic leverage may have helped foster LCY support for Gorbachev's *perestroika* campaign. Indeed, as will be detailed in Chapter 6, during Gorbachev's visit to Yugoslavia in March 1988, Yugoslavia was granted what amounted to new and favourable CMEA terms of trade (despite its non-membership of the CMEA) and increased Soviet credit to deal with the large hard currency debt that had accrued from purchasing oil from the Soviet Union under Western terms of trade since the early 1980s. From the press coverage in the LCY party newspaper, *Komunist*, it would appear that in return for this Soviet financial aid, the LCY offered endorsement of the CPSU's new political agenda, *perestroika*, and specifically the forthcoming Nineteenth CPSU Conference.[115]

Transcripts of discussions from Gorbachev's meetings in Yugoslavia in 1988 explain his reasons for trying to transform the CPSU and encourage reform of the fraternal parties' leaderships. These meetings were held during Gorbachev's visit to Yugoslavia from 14–18 March 1988.[116] He claimed that Western governments had developed a strategy to maximise the chaos resulting from the implementation of *perestroika* and that the purpose of this was to make Central, Eastern and South-eastern Europe vulnerable to Western political influence to bring about regime change in these states. Gorbachev stated at one of these meetings:

> I called this meeting so that I could discuss one question which we touched upon in passing during the course of our meetings. Information has reached us that leading government groups in the West have seriously put their heads together over how best to take advantage of the way things are developing these days in the socialist countries. They start from the premise that the Soviet Union, submerged in *perestroika*, is going through a difficult period and that *perestroika* of the relations between the socialist countries is in line with the principle of independence and self-reliance, and ultimately will result in the rise of centrifugal forces in world socialism. This in their view creates qualitatively new possibilities, which, if squandered, would be for the West a historic mistake. So, making use of the difficulties Poland is experiencing, they are promising to meet Poland halfway under conditions of the recognition of Solidarity and [Poland's] agreement to the [legal] formation of opposition political parties. In Poland, as is well known, there are strong religious feelings so that at any moment an opposition party of a Christian type could form. And Polish comrades decisively deny such a situation [while] in truth they see these [opposition parties] as a direct threat to socialism. There are similar intrigues in Hungary, the GDR and other countries. But above all they have the Soviet Union in their sights. They are developing plans to undermine *perestroika*, having blocked the channels of cooperation with the capitalist countries in the economic sphere, they will not allow us to stand independent.

Gorbachev argued that Western governments were calling his bluff over the real implementation of *glasnost* and democratisation. Indeed, the following extract strongly suggests that Gorbachev intended to maintain the *status quo*, but was being forced into a corner to honour his public statement of non-interference in the case of secessionist republics:

> They make use of the atmosphere of democratisation and *glasnost* to the detriment of the friendship among the nationalities within the Soviet Union by upsetting relations among the nationalities. This stems from the [premise] that if we really take measures to stop these detrimental activities then we will be accused of breaking with and discrediting our process of democratisation and thus they would achieve their desired goal in showing that socialism is incapable of solving its own problems. The main initiator of this strategy was M. Thatcher. At the NATO meeting in Brussels this was the main point – everything else was just a camouflage.[117] It was here that the West fully displayed its intention to undermine the influence of the Soviet Union's peaceful foreign policy in public world opinion.[118]

As he had explained to other fraternal leaders, Gorbachev argued that the West was taking advantage of the fraternal countries' economic[119] and political crises, and was using these as an opportunity to create and support political opposition cells in these states. This was ultimately for the purpose of undermining the monopoly of the ruling communist parties, so that multiparty systems would evolve. As Gorbachev explained to Lazar Mojsov, of the LCY Presidium:[120]

> The essence of the programme is that they are trying to put together a series of measures geared towards making use of the difficulties the socialist countries are going through and influencing them under the pretext that they each should have a different approach. The same theme of stimulating opposition parties has been heard widely. The issue is not limited only to claims but also to attempts at actually founding the cells of such parties. I think that these examples are of interest to you, too, which is why we considered it strategically important to inform the Yugoslav government.

Gorbachev then explained in this context the importance of consolidating the party's leading role, which would serve to maintain the integrity of the Soviet Union, and that they would present their proposed solutions at the forthcoming Nineteenth CPSU Conference:

In this connection, I would like to emphasise two issues: the importance of strengthening the party as the political vanguard of society and of course not by means of command but by methods of political and ideological activity, which should act as a centripetal force in our multinational states. We cannot diverge from that. Life [experience] shows that strong unifying forces are needed to integrate the country into one whole. We will think about these issues, so as to work out a subsequent approach and present it at our forthcoming party conference.[121]

Clearly, at this meeting, Gorbachev sought some advice on how best to deal with the prospect of growing republican autonomy, which would inevitably arise as a consequence of liberalisation. This issue was very familiar to the LCY and one which they had traditionally addressed at the federal conference.

As an institution, the LCY conference was developed in 1973 with the purpose of replacing the CC in preparation for a more confederalist state, which the federal leadership envisaged as the only feasible way to maintain the federation's future integrity. The conference in this format was disbanded when the whole experiment failed, after Serbia refused to ratify the new constitution of 1974 that had granted Vojvodina and Kosovo autonomous status. Consequently, the former rules concerning conference convention were reintroduced into the LCY Party Rules in 1982. Therefore, as an institution, the conference of May 1988 was similar to that held in the other fraternal parties, and similar themes were raised in support of *perestroika*. At the same time, Yugoslavia had not only to deal with the problem of falling party membership, as experienced by the rest of the socialist fraternity, but sought also to increase federal party authority over the federation's increasingly autonomous constituent republics.

Poland

Although Poland had accrued by far the greatest foreign debt during the 1980s, and was therefore in serious economic crisis, it was not particularly adversely affected by the change in Soviet oil allocation as the Soviet Union, aware of the unstable socio-political situation arising from a resurgence of the Solidarity movement in Poland, reduced oil exports to Poland by the least amount. Like Czechoslovakia and the GDR, Poland relied mainly on its own coal industry as a source of energy and so its economy was less dependent on the Soviet Union. Unlike Hungary and Bulgaria, Poland did not re-export Soviet oil as a source of hard-currency earnings, and so was in any event less vulnerable to these policy changes.[122] The Soviet Union at this time did, however, maintain some financial aid to Poland,[123] although not on the same scale as it had done during the early 1980s.[124]

Archival materials detail that between 1987 and 1988, Gorbachev and Jaruzelski discussed their respective forthcoming conferences.[125] In 1987 Jaruzelski stated that the PUWP would be holding the conference in 1988, but then, subsequently, during Gorbachev's visit to Warsaw the following year, a couple of weeks after the Nineteenth CPSU Conference, Jaruzelski offered his excuses for postponing the PUWP conference until 1989.[126] His reluctance to convene a conference appears analogous to Husák's and Honecker's unwillingness in this respect: *glasnost* brought with it revelations that were deeply harmful to all these leaders and Gorbachev's destalinisation policy required admission of these malpractices of socialism, as a precondition for the party's renewed capacity to re-engage society.

At the meeting in April 1987, Gorbachev advised Jaruzelski to strengthen the PUWP's leading role in society, but at the same time Gorbachev warned that the party needed modernising in tune with public opinion, otherwise there was a risk that the 'mood of the masses' might initiate change, which could lead to confrontation.[127] In July 1986 Gorbachev had attended the Tenth PUWP Congress, at which he stated that the events of 1980–81 and the conflict between Solidarity and the party were the fault of the PUWP, and that the working classes had simply been expressing their legitimate criticism against a regime which was practising socialism incorrectly.[128] Gorbachev had therefore already implicitly acknowledged the legitimacy of Solidarity, and publicly declared his own view that the introduction of martial law was the result of the PUWP's failure, instead of a legitimate response by the regime to put down a counter-revolution. As Jaruzelski had established his legitimacy as First Party Secretary around the belief that his step to introduce martial law had averted an even more bloody Soviet invasion, this statement must have damaged Jaruzelski's authority within the party, and raised the question as to whether or not the Soviet Union had had any intention to intervene in 1981.

During their 1987 meeting, Gorbachev and Jaruzelski had signed a joint declaration to investigate and publicise the truth about historical matters concerning both the Soviet Union and Poland, which had damaged relations between the two states.[129] This included the issue of the Katyń Massacre of 1940, which throughout the socialist fraternity had been construed as an atrocity committed by Nazi Germany, but which the vast majority of Poles knew to be a Stalinist crime. Gorbachev's and Jaruzelski's agreement also entailed revealing the truth about martial law, as Chapter 7 will discuss. Revelations concerning both these issues would have been damaging for Jaruzelski and so at the prospect of convening a conference under such circumstances he must have worried that the meeting could result in his removal from office. This could explain why he deferred the event from 1988 to 1989.

Poland's conference was finally held in May 1989 and was convened shortly after the April 1989 round-table talks which had agreed that thirty-five per cent of the seats in the Sejm and all of the seats in the Senate were to be contested. According to Alfred Stepan's typology this conference could be situated at the 'reform-pact' stage of transition, following the 'reform' stage.[130] However, the conference was very far removed from these liberalisation processes, and was so overshadowed by them that it features rather more as a 'non-event'. The meeting nominally espoused the same ideals and policies as *perestroika*, and reaffirmed the party's leading role in society. But in the context of Poland's political situation of 1989, these declarations appeared irrelevant, and did little (if anything) to improve the image of the party. Nor did it offer Gorbachev the timely support he had needed the previous year. Jaruzelski was sufficiently in control at the conference, however, to postpone his own ouster. After the PUWP's unprecedented defeat at the June elections the following month, Jaruzelski resigned as First Party Secretary, and allowed the more reformist Mieczysław Rakowski to take his place.

Conclusion

So far we have focused on the extent to which regime type and varying levels of economic dependence on the Soviet Union induced fraternal party leaders to convene a conference in support of Gorbachev's policies. There was an inherent tension for fraternal leaders in adopting these policies, in particular *glasnost* regarding Stalinist crimes and the renunciation of the Brezhnev Doctrine, which posed a significant threat to all fraternal leaders that had either come to power in the wake of Soviet intervention or had personally supported one of these invasions by sending their own troops. Regardless of whether these leaders themselves embraced Gorbachev's *perestroika*, they were aware that it was only a question of time before they themselves would have to resign, as Gorbachev had already broadcast the new terms of the socialist fraternity worldwide. Moreover, as a leader who had not been personally involved in such military cooperation to maintain the integrity of the socialist fraternity, Gorbachev had an unassailable position. He was innocent of complicity in these 'crimes', but at the same time he held compromising information regarding these leaders' involvement. Those that remained 'untainted' by this issue were Albania, Romania and Yugoslavia. Although the first two clearly did not convene conferences to pursue align-ment with Gorbachevian *perestroika*, Yugoslavia apparently did so.

From the archival material, there is clear evidence that Bulgaria, Czechoslovakia (and perhaps the GDR by analogy), Hungary, Poland and Yugoslavia were in communication about and were responding to Gorbachev's request for a conference. There is, however, no archival evidence of this in the cases of the Albanian and Romanian communist parties.[131] Although both held conferences in November and December 1987 respectively, relations between these parties' leaderships and the CPSU were strained and any Soviet initiative for liberalisa-tion would not have been welcomed by such regimes.

Romania, Albania and Bulgaria respectively did not actively align themselves with CPSU policy – although the BCP made a show of doing so, without making leadership changes or implementing the policies proposed at the conference – and convened their conferences some months in advance of their Hungarian, Soviet and Yugoslav counterparts. Czechoslovakia and the GDR were sufficiently financially independent of the Soviet Union to reject both *perestroika* and the need for a conference, and instead convened regional conferences. At the same time, as will be discussed in Chapter 7, because of their awareness that the CPSU and other fraternal parties held compromising information that could have been used to publicly oust these ageing leaders, both chose to 'jump' before being pushed from office. Since both the Czechoslovakian and GDR leaderships had wholesale rejected *perestroika*, the convention of a conference to align with CPSU policy was in any event anathema. In marked contrast to this, Hungary and Yugoslavia held conferences at which incumbent members of the leadership aligned themselves politically with the CPSU. Since Jaruzelski's regime was the most vocal and active supporter of Gorbachev's *perestroika*, which would suggest a strong coincidence of interests between the regimes, it is particularly surprising that the PUWP conference was convened so late, and produced so little in terms of modernising the regime in terms of personnel change. The PUWP case is particularly interesting as it indicates more clearly than the other cases a reluctant step on Jaruzelski's part to comply with Gorbachev's request, as Chapter 7 will illustrate. This case has therefore been chosen as a counterfoil to the other three cases for in-depth study instead of Bulgaria.

Notes

1   HSWP member in 1988 and HSP parliamentary deputy in 2003.

2   Interview with Zoltán Szabó, Budapest, 2 June 2003.

3   *Ibid.*

4   T. Colton and R. Tucker, *Patterns in Post-Soviet Leadership* (Boulder CO: Westview, 1995), p. 49.

5   V. Mastny and M. Byrne, *A Cardboard Castle: an inside history of the Warsaw Pact, 1955–1991* (Budapest: CEU Press, 2005), p. 79.

6   P. Dybicz and G. Sołtysiak, *Rozmowy dyplomatyczne polityków państw-stron Układu Warszawskiego 1985–1989* (Warszawa: Wyd. Mag, 2009), p. 8.

7   *Ibid.*, p. 7.

8   *Ibid.*, p. 14.

9   *Ibid.*, pp. 77–83.

10 L. Whitehead, *The International Dimensions of Democratization: Europe and the Americas* (Oxford: Oxford University Press, 1996), pp. 382–3.

11 Jacques Lévesque details *informal* sources for Soviet influence over events. See J. Lévesque, *The Enigma of 1989: the USSR and the Liberation of Eastern Europe* (Berkeley CA: University of California Press, 1997), pp. 93–204.

12 Vadim Zagladin was First Deputy Head of the International Department of the CC from 1975–88 and became one of Gorbachev's advisers in 1988.

13   Gorbachev Foundation. Vadim Zagladin's fond. Z86 Nov 10.

14   See Chapter 5.

15   From 1986, Vadim Medvedev was a secretary of the CC and after the Nineteenth CPSU Conference in 1988 was promoted to the Politburo while retaining his CC secretaryship. Between 1986 and 1988 he was in charge of the department of the CPSU CC that 'kept an eye on other communist countries'. See A. Brown, *The Gorbachev Factor* (Oxford: Oxford University Press, 1996), p. 341.

16   Gorbachev Foundation. Vadim Medvedev's fond, M.87.Feb.02.doc.

17   *Ibid.*, M.87.Nov.18.doc; M.87.Nov.25.doc.

18   Jaruzelski formed a coalition leadership with Stanisław Kania to replace Edward Gierek in 1980 and then was appointed sole leader of the PUWP in October 1981.

19   *Życie Partii*, 13 July 1988, p. 5. Similar reports of the new agreement between socialist parties can be found in *Rudé Právo*, 5 January 1988.

20   Gorbachev Foundation. Mikhail Gorbachev's fond, 87.Apr.21.doc; 87.Apr.28b.doc; 88.Jan.11.doc; 88.July.14.doc; 88.Mar.14-18.doc.

21   Yugoslavia had long since dispensed with the social contract of full employment, having experienced high levels of unemployment, from 5 per cent in 1952 to 17 per cent in 1988. See S. Woodward (1995), *Socialist Unemployment: the Political Economy of Yugoslavia 1945–1990* (Princeton NJ: Princeton University Press, 1995), p. 191.

22   A. Smith, 'Economic relations' in Alex Pravda (ed.), *The End of Outer Empire: Soviet-East European Relations in Transition 1985–90* (London: Sage for RIIA, 1992).

23   Interview with György Wiener, Budapest, 4 June 2003; interview with Hungarian civil servant, Budapest, 3 June 2003.

24   Interview with Hungarian civil servant, Budapest, 3 June 2003.

25   Interview with Evgenii Chazov, Moscow, 30 October 2002.

26   See Chapter 3, p. 73.

27   Adhering to article 6 of the constitution maintaining the party's leading role in society.

28   For a discussion of compliance, see: P. Leach, H. Hardman, S. Stephenson and B. Blitz, *Responding to systemic human rights violations: an analysis of the European Court of Human Rights and their impact at national level* (Antwerp: Intersentia, 2010), pp. 4–5.

29   There is earlier evidence of this, too, as is detailed in Chapter 7, pp. 250–5.

30   For an account of global pressures, see B. Geddes, 'What do we know about Democratization after Twenty Years?', *Annual Review of Political Science* 2 (1999), pp. 115–44 and A. Przeworski, *Sustainable Democracy* (Cambridge: Cambridge University Press, 1995), pp. 1–10. For a detailed account of systemic domestic economic collapse in planned economies, see J. Kornai, *The Socialist System: the Political Economy of Socialism* (Oxford: Clarendon Press, 1992) and J. Elliott, 'Disintegration of the Soviet Politico-Economic System', *International Journal of Social Economics* 22:3 (1995), pp. 31–59. For the debate over how and to what extent inflated figures for Soviet growth hid the scale of economic crisis long after the collapse of the Soviet regime, see S. Rosefielde, 'Post-War Russian Economic Growth: Not a Riddle – a Reply', *Europe Asia Studies*

56:3 (2004), pp. 463–6; J. H. Wilhelm, 'The Failure of the American Sovietological Economics Profession', *Europe-Asia Studies*, 55:1 (2003), pp. 59–74; G. I. Khanin, 'The 1950s: the Triumph of the Soviet Economy', *Europe-Asia Studies*, 55:8 (2003), pp. 1187–212 and V. Kontorovich, 'Economists, Soviet Growth Slowdown and the Collapse', *Europe-Asia Studies*, 53:5 (2001), pp. 675–95.

31 L. A. Tarasov, 'The Economy of the Socialist Community', *Problems of Economics*, November (1988), pp. 96–7. For an account of systemic collapse attributed to the institutionalised practice of 'opportunism', see S. Solnick, *Stealing the State: Control and Collapse in Soviet Institutions* (Cambridge MA: Harvard University Press, 1998).

32 Although after Zhivkov's replacement the Bulgarian debt was revealed to be closer to twelve billion dollars, so this figure is a very conservative estimate.

33 Table, 'Eastern Europe, USSR and Yugoslavia: convertible currency debt, WIIW estimates in million US dollar' in *COMECON Data* (London: Macmillan, 1988), p. 379.

34 Smith, 'Economic relations', pp. 73–4.

35 Khanin notes a short-term improvement during the 1970s for the Soviet economy as oil extraction was accelerated from Western Siberia and the economy benefited from the increase in world prices; however, this source was soon exhausted by the 1980s due to the unecological methods of extraction. See G. I. Khanin, 'Economic Growth in the USSR in the Eighties', *Problems of Economics*, April (1992), p. 33.

36 M. Chadwick, D. Long and M. Nissanke, *Soviet oil exports: trade adjustments, refining constraints and market behaviour* (Oxford: Oxford University Press, 1987), pp. 125–6; 136.

37 K. Nyíri, *Inter-CMEA Cooperation in Energy and the New Trends in the World Economy: Proceedings of the Soviet-Hungarian Roundtable, June 22–26 1981, Moscow* (Budapest: Hungarian Council for World Economy, 1984), p. 94.

38 N. Iakhiel, *Todor Zhivkov i lichnata vlast: spomeni, dokumenti, analizi* (Sofiia: M-8-M, 1997), p. 313.

39 Head of the BCP from 1971–89.

40 Smith, 'Economic relations', p. 77.

41 Chadwick, Long and Nissanke, *Soviet oil exports*, p. 136.

42 I. Aboimov, 'Development of USSR relations with the socialist countries', *International Affairs (Moscow)*, 10 (1988), pp. 38–9.

43 Smith, 'Economic relations', pp. 76–8.

44 J. Stern, *Soviet Oil and Gas Exports to the West: Commercial Transaction or Security Threat* (London: RIIA, 1987), p. 19. As non-aligned states, both Yugoslavia and Romania pursued this policy for some time and consequently their economies suffered.

45 *Ibid.*, pp. 48–50.

46 Party of Labour of Albania, *National Conference dedicated to the immortal work of comrade Enver Hoxha, 15–16 October, 1985* (Tirana: 8 Nëntori Publishing House, 1985).

47 R. Staar, 'Checklist of Communist Parties in 1988', *Problems of Communism*, 38:Jan.–Feb. (1989), p. 65.

48 R. Alia, *Always in the Vanguard of Society, Bearer of Progress: Speech at the 8th Plenum of the CC of the PLA, September 25 1989* (Tirana: 8 Nëntori Publishing House, 1989), p. 8.

49 BBC Monitoring Service, *Summary of World Broadcasts*, 25 November 1987.

50 K. Dawisha, *Eastern Europe, Gorbachev and Reform: the Great Challenge* (Cambridge: Cambridge University Press, 2nd edn, 1990), p. 130.

51 Chadwick, Long and Nissanke, *Soviet oil exports*, p. 138.

52 W. Zimmerman, 'Soviet Relations with Yugoslavia and Romania', in S. M. Terry (ed.), *Soviet Policy in Eastern Europe* (London: Yale University Press, 1984), p. 126.

53 Dybicz and Sołtysiak, *Rozmowy dyplomatyczne polityków państw-stron Układu Warszawskiego 1985–89*, p. 82.

54 According to Lévesque, this contrasted greatly with Gorbachev's usually mild speeches about Soviet *perestroika* in other East European countries. See Lévesque, *The Enigma of 1989*, pp. 58–9.

55 Lévesque, *The Enigma of 1989*, p. 192.

56 Chadwick, Long and Nissanke, *Soviet oil exports*, p. 138.

57 Staar, 'Checklist of Communist Parties in 1988', p. 65.

58 Chairman of the Bulgarian Council of Ministers, 1986–90.

59 Gorbachev Foundation. Mikhail Gorbachev's fond, 87.Apr.28b.doc.

60 *Ibid.*

61 *Ibid.*

62 *Ibid.*

63 Bulgarian Communist Party, *Natsionalna partiina konferentsiia: stenografski protokol, 28–29 ianuari 1988 godina*, (Sofiia: Partizdat, 1988), pp. 31–86.

64 BCP, *Natsionalna partiina konferentsiia*, p. 38.

65 Staar, 'Checklist of Communist Parties in 1988', p. 65.

66 Lévesque, *The Enigma of 1989*, pp. 171–2.

67 According to Lévesque, Bulgaria was the Soviet Union's 'most faithful ally until the very end'. See Lévesque, *The Enigma of 1989*, p. 65; J. Lampe, *Balkans into Southeastern Europe: a Century of War and Transition* (Basingstoke: Palgrave Macmillan, 2006), p. 265.

68 Lévesque, *The Enigma of 1989*, pp. 166–8.

69 'The Socialist Way: Party Conferences, Realistic Renewal', *World Marxist Review*, 31:10 (1988), pp. 45–6.

70 *Ibid.*, p. 48.

71 *Ibid.*, p. 49.

72 *Ibid.*, p. 45.

73 Chadwick, Long and Nissanke, *Soviet oil exports*, pp. 138; 140.

74 P. Marer, 'Reforms in the USSR and Eastern Europe: is there a link?' in Aurel Braun (ed.), *The Soviet–East European Relationship in the Gorbachev Era: the Prospects for Adaptation* (Boulder CO: Westview, 1990), p. 91.

75 Alexander Dubček was First Secretary of the CC CPCZ, January 1968– April 1969 and then demoted after the Prague Spring to Czechoslovak

Ambassador to Turkey from 1969–70. He was then a worker in a forestry enterprise from 1975–84 before retiring.

76   B. Hnizdo, 'Czechoslovak-Soviet Relations', in A. Pravda (ed.), *The End of Outer Empire: Soviet–East European Relations in Transition, 1985–90* (London: RIIA, 1992), pp. 170–7.

77   Head of the CPCZ from 1971.

78   Hnizdo, 'Czechoslovak-Soviet Relations', pp. 178–83.

79   Antonín Kapek was a member of the CPCZ Presidium and CC member between 1969 and April 1988, after which he remained just a CC member. Kapek was the prime signatory of a letter which asked Brezhnev for fraternal 'help', which resulted in the Soviet invasion of Czechoslovakia in 1968. Kapek committed suicide in 1990; his letter was presented by the Soviet Union to the new leader Vaclav Havel.

80   Lubomír Štrougal was Prime Minister of Czechoslovakia, 1971–October 1988.

81   František Hanus was a CPCZ CC member at this time.

82   Jan Janík was a CPCZ CC member, elected in 1988 as Vice-Chairman to the Federal Parliament.

83   Karel Hoffmann was a member of the CPCZ CC Presidium, 1971–89.

84   Gorbachev Foundation. Mikhail Gorbachev's fond, 88.Jan.11.doc.

85   *Ibid.*

86   This appears to be the most comparable event to the conference at that time in the GDR.

87   BBC Monitoring Service, *Summary of World Broadcasts*, 15 February 1988.

88   A. Hyde-Price, 'GDR-Soviet Relations', in A. Pravda (ed.), *The End of Outer Empire: Soviet–East European Relations in Transition, 1985–90* (London: RIIA, 1992), p. 155.

89   *Ibid.*, p. 156.

90   91 The first conference which involved personnel changes to the leadership was convened under the leadership of Wilhem Pieck; see Sozialistische Enheitspartei Deutschlands, *Protokoll der Ersten Parteikonferenz der SED 25–28 Januar 1949* (Berlin: s.n., 1949). The second and third conferences were held under the hardline Stalinist Walter Ulbricht.

91   R. Eppelmann, *Lexikon des DDR-Sozialismus: das Staats- und Gesellschaftssystem der Deutschen Demokratischen Republik* (Paderborn: P. Schöningh, 1996), p. 463.

92   Although he was in Moscow between 1955 and 1957, and may thus have been absent from the 1956 conference.

93   R. Staar, *Communist Regimes in Eastern Europe* (Stanford CA: Hoover Institution Press, 5th edn, 1988), GDR chapter.

94   BBC Monitoring Service, *Summary of World Broadcasts*, 17 May 1988.

95   Chadwick, Long and Nissanke, *Soviet oil exports*, p. 138.

96   M. Nagy (ed.), *Magyar külpolitika 1956–1989* (Budapest: MTA, 1993), p. 233.

97   G. Földés, *Az eladósodás politikatörténete 1957–1986* (Budapest: Maecenas Könyvkiadó, 1995), p. 258.

98 Nagy (ed.), *Magyar külpolitika 1956–1989*, pp. 254–55.

99 A summary of what this entailed is cited in Chapter 6, p. 210.

100 See Chapter 5, pp. 155–9.

101 See Chapter 5, p. 166.

102 G. Partos (1992), 'Hungarian-Soviet Relations', in A. Pravda (ed.), *The End of Outer Empire: Soviet–East European Relations in Transition, 1985–90* (London: RIIA, 1992), p. 122.

103 Secretary General of the People's Patriotic Front between 1976 and 1988, Pozsgay was elected a member of the Politburo at the HSWP May 1988 conference.

104 Appointed Secretary of the HSWP CC in charge of ideology and propaganda in 1985, Berecz was elected to the Politburo in June 1987.

105 Appointed Minister of Finance in 1986, Medgyessy became Deputy Prime Minister in December 1987 and was elected a member of the HSWP CC in June 1987.

106 After serving as Hungarian Ambassador to the Soviet Union between 1979 and 1982, Szűrös was made HSWP CC Secretary for Foreign Affairs in 1983.

107 Partos, 'Hungarian-Soviet Relations', p. 121.

108 See Chapter 5, pp. 154–5.

109 See Chapter 5, pp. 170–4.

110 Horn was at this time State Secretary in the Ministry of Foreign Affairs and a member of the CC.

111 MOL KB 288.f.4/230–231.8.December.1987, p. 141.

112 *Ibid.*

113 B. McFarlane, *Yugoslavia: Politics, Economics and Society* (London: Pinter, 1988), p. 94.

114 As detailed in Chapter 6, pp. 207–14.

115 See Chapter 6, pp. 213–14.

116 This was at the height of the Nina Andreeva affair, when Gorbachev and the reformists were experiencing their most severe opposition from hardliners.

117 For Margaret Thatcher's press conferences before and after the Brussels meeting on 2 March 1988, see www.margaretthatcher.org/search/results.asp?startDate=1985-1-1&endDate=1988-12-31&ps=100&w=reagan%20AND%20gorbachev%20AND%20summit (last accessed 1.12.10).

118 Gorbachev Foundation. Mikhail Gorbachev's fond, 88.Mar.14–18.doc.

119 These archival materials appear to support the account proposed by Brooks and Wohlforth that policy changes implemented by Gorbachev were largely motivated by domestic economic conditions and the effects of the changing world economy. See S. Brooks and W. Wohlforth, 'Power, Globalization and the End of the Cold War', *International Security* 25:3 (2001), pp. 5–53.

120 Chairman of the LCY Presidium, May 1987–May 1988 and Serbian Presidium member.

121 Gorbachev Foundation. Mikhail Gorbachev's fond, 88.Mar.14-18.doc.

122 Chadwick, Long and Nissanke, *Soviet oil exports*, p. 140.

123 Gorbachev Foundation. Mikhail Gorbachev's fond, 87.Apr.21.doc.

124 See Chapter 7, p. 253.

125 See Chapter 7, pp. 239–42.

126 See Chapter 7, pp. 240–1.

127 See Chapter 7, p. 240.

128 See Chapter 7, pp. 254–5.

129 See Chapter 7, pp. 255–6.

130 A. Stepan, *Arguing Comparative Politics* (Oxford: Oxford University Press, 2001), p. 124.

131 Whether such conversations were held is not known. Such documents were not available among those lists offered for research in the Gorbachev Foundation.

5

Purging party factions: the HSWP national conference, May 1988

Introduction

This chapter will demonstrate that the HSWP leadership's decision to convene a conference in 1988 equated with a specific policy choice, which was to align the HSWP with CPSU *perestroika* and purge HSWP hardline opposition to Gorbachev's policies. Analysis of previous conference outcomes indicates a pattern that conferences always served to align Hungarian communists with the Russian Bolsheviks and later CPSU and purge members of the party who were considered opponents. As will be illustrated, in the case of May 1988, this entailed purging the party of hardline opposition and consolidating the centrist Gorbachevian line of *perestroika* while maintaining the *status quo* of the regime. The conference as an institution was perceived as a vehicle for Soviet 'normalisation' as is evident from the CC's debate over the choice of institution in 1987 and then later in 1989. As the chapter details, this debate culminated in a petition signed by the local party organisations, objecting to the way in which conferences were convened, and finally, in 1989, the reformists were victorious and secured instead an extraordinary congress.

Identifying the HSWP conference's 'informal constraints'

As outlined in Chapter 1, this chapter reviews Hungarian NPCs, looks at the outcome and conditions under which they were convened, and draws out the common features of these, which can be identified as the institution's 'informal constraints'. The purpose of this is to construct a framework, on the basis of previous outcomes, which helps us to understand the nature of the conference and under what circumstances a leadership might choose to convene one. This in turn then helps us work out what might motivate a leadership to convene a conference and what they would expect to achieve. On the assumption that these 'informal constraints' remained relatively static and so would continue to operate, we can identify what the conference represented to leaderships in terms of a policy choice. Thus previous conferences act as a precedent for future outcomes, and at the same time promise a formula for leaderships, which they can adopt to achieve a specific goal, as tried and tested in the past. Thus the choice of institution for leaderships becomes synonymous with a particular policy choice.[1]

Historical survey of the Hungarian NPC, 1918–57

There is some confusion as to which HSWP conference may be accurately described as the 'first'. Working backwards, the HSWP conference of 1988 has been referred to as the third.[2] Following this numeration, the second conference was in June 1957 and the conference in 1945 was the first.[3] Two earlier conferences of the Hungarian Bolsheviks took place, however, in 1918.

Much as the CPSU retrospectively claimed its first general conference as that of the Bolsheviks at Tammerfors in 1905,[4] the Hungarian communists adopted a similar strategy in the late 1950s. In the party journal *Társadalmi Szemle*, the HSWP dedicated the November 1958 issue to celebrating forty years of Hungarian communism. After some general introductory material, including a speech made by Kádár at a commemorative meeting, there is an article including the speeches of the party leader, Béla Kun, from two conferences of the Hungarian Group of the RCP(B)[5] held in Moscow in 1918. The first conference was held on 25 October 1918, and the second, an 'enlarged' conference, of greater import, was held just two weeks later on 4 November. Although the official party journal did not identify this 4 November conference as the first national conference, it did so by association of idea, which would not have been lost on its readership of 1958, just over a year after the 1957 conference, the first all-party meeting since Kádár had been appointed as First Secretary following the 1956 Revolution.

The conferences of 1918 were clandestine events convened by a small number of Hungarian revolutionary communists with the support of the Russian Bolsheviks. By the end of October 1918, the Austro-Hungarian monarchy's control had weakened considerably, and the revolutionaries planned to exploit this and secure a communist takeover of Hungary. The two Hungarian Bolshevik Moscow conferences were therefore convened for the purpose of planning a revolutionary coup in the wake of the impending collapse of Habsburg authority in Budapest.[6] Russian training and support for this movement has been well documented. The Hungarian Bolshevik group had spent some months training liberated or escaped prisoners of war to become 'agitators' in specially set-up political schools in Moscow and Omsk, with a view to exporting Communism to Hungary.[7]

Delegates at these conferences were drawn mainly from a pool of these Hungarian prisoners of war and the meetings were held in Moscow at a hotel where the headquarters of the Hungarian Group of the Communist (Bolshevik) Party of Russia were based.[8] At the October conference, Béla Kun fleshed out the plan to create a Hungarian communist party in the same mould as the RCP(B) and stressed the need for Hungarian revolutionary action.[9] Just two weeks later, at the November conference, which was a continuation of the first and larger one, the group resolved to make efforts to mobilise support for their cause in Hungary and found the Hungarian Communist Party (HCP),[10] which they decided would work under the leadership of the CC of the RCP(B), and would adopt the Russian Bolshevik Party Rules as their own.[11] A provisional CC was elected at the conference. Soon after these conferences, between 250 and 300 of the participants were dispatched to Hungary to put the plan into effect and by late November, Kun and his associates had allied with other Hungarian socialist groups to found the HCP.[12] By March 1919 they launched the Hungarian Soviet Republic, which only lasted a few months because Kun's party lacked the necessary power base to implement policy.[13]

This brief description of the Moscow conference of 1918 and ensuing events illustrates the extent to which the Russian

Bolsheviks influenced the meeting.[14] As the seminal party meeting, the conference laid the groundwork for central party organisation, and in the process secured a strong Soviet imprint on the party's structure. The number of participants and the clandestine nature of the meeting suggest that, as an institution, the meeting was an unrepresentative forum guided by a minority of actors, reminiscent of the Leninist and Stalinist Soviet conferences.

The next conference of the HCP was held on 20–21 May 1945. The conference adopted the Soviet command economy model and the party's leading role in society, and the 'Muscovite' party leader, Mátyás Rákosi, denounced both 'right-wing deviation' and 'left-wing sectarianism', thus aligning the party with the CPSU.[15] Although the majority of the new CC was made up of Hungarian communists, the Politburo and Secretariat were heavily populated with 'Muscovites' – that is, former Soviet émigrés, to ensure compliance with CPSU policy.[16]

The next national conference was similarly held under Soviet patronage. Following the Soviet invasion of Hungary to put down the anti-Soviet uprising, the Kádár-regime was established in November 1956, under the protection of Soviet troops. A provisional CC to replace Imre Nagy's Hungarian Workers' Party (HWP) government was formed. The first significant party meeting held after Kádár came to power was the national conference of June 1957. Again, the conference shared all the powers of the party congress. CC elections were held, which in essence confirmed the provisional CC that had been imposed by Kádár under Soviet occupation, and amendments were made to the Party Rules. The conference resolution described the events of 1956 as a 'counter-revolution', condemned those responsible and set out strict limits within which party and non-party members were expected to operate. The leading role of the party and the new requirements of party unity were clarified.[17]

The policy choice of the HSWP conference

Although the regime had significantly liberalised by the 1980s, the fourth conference (or second HSWP conference) in 1988 exhibits many of the same characteristics as the previous three. The 1988 conference was held on the same dates – 20–22 May – as that in 1945. Convened with the support of the CPSU, the HSWP conference made far-reaching changes in personnel and agreed radical resolutions. The conference outcome was, as with the previous conferences of 1918, 1945 and 1957, an act of normalisation of the HSWP in the form of an emergency congress, bringing it into line with CPSU policy by removing old-timers who had been in office since 1956 and who served as a reminder of the Soviet military intervention in Hungary. The extent to which the choice of institution can be interpreted as synonymous with a policy choice is very clearly exemplified in the case of the HSWP NPC between 1987 and 1989, by the strong debate in the CC and the Politburo over whether to convene an extraordinary meeting of the CC (a *felező*),[18] an NPC or an extraordinary congress. This bears witness to the perceived advantages that different groups anticipated would be most likely to yield their respective preferred outcome.

This brief account suggests that the HSWP conference consistently acted as an organ to institutionalise and normalise the party under Soviet tutelage. These conferences were convened at similar crisis points in Hungarian history, when the Russian Bolsheviks and later Soviets were providing (military) support for the implementation of Bolshevik and (later) Soviet policy. Although all three conferences, beginning with November 1918, acted as emergency congresses in terms of the powers they enjoyed, they were far from representative of the party, as at each respective meeting the opposition or a major contingent of the party, or both, was absent. Much as the Russian Bolsheviks had claimed themselves (unconstitutionally) as acting on behalf of the entire party at the Sixth Party Conference of the RCP(B) in 1912,[19] the Hungarian Bolsheviks in 1918, the Rákosi 'Muscovites' in 1945 and then the Kádárists in 1957 acted likewise. From these brief sketches, a pattern of informal procedure appears: the conference acted under Soviet guidance, sought to align Hungarian policy with Soviet policy, was unrepresentative (composed entirely or mostly of Soviet protégés) and was empowered to act as an emergency congress electing personnel to the CC. Hence, historically, the chief informal institutional constraint was, in short, *de facto* Soviet 'control' over outcome.

Soviet influence over the HSWP
Comparing relations between the CPSU and HSWP in 1988 with those between the Hungarian and Soviet commu-

nists during the period 1918–57 through the focal lens of a common institution may appear contextually inappropriate, and in research terms, a bit of a stretch. Clearly relations between the two parties underwent significant change during the period 1918–88. However, as will become apparent later in the chapter, Soviet levers remained in place to direct and influence fraternal party affairs. The nature of these levers changed over time in form, but remained in essence the same. Accounts of HSWP history agree that the party's development was greatly shaped by the Bolshevik and then the Soviet model. The organisation officially responsible for this influence, the Comintern, was crafted by the Bolsheviks for the purpose of disseminating policy to the communist revolutionary parties, which were considered outposts of the Russian Bolshevik Party.[20] By mid-1941 the international war effort and the Soviet Union's new relationship with the Western Allies had apparently softened the Soviet grip over the Comintern, and with it Soviet influence over the fraternal parties, by promoting a new 'national line' whereby parties were freed up to devise their own route to liberation from the German occupation. However, 'in the end Comintern and Soviet officials had the last word'[21] and the HCP leader, Mátyás Rákosi, did not doubt that the Soviet leadership continued to direct Comintern activity.[22] Although the Comintern was dissolved in 1943 and fraternal parties were invited by Stalin to determine their own national party identity and policies (no longer as composite sections of the Comintern), Soviet influence was perpetuated through different organisations. The departments which comprised the Comintern survived but were instead made responsible to the Soviet CC, ensuring the command structure remained intact, albeit in a different guise.[23]

According to Vladimir Kriuchkov, who was a senior member of the Soviet diplomatic corps in Budapest from 1955 while Andropov was Ambassador, relations between Hungary and the Soviet Union were 'excellent', as Hungary enjoyed a high material standard of living and good trade relations with the Soviet Union.[24] In his memoirs, Kriuchkov recounted the 'unexpected' impact of Khrushchev's secret speech at the Twentieth CPSU Congress, which was strongly critical of Stalin's regime. Fraternal party leaders were unaware of the content of the speech in advance of the congress, and so could do little to pre-empt its inevitable liberalising effects on their respective parties. The Hungarian party leader at the time, Rákosi, had enjoyed good relations with Stalin and Rákosi's regime had been repressive. Khrushchev's revelations of Stalin's 'mistakes' and deviations from Leninist norms, therefore, by default, cast a shadow over those fraternal party leaders, such as Rákosi, who had thrived under his patronage.[25] Aware of his predicament, Rákosi consulted Andropov for advice. Andropov himself, however, had only received news of the secret speech after the event and had since then received no brief from Moscow, so was ill-equipped to deal with the situation and subsequent unrest in Hungary. Eventually, Moscow advised Rákosi to take a six-month holiday in the Soviet Union, which he did, and where he remained in exile for the rest of his life. Ernő Gerő replaced Rákosi in June 1956, but proved insufficiently charismatic to engage Hungarian society. On 6 October 1956 a commemoration service was held for Lászlo Rajk, a staunch communist in the Rákosi leadership, who had been executed in 1949 and rehabilitated as a martyr of the Stalinist purges. The event began peaceably but soon erupted into a spate of mass demonstrations against the party, the government, the communist regime and Soviet hegemony. Soviet troops and the Hungarian secret police were deployed to put down the unrest.[26] Imre Nagy, who had been invited to join the government as Prime Minister on 24 October 1956, called a ceasefire and began negotiations with the leaders of the insurgency..[27] At the end of October, Soviet troops were withdrawn, but social unrest continued. Although Imre Nagy was committed to maintaining good relations with Moscow, having spent more than twenty-six years in the Soviet Union, within days of taking office he had acquiesced to the insurgents' demands, which entailed withdrawing Hungary's membership of the Warsaw Pact and declaring Hungary's neutrality to the United Nations.[28] Imre Nagy continued to pledge allegiance to the Soviet diplomatic corps, while simultaneously urging the people to remain in a state of revolution. Kriuchkov claimed that the only solution was to send Soviet troops back in to Hungary. The only two possible 'Muscovite' contenders left to replace Nagy were the elderly Ferenc Münnich and the younger János Kádár.[29] When it came to the point, Münnich stepped aside and recommended Kádár.[30] Kriuchkov described Kádár as a gifted politician as well as a 'genuine friend of Moscow'.[31]

Under Kádár, Hungarians enjoyed a materially higher

standard of living and a much more liberal regime. This 'Kádárisation' in domestic policy was tolerated by Moscow in return for strict compliance with Soviet foreign policy.[32] CPSU influence over HSWP personnel changes and policy-making continued, as will be discussed later in this chapter, but Kádár did not form good relations with the new Gorbachev leadership. From 1986 onwards, Gorbachev instead forged strong links with other HSWP would-be first secretaries. In December 1987 the HSWP CC approved the decision to hold a conference, which as the next section will discuss, was a matter that had been subject to much debate over the preceding months.

The felező, conference and congress as three different policy choices

In 1987 the three different factions within the party each advocated a different type of meeting: the conservative Kádárists wanted a felező – i.e. a 'mid-term', or extraordinary meeting of the CC – or nothing at all; the prime minister Grósz and the centrists preferred a conference, in accordance with Moscow; and reformists such as Rezső Nyers and his contingent pushed for a congress and more extensive reforms and personnel change. Nyers, who had introduced a package of liberalising economic reforms (the New Economic Mechanism) in 1968 was removed from the Politburo in 1974 after failing to comply with the Soviet demand to recentralise the economy.[33] Nyers remained in the CC but was still treated with some suspicion by Kádárists and was only later reappointed to the Politburo under Grósz, following the conference. As will be illustrated, each of these meetings constituted a different policy choice, which is reflected in a clear correlation between faction members and their preferences. Evidence suggests that the conference was perceived by the party membership and more reformist circle as an institution less likely to yield a radical outcome. First secretaries, however, preferred the convention of a conference over a congress precisely for that reason. Both Kádár in 1987 and Grósz in 1989 believed that by convening a conference rather than a congress, they were more likely to avoid personnel changes and preserve the existing system.[34] A conference was Kádár's second choice after a felező, when it became apparent he could not garner sufficient support for this. In both 1987 and 1989, reformists argued the case for convening an extraordinary congress instead of a conference. By 1989 the contingent voicing this opinion was strong enough to force Grósz to opt instead for a congress. Unlike in 1987, discussion of the topic in 1989 reached as far as the Politburo. Like a congress, the NPC was a body comprised of a large group of delegates which was ostensibly representative of the entire party membership. Unlike the *felező*, which was an extraordinary session of the CC, held 'midway' between congresses, the NPC was a formal consultation of (nominally) the entire party. NPCs were also convened for the purpose of crisis management, but they were more symbolic events to publicise solutions to a crisis, theatrically staging a discussion with preconceived and approved responses.[35] Kádár used the *felező* as a way of consolidating his power over the party.[36] While the function of the conference was essentially the same, instead of being restricted to a small group, the conference could claim the entire party's approval of the outcome.

Like a conference, a *felező* was traditionally held following a Soviet 'freeze' in order to alter the course of Hungarian policy and to realign with Soviet policy. In November 1972 the *felező* had been convened to introduce a series of measures partially recentralising the economy following Brezhnev's objection to the liberalising economic reforms of the New Economic Mechanism that had been introduced in 1968. Another instance when the *felező* had been called was for the purpose of reaffirming Kádár's authority after the CPSU had requested his resignation from the post of First Secretary.[37] Therefore, on the basis of historical precedent, the *felező* afforded the First Secretary optimal control over outcome and so is the institution we might therefore anticipate that Kádár would have preferred in 1988 – which he did. Archival documents, memoirs and interviews indicate a dispute between Kádár and the reformists over convening a conference. There is some confusion as to when the suggestion of a conference first arose in HSWP circles. György Földés has suggested he might have been the first to propose a conference to Kádár.[38] Professor Földés wrote to Kádár on 30 June 1987 and insisted that a party conference be held to determine the trajectory of the socio-economic reform programme.[39] Kádár's response stated unequivocally that the CC was perfectly equipped to deal with the matter instead.[40]

According to Nyers, however, the possibility of holding a conference was raised as early as 1986, but is only documented in Politburo and CC stenographic reports from 1987.[41] As was discussed in Chapter 4, it is plausible that Gorbachev first raised this topic with Kádár at a meeting in 1986, for example, at the meeting of the fraternal party leaders at the Political Advisory Committee of the Warsaw Pact in Budapest in June 1986 or at the 12 November 1986 bilateral talks, when Kádár visited Moscow.[42] In any event, the topic pre-dates Földés' letter. Certainly by 23 June 1987 there is documentary evidence, which indicates discussion of whether or not a conference should be convened. Members of the HSWP present at the time confirm that, as would be expected, those in favour of holding a conference were those who most benefited from the outcome – Grósz and his supporters – while those who opposed the idea were Kádár and his loyal old guard, who lost their posts at the conference.[43] The First Secretary of the Budapest Eighteenth District HSWP Committee at the time of the conference, Béla Katona, offered a more colourful account of events, stating at interview that the Politburo actually *forced* Kádár to convene the conference.[44]

June 1987: conference or felező?

The need to convene some sort of meeting of the HSWP to review the decisions and plans approved at the Thirteenth Congress in 1985 was expressed by party intellectuals the same year, immediately following the congress.[45] Some considered that the directives approved at this congress were unrealistic and could not be fulfilled,[46] as there was a growing awareness as early as 1985 that 'the party had no influence over social processes'.[47] At a CC meeting on 23 June 1987, Jenő Fock, the former Prime Minister (1967–75) responsible for introducing the New Economic Mechanism, suggested a conference (*pártkonferencia*) be convened. He proposed that Kádár adopt instead an advisory role as President and that a new First Secretary be appointed. Fock outspokenly criticised the hypocrisy of those members who pretended to consult Kádár before making decisions, suggesting that people should admit that Kádár had lost his authority and should therefore be replaced.[48]

At this CC meeting, the former President of the Hungarian

State Radio and Television, István Tömpe, also strongly pressed for personnel changes and that a new leadership be granted greater autonomy in decision making, but that there be more accountability than in the past. Tömpe argued that electing a new leadership would be the only way to restore the masses' faith in the party.[49]

At the meeting, discussion then followed as to whether a NPC or *felező* should be convened. Jenő Fock questioned whether it would be better to convene a *felező* or an even smaller delegation from the CC to minimise the risk of details of the crisis leaking out and alarming the general public. However, at the close of his speech he advocated the hasty convention of the conference in October or November 1987.[50] At this CC session Rezső Nyers pushed even more strongly for a conference, arguing that the leadership should not be concerned by the possible risk to security the conference posed, but instead should concentrate on solving the main problem, which was the lack of transparency within the decision-making process. Nyers complained that there was insufficient debate when forming policy, and argued that decision-making processes were becoming undemocratic: 'We are returning to old practices whereby you hear the suggestion just five minutes before the decision is made.'[51]

Nyers agreed with Fock's proposal that Kádár be transferred to the post of President and that a new First Secretary be appointed.[52] Nyers also proposed personnel changes and the appointment of more independent reformist actors such as the leader of the Patriotic People's Front, Imre Pozsgay,[53] who with Nyers, had supported the controversial report 'Turnabout and Reform' of 1986 that had diagnosed the economy as 'in crisis'. Kádár dismissed the suggestion of discussing Pozsgay's appointment because it was 'not on the agenda'.[54] Kádár naturally objected to his proposed demotion to the (largely symbolic) role of President. He emphatically claimed the country was not in crisis, that a change of leadership could not therefore be justified, and that it would moreover be a great mistake and a 'crime' if the leadership were to be replaced.[55] Kádár received some support from others who agreed with him that the country was not in a state of crisis.[56]

Although the item 'the convention of the national party conference in the first half of 1988 for the debate of current issues concerning socialist work' has been listed in the final section of the archival bibliography for the 20 November 1987 Politburo meeting under the heading 'Verbal Announcements',[57] no discussion about the topic is documented in archival sources. This could suggest that what was discussed was purposely not minuted – for example, if at this Politburo session,[58] there was strong disagreement between Kádár and others over the matter. As already mentioned, Béla Katona stated at interview that the Politburo *forced* Kádár to agree to the convention of a conference,[59] and since this was the last Politburo session before the decision was formally proposed to the CC on 8 December 1987, we could surmise that this was the session at which Kádár was forced to concede.

December 1987: conference or congress?

However, by the time this proposal was presented to the CC in December 1987, the convention of a conference was not a radical enough step for the reformists and instead an argument broke out between reformists and hardliners over whether a conference or a congress should be convened. The old guard stood in the way of the reformists' demand to hold an emergency congress and in the end secured a party conference.[60]

This debate is attested in the minutes of the CC session in December 1987. Nyers disagreed with the decision to convene a conference and said that an emergency congress should be held instead. Kádár interrupted, telling him, once again, that as the matter was not on the agenda, it could not be discussed. Nyers, however, managed to force a discussion about the topic:

Well, would you rather we debated this in private instead? If not then I would like to express my opinion on the topic... at a party conference it will no longer be possible to debate the issue that needs working out. And then I would like us to debate today's politics with the youth, who wants what; therefore we ought now to govern ourselves by turning to [others] outside [the party], so that we will not just be discussing it among ourselves. From this standpoint, I believe that we should prepare a congress, [and that] [by doing] this [we] will achieve far more. Of course, in the realm of the international communist movement at the moment there is the slight fashion that we are supposed to prove our communist worth [*kommunistaságunkat*] by holding a conference... I do not agree with it.[61]

Nyers' comment 'that we are supposed to prove our communist worth by holding a conference' appears to be an allusion to the implicit demand by the Soviet Union that the fraternal socialist states keep in step with Soviet policy and so convene a conference. This would correspond with other accounts, which have suggested that the decision by the CPSU to convene their conference implicitly demanded a comparable step on the part of the fraternal parties, including the HSWP.[62] In the context of Chapter 4, however, Nyers' remark could refer to a more concrete request from the CPSU to the fraternal states that they convene their respective conferences to endorse *perestroika* and, more importantly, that they modernise their respective parties to secure the survival of the socialist model.[63] In any event, by this stage, Nyers clearly opposed the idea that the HSWP should be expected to show loyalty to the Soviet Union by convening a conference.

Secretary of State for Foreign Affairs, Gyúla Horn, explained at this CC meeting why he considered a conference more appropriate than an extraordinary congress. He explained the strategic significance of a conference, in that it would demonstrate support for Soviet *perestroika* in the East, while in the West it would serve as an example that the fraternity was reforming the socialist model. Horn stated that one of the primary aims of the conference would be to bring about personnel change, with the aim of improving the party's popularity in society. Horn alluded to the fact that the problem was systemic, noting that within the socialist fraternity, people in other fraternal states had also become disillusioned with the system.[64] Kádár also alluded to external factors which necessitated that the HSWP hold a conference, in particular the fact that other fraternal parties were convening conferences 'in sequence', which could affect the HSWP:

> The Politburo suggests for the CC's consideration that... in the first half of 1988 the HSWP party conference be called. The draft is clear: we propose it for [your] consideration. I shall briefly give reasons [for convening it]. You know that we first began this particular intermediary meeting and then it gained ground in the other socialist countries. That the fraternal parties are now holding party conferences in sequence could also have repercussions for us, and among the party membership the wish has been expressed in a number of circles that we should also hold one.[65]

By referring to the fact that other fraternal parties' conferences could affect Hungary, Kádár was clearly referring to the existence of some common policy that parties were convening their conferences 'in sequence'. Moreover, as expressed in the case of other fraternal parties, the most pressing issue for discussion was the socialist model. This suggests that, although officially no mention is made of a directive, there is reference to conferences being convened in sequence which could affect Hungary and that the HSWP was expected to follow suit.

Kádár clearly stated that the purpose of the forthcoming conference was not to consult the membership at large and sound out public opinion, but instead to discuss the leading role of the party in society. He offered a clear statement of his intent that the party consolidate its power and secure greater control over society:

> I believe that there is not much here that needs discussing, either with the public at large, or with the party membership. Otherwise it could also spread to ideological questions, because these are issues which have also surfaced. [Instead] we should engage with [the matter of] the leading role of the party, as has been said many times here already, in relation to the political activities of our society.[66]

Despite the disagreement among party members over whether to call a conference, by the end of the December CC session, when Kádár requested a show of hands to see how many were in favour of a conference, he was able to say, 'I note the vast majority.'[67] As has been attested at interview with HSWP officials, Kádár did not intend personnel changes at the conference. The fact that the only tangible outcome of the conference was widespread personnel change and a confirmation of existing policies further demonstrates that the agenda was set by Grósz and the centrists.[68] Like Gorbachev, they achieved this strong support by selecting delegates who they considered would be more likely to support their agenda.

The HSWP conference, 20–22 May 1988

Textual analysis of the conference indicates that the meeting was not representative in terms of its delegates. Speeches were dominated by a demand to consolidate the party's power and proclaim the importance of *perestroika* in the party, and personnel changes were on the conference agenda, albeit unofficially.

Representation

At the May 1988 conference, a researcher from the Hungarian Academy of Sciences, Judit Timár, pointed out that delegate selection for the conference was not sociologically representative and concluded therefore that delegate selection had not been performed according to the usual procedure, whereby individuals were selected by social class and region, as delegates were not representative according to either criteria. Timár noted that there were proportionally too many managers and insufficient workers, the youth was significantly under-represented and there were insufficient delegates from villages.[69] Her main complaint was that large numbers of the population, mainly workers and peasants, were therefore not represented, thus invalidating the conference's claim to be nationally representative.[70] This factor was noted also in the case of the CPSU conference, where insufficient workers were invited to speak, as discussed in Chapter 3, and was also apparent in the Polish case, as will be discussed in Chapter 7.

It seems logical to assume that those with the greatest influence over the conference would have recruited a majority of delegates who would be sympathetic to their agenda. Grósz and the conference organisers apparently achieved this in selecting those individuals and sectors of society most likely to be in favour of his centrist policy and personnel changes. This is borne out by textual analysis of delegates' speeches, which indicated very little criticism at the conference of economic liberalisation; this appears counter-intuitive for the following reason.

Economic liberalisation entailing the introduction of wage differentials as a way to encourage productivity and meritocracy under conditions of little economic growth would understandably have been unwelcome to large sectors of society, especially workers. We might surmise that those most in favour of economic liberalisation would have been those most likely to benefit from it: managers, intellectuals and skilled workers – those sectors of society by far best represented at the conference in May 1988. The leadership had expressed concerns regarding the workers' diminishing support for reform and trust in the party, and that without this support the party could not continue.[71] Hence by minimising worker presence at the conference, any potential worker malaise at the meeting could be contained. Delegates would be less likely to voice criticism at the worsening economic conditions and expected loss of social security following the possible introduction of further market forces if they were those who were most likely to benefit from these policies. This theory is supported by the fact that three of the four people who advocated retaining state control over industry and agriculture, which was the strongest criticism voiced at the conference against economic liberalisation, were workers. Only six workers were invited to speak. We could infer from this that industrial and agricultural workers – the most likely defenders of the *status quo* – were purposely excluded from the conference.

One interviewee stated that Grósz and the organising committee would have been able to direct the delegate selection procedure to maintain party control of the event and that they had not wanted 'reformists' advocating the transition to a multiparty democracy.[72] Since elections were 'directed' and Grósz did not want 'reformists', we may conclude that Grósz and the organising committee selected delegates most likely to support his stance.

Centrist policy

Those with a voice at the conference were overwhelmingly from the centrist camp led by Grósz. Although a small number of more reformist delegates were invited to speak, views expressed rarely diverged from the centrist line. However, as was pointed out at the conference itself, those views expressed were not necessarily representative of the entire party's views.

Textual analysis of the conference speeches bears out that there was overwhelming support for Grósz, which clearly favoured that the party maintain its leading role in society. Although well over half of the delegates advocated some form of 'democratisation' within the party, from the context it is clear that what they were advocating was far from 'democratisation' *per se*. What they proposed varied from maintaining the *status quo* to major reform of party structures within the one-party system. More than two thirds of the speakers advocated *perestroika* and just over half demanded more *glasnost*.

Clearly what was advocated in delegates' speeches corresponds closely to CPSU modernisation, consisting of some liberalisation of party structures, a purge of corruption, and further economic liberalisation. Conspicuously, the mostly widely expressed view was that the *status quo* should be maintained in terms of party policy. A majority contingent of twenty-three speakers, composed of hardliners, Grósz and the centrists advocated maintaining the monolithic unity of the party and that any divergent views expressed by a minority or faction within the party continue to be outlawed. Two veterans, the Politburo member, Sándor Gáspár and the Chairman of the Central Control Commission, András Gyenes, both referred to 1956 as a counter-revolution, and spoke favourably of the policies introduced under the new Kádár leadership following 1956.[73] Similarly, Kádár stated that the party had successfully overcome the crisis of 1953–57 and that this should serve as encouragement to the party in the present (in1988).[74] Kádár might, therefore, have been advocating that the 1957 conference should be used as a model for the 1988 conference. Given the circumstances and nature of the 1957 conference, as was discussed earlier in the chapter, this was a clear call for a crackdown on the opposition in favour of a consolidation of the party's power.[75] More importantly in the context of 1988, these individuals were claiming that the Soviet intervention of 1956 was justified, whereas instead relevant individuals were expected to own up to past crimes, in the spirit of *glasnost*, to renew society's faith in the party.

Only seven delegates spoke in favour of the democratisation of the decision-making process by taking into account the opinion of the minority. Of those seven, however, only one speaker, an economics graduate student, Csilla Fejesné Jenei, queried whether or not other political parties should be legalised: 'It is a similar scenario with the recently formed political youth organisation. All that we know is that the organisation has been labelled "unlawful". Whether it's illegal or not, the judges should decide…'[76]

Grósz's final words at the conference reiterated Gorbachev's message to the socialist countries' leaders:[77] that the HSWP needed to consolidate power by reforming the party from within, so as to make the existing model viable:

I agree with comrade Kádár that the most pressing task is that we should consolidate our power. The most important condition of this is to renew our party. According to many, the one-party system has not worked and [they] consider today's problems as confirmation of this. They therefore think there should be more parties.[78]

Grósz was therefore not diverging from what Kádár had espoused at a CC meeting in June 1987, when he proposed that Hungary adopt the same position as the Soviet Union. This policy did not challenge the existing ideology underpinning the system; it affirmed the main principle of retaining the leading role of the communist party in society, but sought to broaden the party's horizons to bring in more support from society, as defined by seeking 'more, not less socialism'.[79]

Vote of 'no confidence'

Beyond a show of strength for the party and retention of the one-party system, the main subject of conference speeches was the pressing need to change the CC and Politburo personnel as a means to winning back the people's and party's faith in the HSWP. At a meeting of the Politburo in November 1987, the First Secretary of the Communist Youth League (KISZ), Csaba Hámori presented a long account detailing how the youth were falling away from the party, that membership to KISZ had dropped by seventy-five per cent between 1980 and 1987, and that in academia stagnation had set in due to insufficient funds. Party membership had declined among intellectuals, and disillusionment with the party was growing as economic conditions worsened.[80] At the 8 December 1987 CC meeting, Gyúla Horn similarly stressed society's growing disenchantment with the party:

> I think the fact that there is no unity in the party has some bearing on the issue of the political system. At the same time, society is taking great advantage of this [state of affairs]. Moreover, it needs to be said that regarding the way the system works there has been a lot of tough criticism, certain kinds of disillusionment are also experienced with regard to the system, not just in Hungary but in the other socialist countries as well.[81]

This concern was expressed at the conference. Thirteen speakers referred to society's and the membership's growing mistrust of the party. Nine speakers demanded greater inclusion of intellectuals and non-party members.

Unlike the CPSU conference, where there was a more visible defeat of left and right factions in terms of political debate, the main thrust of the HSWP conference was to purge the old guard by means of sweeping personnel changes at the conference. Significantly, fifteen speakers voiced their approval of personnel changes. Although officially only four of the hardliners were earmarked for 'resignation' (János Kádár, László Maróthy, György Aczél and István Sárlos), a covert plan known only to some delegates had been hatched to oust others as well: Sándor Gáspár, Ferenc Havasi, György Lázár, Miklós Óvári and Csaba Hámori.[82] One delegate present said that he knew nothing of what was to happen and thought the conference was a meeting held according to the usual protocol, where delegates were expected to approve obediently all decisions taken.[83] Another delegate indicated in her speech that she had heard rumours of personnel change circulating at the conference, but that nothing had been officially announced.[84] The secretary of a university party committee, György Barta, made a very vocal demand for personnel change: 'We are waiting for new faces, new words, and new deeds…'[85] Although Kádár had been diametrically opposed to the plan of personnel change in the run-up to the conference, as has been discussed earlier, by the time of the conference he had been forced to acquiesce. In his opening speech to the conference, Kádár stated that both the CC and CCC had proposed personnel changes in the leadership and that this was now considered timely.[86]

Aware of this, some of the old guard lobbied delegates during their conference speeches, arguing that existing officials should remain in post as they were best equipped to continue the reform process.[87] Two CC members, the reformist Miklós Németh, who replaced Grósz as Prime Minister at the end of 1988, and the eminent physicist, Pál Lénárd, suggested a greater proportion of intellectuals should be appointed to the leadership.[88] The secretary of the Szigetvár town committee, József Gráf, advocated more widespread changes, and demanded a complete re-election of the CC and CCC because of the lack of confidence in the leadership.[89] Two delegates representing different industrial enterprises expressed the same sentiments. The chief dispatcher of a machine factory, József Tavaszi, demanded that the new leadership comprise more dynamic personnel:

It's not just a question of the membership wanting to see new faces in the CC and Politburo. The spirit of the time requires a leadership which arouses dynamic and progressive thoughts, tolerates divergent opinions and is both decisive and consistent.[90]

Similarly, the secretary of the Gagarin power station's party committee, Sándorné Rajki, insisted that those elected must effect party modernisation at every level.[91] One Politburo member, György Aczél, a veteran who had served the party since the 1930s, was aware of the planned leadership changes[92] and graciously bowed out, having accepted responsibility, as a long-serving member of the leadership, for the crimes the party had committed since 1956, even claiming 1956 'a tragedy':[93]

> What does the future bring? Nothing from me. What should we bring our future? Perspective. We should restore our people's trust in us... so that we should not just hand on the reputation but the reality of a socialist country to our successors.[94]

Those who were more reformist than Grósz's contingent strongly sensed his orchestration of events at the conference and, although in favour of ousting the old guard, were resentful of the centrist line Grósz's government adopted. The party very soon outgrew Grósz and began demanding leadership change. In response to this Grósz proposed another conference be held the following year, in 1989. Aware that the Party Rules did not specify the procedure for delegate selection to the conference, and that Grósz and his supporters had taken advantage of this loophole to hand-pick delegates for the 1988 conference, local officials banded together to sign a petition demanding a change in the Party Rules that would ensure wider representation of the party membership.

Spring 1989: conference or congress?

The argument over whether a conference or a congress should be convened was more acrimonious in 1989. At the Politburo session on 21 March 1989 there was strong debate between the reform circle and the Grószists over the issue. Grósz's rationale for preferring a conference was that the outcome of a congress could not be guaranteed. He supported this argument with exactly the same explanation that Gorbachev had presented when arguing that the Nineteenth CPSU Conference be convened: an extraordinary congress could raise unnecessary alarm among the party membership and general public. We may infer from Grósz's statement that the outcome of a congress was unsure, while the outcome of a conference could be more easily directed:[95]

> What could we expect from a congress? If a [congress] works to our advantage politically then we know what we can expect, but if it doesn't work, then we don't know what the outcome will be and besides we might then alarm the party membership, which we do not want to do.[96]

Leading on from this, the next topic Grósz remarked upon was the worsening relationship between Hungary and the rest of the 'socialist fraternity' and the subsequent need to follow Moscow rather than the West:

> Regarding our international relations, I see that a new situation has arisen whereby our allies – our socialist friends – have begun to view us with increasing suspicion and with increasing fear. ... The source of this is none other than our fraternising with the West, we have begun changing erratically, [our socialist friends] don't really understand where we are trying to go, because they do not understand the meaning of our catchphrases. ... From this point of view, the Moscow way will be of particular interest to us, just as comrade Németh's meeting in Moscow, and others' [meetings] too, will be of interest.[97]

The HSWP's petition to change the NPC's 'informal constraints'

As a countermeasure to Grósz's plan of convening the NPC a second time in 1989, local party organisations petitioned the CC to change the *de facto* rules of conference convention, in a bid to curb the General Secretary's power to select delegates freely. This appears to have been part of a two-pronged attack by the reformists to ensure a congress rather than a conference be held in October 1989. The first strategy was widespread demand for congress convention; the second was a signed petition that the conference rules be changed to prevent Grósz orchestrating the outcome as he had done at the May 1988 conference. It was at the height of this dispute, at a 16 May 1989 session of the CC, that the representatives of the county and town party leaderships presented their petition demanding radical changes to the rules governing conference convention. This declaration described the previous year's conference model as *'unsuitable'* and requested new legislation be introduced to systematise delegate selection and make it more democratic. They subsequently demanded one representative for every 1,000 of each county's population. Other requests made in the declaration included equal representation from the Hungarian Democratic Youth Union (MADISZ).[98] The opening paragraph of the declaration clearly stated the problem:

> The overwhelming experience following consultations with the district and town party leaderships, and the majority of CC members respectively, was that neither delegate selection nor the preparations of proceedings for the organisation of the conference according to the 1988 model are suitable. The manner of delegate selection was the main issue. Last year's model (the district party committees delegated) is unacceptable; there was much criticism of this already, last year.[99]

This confirms that there was widespread dissatisfaction with the process of delegate selection for the May 1988 conference and the perception that mainly those adhering to Grósz's centrist policies had been selected as delegates. Rezső Nyers confirmed this at interview, stating that Grósz invited larger numbers from his own county (Borsod-Abaúj-Zemplén) to the conference to ensure sufficient support for him and the personnel changes he had endorsed. This manifested itself in the attendance of a significantly larger proportion of representatives per capita from the Borsod-Abaúj-Zemplén County.

In turn this supports the 'informal constraints' of the CPSU conference outlined in Chapters 2 and 3, which identified the conference as an unrepresentative forum where purges of the opposition were staged. Another informal mechanism guiding conference convention was that of Soviet 'control' or influence over conference outcome. As the next section details, this mechanism also applied to the 1988 conference.

Soviet 'control' over conference outcome

Most Hungarian respondents agreed that Gorbachev and the CPSU had certainly been informed of the intended personnel changes that were to take place at the HSWP conference in 1988, and that they had expressed approval of these proposed appointments. According to some accounts the CPSU actively helped orchestrate events to facilitate the conference outcome, as also attested in some published memoirs.

According to one respondent, the forthcoming CPSU conference would most certainly have been an informal topic of conversation among delegates at the HSWP conference, because Hungary was still an 'occupied country' and the possibilities for reform in Hungary depended on what happened in the Soviet Union, and the outcome of the CPSU conference.[100]

Respondents either did not know, or declined to answer the question of whether Gorbachev directly requested a conference be called. Zoltán Szabó conceded that it is possible that Gorbachev encouraged the convention of conferences in the fraternal parties.[101] Valerii Vorotnikov declined answering the question, explaining, 'I cannot comment. I fear that I am unable to give an objective answer to that question.'[102] Nyers remarked that the collaboration between Grósz, Gorbachev and others might prove to be more significant than was currently documented when Soviet archives are declassified.

Hungarian archival documents shed more light on this. Firstly, there is at least an acknowledgement by Kádár, Nyers and Horn that the other fraternal socialist parties were convening conferences in sequence and that the HSWP was expected to follow suit.[103] Secondly there is some implication that convening a conference indicated loyalty to the communist cause,[104] and thirdly that conference outcome in one socialist party could affect the other socialist parties.[105]

Both Russian and Hungarian archival materials and published memoirs indicate the CPSU's role in influencing the HSWP conference outcome in May 1988 and the ouster of Kádár and most other hardliners from the CC and Politburo. Archival documents show that this was on the agenda by 11 April 1988, when the HSWP Secretariat issued a statement that the planned leadership changes and high-ranking personnel changes in the CPSU would be followed by similar changes to the CC in the HSWP.[106]

The existing literature testifies active CPSU involvement in preparing these changes and in helping engineer Grósz's replacement of Kádár. Grósz's rise from first secretary of the B-A-Z County to the party's CC in 1984 has been attributed to the support of one of Gorbachev's rivals for the position of CPSU General Secretary, Grigorii Romanov.[107] Following Gorbachev's dismissal of Romanov from the Politburo in 1985, Gorbachev forged links with Grósz. Kádár had openly expressed to Gorbachev his disapproval of the new policies of *perestroika* and *glasnost*, while Grósz appeared to Gorbachev a cooperative alternative to Kádár.[108] By 1987 Grósz was already the CPSU's preferred candidate because of his pragmatism, his hard line against nationalism and liberalism, and his proven loyalty to the Soviet cause.[109]

Published memoirs detail how the CPSU acted to secure Grósz as Kádár's replacement. During a visit to Budapest in February 1988, Chairman of the Presidium of the USSR Supreme Soviet, and former foreign minister, Andrei Gromyko, tried to persuade Kádár to resign. When Kádár refused, the CPSU sent Kriuchkov to Budapest four days before the conference to ensure a 'positive' outcome.[110] According to Tibor Huszár, 'Kriuchkov fortuitously ensured a "positive" outcome to the question during his visit to Budapest four days before the conference.'[111] Berecz has supported this claim:

> Between Gorbachev and Kádár there had been no exchange of words concerning internal matters since the summer of 1986, or at least there is no written evidence as such. The 'last man' from Gorbachev's contingent with whom Kádár had officially spoken prior to the conference was Andrei Gromyko – at that time in his capacity as head of state. But Kádár was not willing to negotiate on the matter of 'internal affairs'. According to Berecz, he [Kádár] was extremely disturbed by the timing of the visit, as it looked, perhaps, like the Soviets would 'interfere' in the planned changes. ... Gorbachev had already [committed himself] to a policy of non-intervention, but he nonetheless agreed with the idea of Kádár's replacement (by the spring?) ... The commissioned task ... was to send someone [else] for this purpose to Budapest before the May conference. Since he spoke good Hungarian, in his capacity as head of the KGB [State Security Committee (Soviet Union)] Kriuchkov was the one [chosen]. He arrived here [in Budapest] incognito. He negotiated with three people, Kádár, Grósz and Pozsgay. He was interested in them. The CPSU agreed that Grósz was an energetic politician, that Kádár should step down for good, and that beside him were 'men of the future' (probably a potential prime

minister), referring also to Pozsgay. Those with whom Kriuchkov did not meet were those not to succeed Kádár.[112]

Precisely what happened at the meeting that secured the outcome was not documented. Kádár may have been persuaded to resign in response to the possible threat that the press would publish Imre Nagy's death warrant, which Kádár himself had signed.[113] Since Kádár's legitimacy with society had been forged on the basis that he had not been responsible for Nagy's execution, the revelation of such a document would have caused public outrage. The fact that only a few months later Grósz happened upon the document and publicised it could suggest that he had had it for longer. In any event, the fact that Kádár did not resign until the eve of the conference[114] (around the time of Kriuchkov's visit) could suggest that Grósz had been given this document by Kriuchkov as leverage over Kádár.

Kriuchkov's own memoirs indicate that the CPSU had other leverage over Kádár and then ultimately Grósz in the form of documents only handed over to the Hungarian government in 1990. These were documents implicating Nagy as an informer against fellow Hungarians which had resulted in over 200 false convictions in Moscow during the 1930s. Kádár, evidently aware of the existence of these documents, had requested them from the CPSU. Kriuchkov, however, stated in his memoirs that 'unfortunately' for Kádár they were only 'discovered' in KGB archives later and given to the HSWP government in 1990:

> János Kádár called the story with [Imre] Nagy his personal tragedy. Kádár only just lived to the day when it became known that there existed authentic material about the participation of Nagy in the repression of a group of Hungarian émigrés in the Soviet Union in the 1930s. As the material showed, handed over to the Hungarian side in the 1990s, Nagy, as an NKVD [People's Commissariat for Internal Affairs] agent (under the pseudonym Volodia), bore false witness about some incidence of anti-Soviet activity by a group of Hungarian émigrés (in this group were more than 200 people). Many of these people were convicted and some even shot. Nobody would dispute the fact that this very important feature in Nagy's biography puts his whole life-story in a very different light. I would like to emphasise that neither Rákosi nor Kádár nor any of the other Hungarian allies had any knowledge about this secret biography of Nagy until recently, although some rumours about this had

already been circulating in Budapest before then. Kádár himself at some point spoke to me about it. In the Soviet Union the relevant documents were only discovered in the archives in 1990.[115]

Such evidence would have helped exonerate Kádár for having authorised Nagy's execution and could possibly, therefore, have served as an 'antidote' to Kádár's signature on Nagy's death warrant. Grósz may also have requested this from the CPSU. Grósz's interest in publicising such evidence about Nagy was probably motivated by his growing need to discredit the new political parties, the Alliance of Free Democrats and the Hungarian Democratic Forum (HDF), that were using Nagy's rehabilitation as a platform, and were gaining very significant support by early 1989. A portion of a memo from Anatoly Cherniaev to Grósz and copied to Shakhnazarov in February 1989 could support the claim that Grósz had requested the document.[116] If this is the document referred to in the memo, then apparently the CPSU decided against disclosure as they considered publication might have been damaging for both the CPSU and HSWP:

> Among the bundle of telegrams there are three from Budapest on this question. I agree that we need to entrust [them with information] to prepare their position on the topic of 1956. But at the present moment, as Georgii [Shakhnazarov] suggests, putting something in writing to Grósz is a problem. Above all, what Georgii proposes saying to Grósz is more reminiscent of a 'warning' rather than a report. Moreover, Grósz himself, as is apparent from the telegram, has already disavowed Pozsgay's declaration. And thirdly, even if Grósz agrees with our appraisal, he will not be able to implement it because he is barely still in charge of the political ideological situation. Moreover, we will put ourselves and him in a difficult position, which is especially important at the moment in the context that there is a danger of the country's collapse. And we will not look very strong if at that moment at the highest level we 'show our concern' over any concrete instance concerning our history. And overall it would be best to follow [Miklós] Németh's idea and try to keep the problem of 1956 to the level of a scientific discussion and not allow it to turn into a political argument with anyone.[117]

This memo in any case indicates continuing active (although increasingly unofficial) CPSU influence over HSWP policy. Documentation from the Gorbachev Foundation indicates this relationship continued until at least late 1988;[118] Hungarian sources show it continuing much longer until the one-party system could no longer be sustained. As mentioned earlier, at interview Nyers conceded that Soviet influence over Hungarian policy at this time might well prove to be much more significant than is now documented in published works, once the Russian archives are fully declassified.[119]

Grósz continued to receive CSPU support for his centrist position beyond 1988. Pozsgay recounted in his own memoirs that in April 1989, when Grósz was at risk of being ousted by the reformists after his unsuccessful attempt to call a conference once again to consolidate his position, Yakovlev tried to persuade Pozsgay to support Grósz: 'In April, by means of Yakovlev – whom I met in Rome – I was advised to support Grósz.'[120] By 1989 the reform circle had outgrown the HSWP and was pushing to oust Grósz. In September 1988 the HSWP and CPSU leaderships were aware of this growing problem. Transcripts of György Aczél's and János Berecz's meetings with one of Gorbachev's advisers on foreign affairs, Vadim Zagladin, indicate this. Aczél explained how the removal of hardliners at the May 1988 conference had only briefly appeased the party and general public. Craving yet greater liberalisation at a time when the economic situation was perceived as worsening, the HDF had demanded Grósz's resignation as he was considered unable 'to bring the country in to the international arena'.[121] Berecz voiced his concern at the increasing influence of the US, 'courting Hungarian academics' and the subsequent loss of Soviet influence over the intelligentsia. Berecz demanded that the HSWP consolidate its power and re-establish its authority over society:

> People require from us direction, and if we turn out to be unable to do that then they will turn to religion or even worse, to some demagogue or other. ... We have always promised the people a better future – our ideology is based on that. But time has passed and no better future has arrived. Certain comrades who have left active office in the party (including those who received insufficient votes to stay in the CC) are backbiting and slandering us. This cannot just be contained to their influencing small groups of people. The Youth are looking for direction, but have not found one. Our way out of this is to consolidate the party as much as we can... In this regard we need to continue our mutual [HSWP and CPSU] discussions for working out solutions to new problems as they arise. Otherwise, both our parties – and even the other fraternal parties in the end– will lose out.[122]

At the 21 March 1989 session of the HSWP Politburo, Grósz alluded to Soviet disapproval at the increasingly evident factions within the HSWP and the rise of opposition parties. Grósz emphasised the importance of CPSU policy in determining HSWP policy and the need for continued collaboration with the CPSU: 'From this point of view the new Moscow way will certainly be interesting as will the results of [Miklós] Németh's meeting in Moscow.'[123] This corresponds with Yakovlev's remark to Pozsgay in April 1989, that the CPSU was aware of growing factionalism in the HSWP and that Yakovlev requested Pozsgay to support Grósz and centrist Gorbachevian policy.[124]

Conclusion

From the survey of conference outcomes and the conditions under which they were called throughout the party's history, this chapter has reconstructed the conference's 'informal constraints' and what policy choice this represented. The pattern which emerged suggests that the most significant 'informal constraints' were the harmonisation of HSWP policy with CPSU policy. Evidence of acrimonious debate between hardliners and reform communists confirms that the conference and congress were perceived as two very different policy choices. Demands by the reform communists in 1989 that the provisions in the rules regarding conference procedure be modified further to ensure better representation serves as further evidence of a 'struggle over the rules'.

More specifically, speeches at the 1988 conference indicate that some speakers were aware that delegates selected to attend the conference were not representative of the party. Interviews bear out that a disproportionate number of centrists – those supporting Grósz – were selected to attend. Textual analysis of delegates' speeches further demonstrates an overwhelming expression of support for centrist policies. The policy which Gorbachev requested the fraternal parties implement, as detailed in Chapter 4, was consistently advocated by delegates at the HSWP conference in their widespread demands for HSWP leadership change and party modernisation. At the same time, the leading role of the HSWP was underlined at the conference, indicating an alignment with CPSU policy that fraternal parties should consolidate their power. Textual analysis further bears out that the burning issue was indeed personnel change; delegates' speeches otherwise discussed very general topics or gave vent to emotional outpourings against the leadership for current ills. Although in some speeches hardliners in the leadership attempted to defend themselves, there was an overall admission that modernisation of the party was essential for the party to regain its legitimacy in society. Nyers confirmed that the sole purpose of the conference was leadership change, and he explained that when the decision was made in December 1987 to call the conference, two items were put on the conference agenda: the first was ideological issues, the second personnel change. Nyers stated, however, that ideological issues were never fleshed out in preparation for the conference, and that instead the main focus had been personnel change.[125]

This chapter demonstrated how Grósz and the centrists at the conference acted together with Gorbachevian centrists in the CPSU to espouse *perestroika* and effect the ouster of all those that were implicated in the 1956 repression. This was a clear statement, on the part of the HSWP leadership, that Hungary was also culpable for the Soviet military intervention, contrary to how Kádár's cohort had conveyed these events. This was particularly important to Gorbachev, who wished to signal the end of the Brezhnev Doctrine. Moreover, he wanted fraternal party leaders to debunk the myth, in the spirit of *glasnost*, that the Soviet Union had unilaterally intervened, when instead leaders in these states had collaborated with the CPSU, and actively requested Soviet intervention, as will be detailed further in Chapter 7. Although this was not explicitly stated at the conference, the ouster of the old guard was sufficiently symbolic to impute to the HSWP some complicity with the CPSU in this repression and for a short while this action served to improve the HSWP's reputation. At the same time, by ousting the old guard in the HSWP, Gorbachev was securing his goal of 'making *perestroika* irreversible', as CPSU hardliners had a diminishing pool of possible support among the leaderships of the fraternal parties.

Notes

1   Chapter 1, pp. 37–49.

2   R. Tőkés, *Hungary's Negotiated Revolution: Economic Reform, Social Change and Political Succession* (Cambridge: Cambridge University Press, 1996), p. 284.

3   M. Molnár, *From Béla Kun to János Kádár: Seventy Years of Hungarian Communism* (New York NY: Berg, 1990), p. 124; B. Kovrig, *Communism in Hungary: from Kun to Kádár* (Stanford CA: Hoover Institution Press, 1979), p. 175.

4   Chapter 2, p. 58.

5   *Társadalmi Szemle*, no. 11 (1958), pp. 92–8.

6   R. Tőkés, *Béla Kun and the Hungarian Soviet Republic: the Origins of the Communist Party of Hungary in the Revolutions 1918–1919* (Stanford CA: Hoover Institution on War, Revolution and Peace, 1967), p. 79.

7   *Ibid.*, pp. 69–75.

8   Molnár, *From Béla Kun to János Kádár*, p. 11.

9   *Ibid.*, p. 12.

10   Tőkés, *Béla Kun and the Hungarian Soviet Republic*, p. 238.

11   *Ibid.*

12   Molnár, *From Béla Kun to János Kádár*, pp. 10–12.

13   R.J. Crampton, *Eastern Europe in the Twentieth Century* (London: Routledge, 1995), p. 82.

14   Much as the CPSU, through the actions of the Comintern, influenced the Bulgarian Vitosha conference of 1924, entitled 'Vitoshka nelegalna konferentsiia na BKP' – the first illegal BCP conference (see *Éntsiklopediia Bŭlgariia* (1978–96), BAN, Sofiia, v.1, p. 691; N. Oren, *Bulgarian Communism: the Road to Power 1934–1944* (New York NY: Columbia University Press, 1971), pp. 49–64; J. Rothschild, *The Communist Party of Bulgaria: origins and development 1883–1936* (New York NY: Columbia University Press, 1959), p. 154; J. D. Bell, *The Bulgarian Communist Party from Blagoev to Zhivkov* (Stanford CA: Hoover Institution Press, 1986), p. 45.

15   Kovrig, *Communism in Hungary*, p. 175.

16   Molnár, *From Béla Kun to János Kádár*, p. 125.

17   *Népszabadság*, 30 June 1957.

18   *Felező* does not translate neatly into English; it translates roughly to the word 'mid-term' which in English conveys something regularly held, which it was not; like the conference there were only a handful of *felező* convened during the history of the party.

19   See Chapter 2, pp. 59–61.

20   Molnár, *From Béla Kun to János Kádár*, pp. 84–99.

21   M. Mevius, *Agents of Moscow: the Hungarian Communist Party and the Origins of Socialist Patriotism* (Oxford: Clarendon Press, 2004), p. 29.

22   Mevius citing Rákosi from *Visszaemlékezések*, see *Ibid.*, p. 27.

23   *Ibid.*, pp. 37–42.

24   V. Kriuchkov, *Lichnoe delo* (Moskva: Olimp, 1996), pt. 1, pp. 38–9.

25   *Ibid.*, pp. 44–7.

26   G. Litván, *The Hungarian Revolution of 1956: reform, revolt and repression, 1953–1956* (London: Longman, 1996), pp. 63–5.

27   *Ibid.*, p. 72.

28   *Ibid.*, p. 80.

29   Münnich and Kádár had gone to the Soviet Embassy in Budapest on 1 November 1956 and the following day had been flown to Moscow, where Budapest's future leadership was agreed. See Litván, *The Hungarian Revolution of 1956*, p. 81.

30   C. Gati, *Hungary and the Soviet Bloc* (Durham NC: Duke University Press, 1986), p. 156.

31   Kriuchkov, *Lichnoe delo*, pt. 1, p. 62.

32   Gati, *Hungary and the Soviet Bloc*, p. 173.

33   N. Swain, *The Rise and Fall of Feasible Socialism* (London: Verso, 1992), pp. 116–17.

34   Interview with György Földés, Budapest, 4 June 2003; interview with Zoltán Szabó, Budapest, 2 June 2003; interview with Béla Katona, Budapest, 28 May 2003.

35   Interview with Péter Heves, Budapest, 5 June 2003.

36   Interview with György Földés, Budapest, 4 June 2003.

37   T. Huszár, *Kádár János politikai életrajza* (Budapest: Szabad Tér Kiadó, Kossuth Kiadó, 2003), vol. 2, pp. 238–49.

38   Interview with György Földés, Budapest, 4 June 2003. Professor Földés kindly gave me a photocopy of the letter and Kádár's response.

39   Földés' letter to Kádár, 30 June 1987.

40   Kádár's reply to Földés, 2 July 1987.

41   Interview with Rezső Nyers, Budapest, 5 June 2003.

42   As detailed in Chapter 4, pp. 111–12; 132.

43   Interview with György Wiener, Budapest, 4 June 2003

44   Interview with Béla Katona, Budapest, 28 May 2003

45   Interview with Hungarian civil servant, Budapest, 3 June 2003.

46   Interview with Zoltán Szabó, Budapest, 2 June 2003.

47   Interview with Hungarian civil servant, Budapest, 3 June 2003.

48   MOL KB 288.f.4/425, 23 June 1987, pp. 33–7.

49   *Ibid.*, pp. 39–41.

50   *Ibid.*, pp. 33–7.

51   *Ibid.*, p. 42.

52   *Ibid.*, p. 36.

53   *Ibid.*, p. 42.

54   *Ibid.*, p. 83.

55   *Ibid.*, pp. 79–80.

56   *Ibid.*, p. 42. Imréné Takács and Péter Rényi.

57   Magyar Országos Levéltár, 'A MSZMP Központi vezető szervei üléseinek napirendi jegyzékei' in *A MOL Segédletei* 4:1, 1–2, (Budapest: MOL, 2001), p. 178.

58 MOL PB 288 f.5/1013 őe, 20 November 1987

59 Interview with Béla Katona, Budapest, 28 May 2003.

60 J. Berecz, *Vállalom* (Budapest: Budapest-Print Kft, 2003), p. 500; interview with Rezső Nyers, Budapest, 5 June 2003.

61 MOL KB 288.f.4/230–231, 8 December 1987, pp. 52–3.

62 G. Schöpflin, R. Tökés and I. Völgyés, 'Leadership Change and Crisis in Hungary', *Problems of Communism*, 37:5 (1988), p. 34.

63 As detailed in Chapter 4, pp. 109–16.

64 MOL KB 288.f.4/230–231, 8 December 1987, p. 141.

65 *Ibid.*, p. 138.

66 MOL KB 288.f.4/230–231, 8 December 1987, p. 138.

67 *Ibid.*, p. 148.

68 Nyers conceded that although there is no documented evidence, it is more than likely that Grósz wielded the most influence over the conference and that personnel issues were far more important than ideological or political issues. Interview with Rezső Nyers, Budapest, 5 June 2003.

69 This forceful criticism was also made at the CPSU party conference. Cf. Chapter 3.

70 Hungarian Socialist Workers' Party, *A MSZMP országos ertekezletének jegyzőkönyve 1988. május 20–22* (Budapest: Kossuth Kiadó, 1988), pp. 120–1.

71 MOL KB 288.f.4/225, 23 June 1987, pp. 39–41. This is also of course well documented in the CPSU archival documents: RGANI fond.89. Perechen'.42.dokument.22.

72 Interview with Zoltán Szabó, Budapest, 2 June 2003.

73 HSWP, *A MSZMP országos ertekezletének jegyzőkönyve 1988*, pp. 80; 54.

74 *Ibid.*, p. 15.

75 *Ibid.*, pp. 80; 11–26; 75–78; 37–40.

76 *Ibid.*, p. 87.

77 See Chapter 4, pp. 123–4; 137.

78 HSWP, *A MSZMP országos ertekezletének jegyzőkönyve 1988*, p. 115.

79 MOL KB 288 f.4 225 23 June, p. 74.

80 MOL PB 288.f.5/1011, 3 November 1987, pp. 12–50.

81 MOL KB 288.f.4/230–231, 8 December 1987, p. 141.

82 However, one interviewee – Professor Heves – who was not present at the conference claimed he had been informed by his boss, György Aczél, of the intended personnel changes. Interview with Péter Heves, Budapest, 5 June 2003.

83 A Hungarian member of parliament remarked this during a conversation with the author (May/June 2003).

84 HSWP, *A MSZMP országos ertekezletének jegyzőkönyve 1988*, pp. 88–9, Csilla Fejesné Jenei speaking.

85 *Ibid.*, p. 45.

86 *Ibid.*, p. 12.

87 Ferenc Karvalits, Imre Olajos and Gáspár Sándor. *Ibid.*, pp. 216–17; 54–8; 75.

88   *Ibid.*, pp. 160; 97.

89   *Ibid.*, p. 171.

90   *Ibid.*, p. 204.

91   *Ibid.*, p. 45.

92   Interview with Péter Heves, Budapest, 5 June 2003.

93   HSWP, *A MSZMP országos ertekezletének jegyzőkönyve 1988*, p. 198.

94   *Ibid.*, p. 201.

95   G. Shakhnazarov, *Tsena svobody: reformatsiia Gorbacheva glazami ego pomoshchnika* (Moscow: Rossika; Zevs, 1993), p. 46.

96   MOL PB 288.f.5/1058, 21 March 1989, p. 134.

97   *Ibid.*

98   MOL PB 288.f.5/1065, 16 May 1989, pp. 28–33.

99   *Ibid.*, p. 28.

100 Interview with Zoltán Szabó, Budapest, 2 June 2003.

101 *Ibid.*

102 Interview with Valerii Vorotnikov, Moscow, 30 October 2002.

103 MOL KB 288.f.4/230–231, 8 December 1987, Kádár, pp. 137–9.

104 *Ibid.*, Nyers, pp. 52–53, as cited above.

105 MOL KB 288.f.4/230–231, 8 December 1987, Kádár, pp. 137–9 (cited above); *Ibid.*, Horn, pp. 140–1.

106 MOL T 288.f.7/803, 11 April 1988, p. 7.

107 J. Kis, *Politics in Hungary: for a Democratic Alternative*, Atlantic Studies on Society in Change; no. 60 (Highland Lakes NJ: Atlantic Research and Publications, 1989), p. 133.

108 E. Aczél (ed.), *A puha diktatúrától a kemény demokráciáig* (Budapest: Pelikán Kiadó, 1994), pp. 52–4.

109 P. Lendvai, *Hungary: the Art of Survival* (London: Tauris, 1988), p. 137.

110 Aczél, *A puha diktatúrától a kemény demokráciáig*, pp. 54–5. Kriuchkov declined an interview (email: S. Ignatchenko, deputy director Public Relations FSB [Federal Security Service] 2003 18 03).

111 Huszár, *Kádár János politikai életrajza*, vol. 2, p. 307.

112 Aczél, *A puha diktatúrától a kemény demokráciáig*, pp. 54–5.

113 A UK journalist present in Budapest at the time of the conference claims this was the case.

114 Lendvai, *Hungary: the Art of Survival*, pp. 147–8.

115 Kriuchkov, *Lichnoe delo*, pt. 1, p. 62.

116 Gorbachev Foundation. Anatoly Cherniaev's fond, Ch.89.Feb.01.a.doc.

117 *Ibid.*

118 Gorbachev Foundation. Vadim Zagladin's fond, Z.88.Sep.07.doc; Z.88.Sep.08.doc.

119 Interview with Rezső Nyers, Budapest, 5 June 2003. This could suggest that until Russia declassifies these archival documents, the Hungarian Socialist Party (HSP) would feel unable to comment officially on the matter.

120 I. Pozsgay and T. Polgár, *A rendszerváltás (k)ára nyílt párbeszéd a sorsfordító évtizedről* (Budapest: Kossuth Kiadó, 2003), p. 31.

121 Gorbachev Foundation. Vadim Zagladin's fond, Z.88.Sep.08a.doc.
122 *Ibid.*, Z.88.Sep.07.doc.
123 MOL PB 288.f.5/1058, 21 March 1989, p. 134.
124 As cited above in this section, p. 174.
125 Interview with Rezső Nyers, Budapest, 5 June 2003.

6

Consolidating federal party unity at the LCY conference, May 1988

Introduction

The LCY leadership convened the conference in 1988 to revive what had become a largely impotent federal power,[1] to try to preserve Yugoslav unity by re-establishing federal party control of the republican parties[2] and reassert the party's leading role in society. The same issues that had given rise to the preceding four conferences of the 1970s were once again on the agenda: the workers' and the youth's disengagement from politics; the recurring problems of unfulfilled congress directives; economic crisis and conflict in Kosovo. From the review of conference outcomes in this chapter, a clear pattern emerges that the LCY conference was a federal institution convened to reassert federal party authority over the republics by urging republican leaders to quell rising nationalism, implement unfulfilled federal directives and mobilise greater support for the party among an increasingly disenchanted society.

By 1986 the growing impotence of federal institutions and the increasingly evident economic crisis had polarised republican politics particularly in Serbia and Slovenia, whose new leaderships adopted policies that further threatened the unity of the federation.[3] In Serbia, Slobodan Milošević's appointment as head of the League of Communists (LC) in September 1987 had quickly led to the party's greater emphasis on a republican national agenda.[4] Milan Kučan's rise to power in Slovenia in 1986 had allowed the growth of a strong anti-federal student opposition, which received tacit support from the CC of the Slovenian LC.[5] One of the main purposes of the LCY conference in May 1988 was therefore to bring these parties into line, according to the conference formula of the 1970s. Most unusually, however, the conference of 1988 was organised in collaboration with the CPSU and was synchronised with other fraternal party conferences, with the aim of affirming a centrist line in support of Soviet *perestroika*. This marked a very significant change in policy for non-aligned Yugoslavia, following a new rapprochement between the CPSU and LCY, which Gorbachev formalised with the LCY leadership in March 1988.

This chapter demonstrates how the LCY conference was thus part of the same socialist fraternity initiative and therefore constituted the same policy choice as for the leaderships of the CPSU and HSWP. This common fraternal policy was the consolidation of party power and the liberalisation of party structures to modernise the party, thereby attracting the disaffected youth whose membership levels had fallen, on average throughout the federation, from ninety to only fifty two per cent in just over a decade, as shown in Table 3. The conference therefore had the same function as those of the CPSU and HSWP, i.e. to affirm the leading role of the party in society and to consolidate the leadership's power over party factions. In the case of the LCY, these factions constituted strong-willed republican parties. All such policies were geared towards maintaining the one-party state, the party's leading role in society, and reforming the economy to improve efficiency with a view to releasing Yugoslavia from increasing financial dependence on the West.

Table 3 *Percentage of youth membership in the League of Communists*

Republic/ Province	% of youth **not** belonging to LC		Republic/ Province	% of youth **not** belonging to LC	
	1974	**1985**		**1974**	**1985**
Slovenia	32	88	Bosnia and		
Croatia	13	70	Herzegovina	5	36
Vojvodina	4	54	Kosovo	4	35
Serbia	6	40	Montenegro	8	18
Macedonia	7	40			
			Average	10	48

Reproduced from Komunist 20 May 1988, p. 11.

Historical institutional analysis of the LCY conference

'Formal constraints': institutionalising federal unity

During the 1970s the LCY conference was an entirely different institution from those of the other Central, Eastern and
South-eastern European communist parties.[6] The LCY conference had been designed in the wake of federal institutional
and economic reforms during the mid to late 1960s as part
of an envisaged solution to maintain federal unity in a post-
Titoist Yugoslavia.[7] Tito had pursued reforms during the mid
to late 1960s to defuse republican nationalism by devolving
greater federal powers to the republics, but declining living
standards and inter-republican rivalry over securing federal
subsidies created tensions among republics.[8] By 1970 republican nationalism and growing inter-ethnic tensions within all
the republics threatened the integrity of the federation.[9] Yugoslavia's unity and the legitimacy of the regime had largely been
maintained by the elderly Tito, whose charisma, and hero
status as communist liberator during the Second World War
had sustained the federation. Aware that with Tito's passing
such unity would be increasingly difficult to maintain through
the leadership of one individual, a new institution, the LCY
conference, was designed to replace the federal CC, and would
cement republican leaderships within the federation.

In July 1968 the LCY CC was replaced with the LCY conference, which was to meet at least once a year.[10] The immediate
policy-making organ behind the conference was the executive
bureau that was comprised of the most senior members of all
the republican parties and equally represented the republics.
This was designed to aggregate republican interests, which
would then be passed on as proposals to the newly created
Presidium,[11] which was to meet monthly to discuss these
proposals. Members were to be elected at the regional party
conferences.

The rules specified, as did the CPSU Stalinist rules and
those amended under Gorbachev,[12] that up to one third of the
membership of the Presidium and LCY organs could be replaced
at a conference.[13] Unlike the other parties' rules, however, the
guidelines for delegate selection were very clearly defined in
the LCY rules.[14] The 1970 Rules specified that the Presidium
could call the conference, or in the event of an inter-republican

disagreement, any of the republics could also request one.[15] One provision in the Rules furthermore specified that in the event a solution was not found to a 'serious problem' discussed at a conference, then it was mandatory that the Presidium call an extraordinary congress within six months.[16]

Since the conference was to meet regularly – annually – it was designed, in part, as a standing committee of permanent members, elected at each five-year congress; the remainder of delegates were elected at regional and local conferences.[17] Thus the LCY conference, unlike those in the rest of the socialist fraternity, was designed *de jure* as a regular and established institution rather than an emergency measure for crisis.

'Informal constraints' of centralisation and normalisation

Nevertheless, *de facto*, the conference appears to have been designed for the purpose of crisis management. At interview, historians Latinka Perović and Aleksa Đilas both agreed that historically the federal conference acted as a forum to normal-ise the party at moments when republican nationalist tensions were rising.[18] They agreed that at these events the LCY federal leadership hoped to consolidate federal power over the repub-lics and solve republican differences. According to Aleksa Đilas, Tito, like Stalin, feared congresses[19] and considered that he had more control at conferences.[20] As will be illustrated, the conference dealt with the same recurring issues: nationalism, inter-republican inequalities, economic inefficiency and the ongoing failure to implement correctly reforms approved at the Ninth Congress. Each of the four conferences, held between 1970 and 1973, focused on these issues, although republican implementation of resolutions approved at these meetings remained problematic, as Tito said at the Third Conference:

> I would not like this resolution to suffer the same fate as the reso-lutions of the Ninth Congress and of the First and Second LCY Conferences, to which many people did not pay any attention, nor did they respect them.[21]

At the Fourth Conference a special report was presented about the continued failure to implement party policy.[22] Tito, nota-bly, did not attend this conference.[23] All four conferences were held between the Ninth and Tenth Congresses, between 1969 and 1974. At these events, the federal leadership struggled to maintain the reformist policies from the mid-1960s, encouraged their proper implementation, and finally attempted to institutionalise them in the new constitution of February 1974.

The First LCY Conference, held in October 1970, reiterated the unfulfilled directives approved at the Ninth Congress. These entailed the development of economic self-management and the further decentralisation of power from the federal to the republican level. Equality among the nationalities,[24] but nonetheless strong unity among the republics, was encouraged.[25] Tito criticised the party's slow resolution of economic problems and demanded that a long-term economic programme be developed to pre-empt crisis. He expressed his concern at the rise in 'anti-social' nationalist elements and rejected the foreign press's pessimistic forecast of Yugoslavia's impending break-up and reports of the failures in economic self-management.

The Second Conference in January 1972 discussed the same issues of disunity and inefficiency and approved directives, which were formalised into an 'Action Programme'.[26] Tito stated on the opening day of the conference that Yugoslavia was a strong federation and that there was no systemic crisis.[27] Despite his words, federal unity was clearly under strain since increased autonomy in the republics had resulted in a rise in republican nationalism, especially in Croatia. There, the politicisation of the cultural society *Matica Hrvatska* and its transformation into a nationalist movement had culminated in the 'Croatian Crisis' or 'Croatian Spring'. Embittered by the perception that Croatia was subsidising the poorer republics, anti-Serb feeling flourished in Croatia,[28] which provoked Serbs into publicising rumours that senior Croatian politicians had strong links with fascist *Ustaše* émigrés. By 1971, *Matica Hrvatska* had a greater 'leading role in society' than the Croatian LC, as strikes and student demonstrations in Zagreb in November 1971 were met by the Croatian authorities with ambivalence and even some endorsement.[29] Much of the ill-feeling had arisen from the positioning of central federal economic institutions in Belgrade, which had raised concerns of Serbian economic and political hegemony.[30] Latinka Perović, a member of the Serbian LC leadership present at the conference, described how proceedings were conducted with excessive security measures, intended to intimidate delegates and encourage republican leaders to toe the party line,[31] and sweeping personnel changes were made in the replacement of the entire executive bureau. At the conference, Tito denounced Serbian university professors for inciting students to take part in demonstrations. After the conference, the LCY leadership declared that the Serbian LC had not taken sufficient measures to root out 'nationalist' elements and consequently Tito and the Secretary of the Executive Bureau, Stane Dolanc, published letters in the press demanding the resignation of particular members of the Serbian LC.[32] In the wake of these demonstrations, it is not surprising that the issue of 'problems with the youth' subsequently became the main focus of the Third LCY Conference.

There had been a significant decline in LCY membership since 1950.[33] The relaxation of central federal party control had allowed more liberal republican leaderships to exercise greater religious tolerance, and nationalist and religious groups had begun to flourish at the expense of the LCY. The Third Conference, held in 1972, addressed these issues.[34] The conference resolution determined that political, cultural and religious groups should not be allowed to influence the young and demanded more 'ideological work' to engage the young in the LCY.[35]

The Fourth LCY Conference, held in 1973, evaluated the results of the Action Programme from the Second Conference and prepared for the forthcoming Tenth Congress.[36]

As the executive bureau increasingly failed to reconcile republican parties' interests,[37] the Presidium met less regularly. Splintered by the nationalist tensions of the early 1970s, the LCY conference was unable to function as a replacement for the LCY CC as it had been designed. The LCY conference was consequently dissolved and the LCY CC reinstated.[38]

Changes to the conference's 'formal constraints'

In light of these failures and the dissolution of the LCY conference, provisions regarding the conference were consequently removed from the Party Rules until 1982, when new provisions were introduced, which defined the LCY conference in the same terms as articulated in the rules of the other fraternal parties.[39] Although the fraternal parties provided fewer and less detailed guidelines, the LCY essentially ascribed the same functions to the conference: between five-yearly congresses the conference could be convened to discuss important issues.[40] The article that provided the conference with the power to re-elect some of the party organs' personnel was removed from the rules. Similarly, the proviso that the conference could assume the powers of the congress did not appear in the 1982 version of the rules.[41]

These amendments appear to have been designed to make provision for a possible future crisis. Certainly, by 1982 Yugoslavia was in economic crisis. The price of Yugoslav mineral exports plummeted in 1979, bringing the federation's trade deficit to an all-time high, which threatened domestic industry with wholesale bankruptcy.[42] Very sizeable hard currency debts, in the form of IMF loans, had grown as US dollar interest rates soared. Additionally, unlike the other fraternal countries, Yugoslavia was subject to price rises on oil imported from the Soviet Union, as this was paid for in hard currency.[43] In 1982 Brezhnev had implemented a reform programme to move the Soviet economy away from the crippling practice of 'import delirium' which was increasingly indebting the Soviet Union to the West. The Yugoslav leadership, at this time, tried to change the federation's energy profile by developing nuclear power, so as to be less dependent on expensive oil imports.[44] Such pressures may have encouraged the LCY leadership to make provision for an emergency forum between congresses.

In 1986, the provisions regarding the conference were again amended to resemble more closely those in the other fraternal parties' rules, which defined the function of the conference as a plebiscitary forum held between congresses:

> To seek the input of the membership, the primary party organisations and other organs of the LCY in reviewing and deciding the position and policy of the LCY on significant ideological-political, socio-economic and other issues between two congresses, the CC of the LCY may convene as necessary, but only once during a term of office, the conference of the LCY.[45]

Amendments were also made to the 1982 version of the rules with respect to delegate selection. As articulated in the other fraternal parties' rules, the LCY rules were changed in 1986 to grant the LCY CC control over delegate selection.[46] These changes reflected the federal leadership's growing concern that LCY authority had been seriously eroded. In 1984 federal directives were described by the LCY Presidium as carried out by republican leaderships 'half-heartedly' and only when republican interests coincided with federal policy. Although this Presidium report was submitted to the LCY CC in 1984 for immediate action, the CC decided to delay action until the Thirteenth Congress of 1986.[47] The amendments to the rules, which granted the federal party leadership control over delegate selection to the federal conference, suggest the federal party considered that delegate selection was an important factor in determining outcome, and we might surmise that the CC would have been eager to select delegates more likely to embrace federal unity.

The policy choice of the LCY conference in 1988

Interviewees claimed that the conference was convened in 1988 for the same purpose as during the 1970s: to deal primarily with republican nationalism and inter-republican tensions. The economist Jurij Bajec (present at the conference in 1988 in his capacity as a member of the Politburo) stated that the rise in Serbian nationalism and conflict in Kosovo were the chief reasons the conference was convened.[48] Milošević's views on the Kosovo conflict were widely known by the time the decision was made to call the LCY conference in December 1987. In April 1987 Milošević, in his address to a gathering of some 15,000 Serbs in the cultural centre hall of Kosovo Polje,[49] had made the inflammatory declaration that the '[Serbs] would never be beaten'.[50] In September 1987 the Kosovo Presidium wryly commented on the Kosovo conflict that 'the communist paradise of brotherly relations between the nationalities has not yet materialised'.[51] Within liberal circles of the Serbian LC, concern was expressed at Milošević's appointment and his nationalist agenda,[52] and other republican leaders expressed similar misgivings.[53] Just before the LCY conference, Stipe Šuvar, member of the Croatian and LCY Presidium, announced to the LCY Presidium on 24 May 1988 his strong disagreement with the Serbian CC proposal to change the Serbian Constitution to subsume the autonomous provinces of Kosovo and Vojvodina into Serbia.[54] According to Professor Bajec, it is likely that Milošević signalled his discord with federal policy by choosing not to attend the conference in 1988,[55] and his absence would have been particularly conspicuous, given that the event was held in Belgrade. According to Bajec, Milošević resented taking directives from President Boško Krunić because he was from Vojvodina – one of the areas Milošević and his supporters contended was Serbian.[56] Whereas during the conferences of the 1970s, Tito and the LCY leadership had been able to influence republican policy by enforcing federal purges of the republican leaderships to exclude nationalist elements, by 1988 the federal party no longer had the authority to exert such influence.

The ongoing impact of the economic crisis and the failure to attract and engage the youth were equally considered central to the conference's purpose. CC member Ivan Brigić stressed at the LCY CC meeting in December 1987, when the decision to convene the conference was endorsed, that the conference should be used to transform the LCY to make it relevant to society before the party was wholesale rejected by society:

> At the forthcoming conference of the LCY we should act on Tito's words: 'We need to listen to one another, and eliminate the many weaknesses in our work. Because, when a political organisation does not grasp what the times require of it and fails to notice the changes in society around it, then such an organisation is simply pushed from the stage of history.'[57]

Conference or congress?

As early as 1984, party members had been demanding an extraordinary congress to overcome the impasse that the federal government had reached through its disunity and inability to implement the directives of the Twelfth Congress of 1982.[58] In order to deal with the escalating crisis, the LCY discussed whether to hold a congress or conference, and for some months a congress appeared unavoidable.[59] The decision to hold a conference was formally agreed at the Eleventh session of the LCY CC on 7–8 December 1987.[60] At this meeting there was much disagreement over how the conference should be convened, how delegates should be selected and whether it should include a large group of rank-and-file members or just the leadership.[61] At this CC session Radovan Radonjić, a social science professor from Montenegro, stated 'We do not need a conference in the style of an extraordinary congress, but neither do we need a meaningless session that would just constitute yet another meeting.'[62] There does not appear to be, however, any evidence of acrimonious debate within the party in 1987–88 over whether to convene the LCY conference or the congress, as was the case with the CPSU and HSWP, discussed in Chapters 3 and 5. Several reasons for this may be advanced. As already stated, the LCY as a federal organ only exercised limited control over republican policy. Therefore given the federal party's impotence, the federal conference was largely perceived as a symbolic event, one more likely to influence than actively enforce implementation. Although demands were publicised that conference resolution directives had to be implemented immediately following the conference, and that these directives were legally binding,[63] there was, nonetheless, an uneasy awareness that federal directives were often flouted.[64] In preparation for the LCY conference, LCY members demanded that should the conference fail to come to an agreement over how to solve the crisis, an extraordinary congress must then be convened.[65] This demand was reiterated in the Serbian report at the conference.[66]

Press coverage at the time clearly referred to the situation as a 'crisis' and the consequent need for a conference, unlike reportage of the conferences by the press in the Soviet Union and Hungary, where leaders publicly denied that the situation was critical.[67] We can therefore conclude that in preparation for the conference in 1988, the LCY publicly acknowledged the function of the conference as an emergency meeting to solve a crisis, which is how a delegate at the conference, former Serbian CC member Ljubinka Trgovčević, described the event.[68]

Preparations for the LCY conference, May 1988

Delegate selection for the LCY conference

The press conveyed their low expectations of any form of democratic practice in terms of delegate selection to party meetings, as corrupt practice among the *nomenklatura*, such as the Agrokomerc enterprise scandal in 1987 that nearly resulted in the economic collapse of north-west Bosnia,[69] had become highly publicised by this time. The perception of such corruption among officials as epidemic in proportion was captured in the press by a cartoon in *Politika*, entitled 'immunology'. The cartoon alluded to the *nomenklatura*'s belief in their right to (political) 'immunity', as well as capturing the sense that delegates were guinea pigs:

> **Patient** [objecting to doctor's approaching needle]: What's this? I have delegate's immunity!'
>
> **Doctor** [reassuring patient]: Don't worry; we are just testing whether you are HIV positive to agro-commercial syndrome.[70]

In contrast to this perceived corruption, the press had dispassionately reported that the selection procedure for delegates to the federal LCY conference would be according to democratic practices. Originally the federal conference was to take place in March 1988;[71] candidate delegates were to be proposed by 15 February and one delegate for every 5,000 members would be elected by secret ballot. Selection was to be made from a choice of candidates.[72] The press announced that delegates would be selected for the conference in such a way as to ensure adequate representation in terms of nationality and social strata. Although there was no direct reference at the conference to the way in which delegate selection was conducted, interviewees confirmed that selection was certainly not representative of the party, nor left to chance. One interviewee present at the conference confirmed that the federal conference did not comprise a wide range of delegates in terms of social stratification and therefore was certainly not representative of the party at large. Jurij Bajec stated that all the delegates present at this conference were high-ranking party members and that he himself had been selected to attend in his capacity as a senior Politburo member, rather than as a university professor. Consequently, he stated, delegates comprised only the most senior party officials.[73] Serbian CC member Ljubinka Trgovčević remarked that delegates to the republican-level conferences and other party forums were always hand-picked by the 'cadre commission', to ensure that delegates would be compliant, but also appear, as far as possible, to be representative in terms of social stratification.[74]

The federal party issued directives in December 1987 to each of the republican and provincial parties that they hold their own respective conferences in preparation for the federal conference.[75] As the next section will detail, certain leaderships were reluctant to comply fully with this directive, and the fundamental differences in tenor of these meetings denoted the extent of the range of perspectives among the parties.

Republican and provincial LC conferences

The first conference was convened by the Bosnian LC in Sarajevo, on 16–17 April 1988. The central theme of the conference discussion was corruption manifest in the very disparate standards of living between the LC elite on the one hand and in society generally on the other.[76] Milan Škoro, a Presidium member of the Bosnian LC, made a scathing attack on the LC for the Agrokomerc financial scandal, and stated that corruption on such a scale was by no means limited to that instance.[77] Škoro ended his speech with the demand that personnel changes be made throughout the LC, at all levels, to remove those responsible.[78]

Shortly after this, on 22–23 April 1988, the Slovenian LC held its conference,[79] which was entirely geared towards maintaining the unity of the federation, 'with its Yugoslav orientation'.[80] Although conference speeches demanded the greater engagement of the youth, the scale of disaffection with the LC was such that the leadership knew they were fighting a losing battle. In the case of Slovenia only twelve per cent of the youth in 1985 were members of the LC, as opposed to sixty-eight per cent in 1974.[81] In 1986 the youth had created an alternative political organisation, the 'Union of Socialist Slovenian Youth', whose primary demand was the legalisation of other political parties.[82] At the Slovenian conference, President Milan Kučan said that the crux of the forthcoming LCY conference was the issue of how the LC would remain in power, and said that only the politically naïve and short-sighted would fail to see this.[83] Indeed, just a few weeks earlier, on 25 March 1988, the LCY CC had discussed how to deal with these new political movements and had decided that the Yugoslav People's Army (JNA) should arrest the editorial team of the Slovene youth organisation's newspaper, Mladina.[84] The more liberal approach of the Slovenian LC from the beginning of the 1980s had resulted in a more relaxed, open and pluralist society than elsewhere in Yugoslavia.[85] Consequently, although speeches at the Slovenian conference indicated a pro-federalist stance demanding, as did the other republics, greater unity within the LC, the use of the words 'pluralist society' by Kučan in reference to Slovene society belied the vision of monolithic unity imposed by the one-party state as desired elsewhere in the federation. Similarly, Kučan used conditional terms to express the LC's plan to win over society, which suggested that should society not have been convinced by the LC's proposals, then these would not be imposed; instead the future path would be determined by the people:

> The LC is also interested in acting as a leading force in a pluralist society which is *as far as possible* capable of drawing the path of development that is objectively and historically necessary, *as far as possible* on the level of ideology, theory and practice in society. That means that *as far as we are able* to gain people's faith and trust then this is precisely the path that the LC needs to take.[86]

However, such pluralism was not approved at the May LCY conference. Following the conference, at the Twentieth Session of the Slovenian LC CC, on 27 June 1988, Kučan strongly objected to the proposal that the JNA intervene in Slovenia against 'anti-Yugoslav' and 'anti-socialist' forces;[87] these forces constituted, in the main, the new politicised youth group that had formed around the newspaper *Mladina*.

The Macedonian LC conference was held in Skopje, on 26–27 April 1988. The conference endorsed the proposed federal conference resolutions to engage more of society in LC activity and implement the socio-economic reforms that had been approved at the Thirteenth LCY Congress.[88] Jakov Lazarovski, Presidium Chairman of the CC of the Macedonian LC, berated the party's statism, bureaucracy and all divisive nationalist elements that could lead to the (further) 'federalisation' of the LC.[89] He demanded that the working class be restored as the vanguard of the party and that living conditions for the working classes be improved.[90]

On 21–22 May 1988, the Montenegrin LC conference was held in Titograd and endorsed the proposed federal conference resolutions. The Chairman of the Montenegrin LC CC Presidium, Miljan Radović, affirmed that without substantive personnel and organisational changes, the LC would be unable to overcome the socio-economic crisis and that republican leaderships must be made more accountable.[91] In preparation for this republican conference, in April, primary party organisations discussed the ideological-political crisis and inertia within the party, and how to maintain the working class as the vanguard of the party.[92]

The Croatian LC held two CC sessions on 5 May 1988 to discuss the proposed LCY conference theses.[93] The main theme of the meetings was 'breaking down barriers' to allow the LC to function properly. At these meetings they stressed the importance of maintaining the unity of the federation and personnel changes were made.[94] The Croatian LC held its conference at the end of May, which finished on 26 May 1988, just a few days before the federal conference. This meeting focused on the youth's disengagement from the LC, since the drop in their membership had been particularly acute in Croatia.[95] The figure for 'those young people not wishing to belong to the LCY' had risen in Croatia from thirteen per cent in 1974 to seventy per cent in 1985.[96] Croatian Presidium member Stjepka Gugić demanded radical changes to the party, including the eradication of bureaucracy, democratisation of party structures, and the endorsement of the workers' role as the party's vanguard. Gugić insisted that the gap between the living standards of the party elite and the people be closed.[97]

At the end of May 1988, the JNA announced their intention to hold their party conference in the second half of June after the federal conference;[98] they held their conference on 21–22 June 1988.[99] At the meeting, the Chairman of the Presidium of the JNA LC, Petar Šimić, expressed the JNA's concern at the 'coordinated, open attacks, through means of special warfare, with the aim of subverting and compromising the JNA... and discouraging the youth from doing military service by stuffing them full of a narrow nationalist spirit, thereby compromising Yugoslav socialist patriotism'.[100]

Šimić expressed the need, in light of the crisis in Kosovo and the rise in anti-communist activity, for the unequivocal leading role of the LCY in society.[101]

The conference of the Kosovan LC, held in Priština on 24–25 June 1988, focused on ethnic tensions and the mass migration of Serbs and Montenegrins from the province.[102] A petition, signed by 50,000 Serbs and Montenegrins resident in Kosovo, was presented to the conference demanding greater protection from Albanian aggression.[103]

At the Tenth CC Session of the Serbian LC on 14 April, Milošević demanded that the party concentrate on restoring workers' rights, root out bureaucracy, modernise the party, change personnel and implement the stabilisation plans, which had long since been endorsed.[104] Serbian LC CC members who had been selected as delegates to the federal conference spoke out against opportunism and bureaucracy in the party, and demanded greater accountability from party leaders.[105] At the end of April 1988, many of the primary party organisations of the Serbian LC held conferences throughout the republic to discuss the preparations for the federal conference.[106] At the end of July 1988, *Komunist* published articles that declared preparations for a forthcoming Serbian party conference.[107] There is, however, no further indication that such a conference ever took place. Similarly, although the CC of the Vojvodina LC held meetings to discuss the forthcoming federal conference, there is no indication that a provincial party conference *per se* was convened.

These rather disparate responses by the republican/provincial leaderships to the federal directive indicate a lack of unity over crucial issues. Shortly after the intended LCY conference was publicised in December 1987, senior CC member of the LCY Stipe Šuvar, who was appointed President in June 1988, denied the rumour that the forthcoming conference was to discuss regime change and the introduction of a multiparty system as a solution to the crisis. Instead he affirmed the leading role of the LCY in society and stated that the introduction of a multiparty system was considered by the party as a retrograde step.[108] However, despite this bold public statement, the issue still clearly worried the LCY leadership in the run-up to the conference. During his meeting with Gorbachev in March 1988, Lazar Mojsov, from the LCY Presidium, claimed that Western powers were helping found new political parties to introduce a multiparty system into Yugoslavia.[109]

> We also have conscientious objectors to national [military] service and in our country there are certain groups of individuals who adopt an inimical position towards socialism and who, with the support of the West, are fighting to found other [political] parties in Yugoslavia and [to bring about] the introduction of a multiparty system.[110]

The laissez-faire attitude towards the leading role of the party, which the Slovenian leadership displayed at their republican conference in April 1988, rather undermined the federal party's statement that the purpose of the conference was to strengthen the party's authority over society. The Slovenian delegation reiterated this standpoint at the federal conference, as the next section will discuss.

The LCY conference, 29–31 May 1988

A multiparty system as a possible solution to the crisis?

At the conference, LCY President, Boško Krunić, confirmed that there was no intention of regime change and that the leading role of the LCY in Yugoslav society was still sacrosanct. In his opening speech, he conceded that the issue of introducing a multiparty system had been a dilemma since the Eleventh Congress of 1978 but that the party's position on this issue had not changed.[111] Notably, the Slovenian republican delegation was the only one to advocate the end of the communist party's monopoly of power and to propose the legalisation of other political parties.[112] The Montenegrin delegation advocated some pluralism of the press and demanded more tolerance towards journalists who criticised the regime, the JNA or party ideology.[113] The JNA and Vojvodina reports, at the other extreme, demanded the re-establishment of monolithic unity within the party, while the Bosnian, Federal, Kosovan, Macedonian and Serbian reports, and that of the delegates' select working committee, adopted a more pragmatic position, demanding that the vanguard role of the LCY in society be increased, but that plurality of opinion within that vanguard be permitted.

All the reports proposed changes to party electoral processes. Suggestions included changes to the cadre system of appointments, proposing more candidates than mandates contested, secret ballots and direct elections.[114] The resolution endorsed by the conference included the proposed changes to the electoral system, and although the resolution did not advocate a return to monolithic unity, it clearly dismissed the notion of a multiparty system.[115]

Personnel change

Demands for personnel change were made repeatedly at the conference. Boško Krunić, in his opening presidential speech, commented on the conservative resistance to reform.[116] This is reminiscent of Gorbachev's update on the purge within CPSU ranks, made at the Nineteenth Party Conference, just a few weeks after the LCY conference, when he declared that hardliners ('ballast'), standing in the way of reform, had been ousted.[117] Krunić also stressed the need for personnel change, and that there should be free competition in appointments for every post,[118] and commanded that those officials responsible for criminal acts and serious mistakes should be removed from office:

> We cannot have those people who have made mistakes in the leadership [acting] as the moral vanguard of the people, nor those people who have looked after their own interests, who have enriched themselves through cold calculation or abuse of office let alone those who have committed criminal acts. When we talk about renovation in terms of radical changes to the LC, we mean a radical purge of the LC of all such features brought in by the perpetrators [of such acts].[119]

The summary of the delegates' working group was particularly critical of the CC and Presidium, and demanded radical personnel changes.[120] All reports advocated personnel change.[121] This issue was publicised by the LCY in synchronism with the CPSU time frame, in December 1987. For example, in an interview in December 1987 with the popular Serbian political magazine *NIN*, Radoš Smiljković, who attended the conference as a delegate for the Serbian LC, advocated the need for radical personnel changes in the Belgrade leadership. He stated that society's loss of faith in the party necessitated such changes and that they should be made on the basis of merit, rather than according to *nomenklatura* selection protocol.[122]

LCY conference reports reflected an overwhelming preoccupation with the loss of LCY legitimacy in society, as had speeches at the CPSU and HSWP conferences. Similarly, those sectors of society identified as most alienated from the LCY were the youth and workers.[123] This is evident in all reports presented at the conference which demanded measures be taken to combat the loss of faith in the party and re-engage these sectors of society.[124] Some months prior to and following the conference there was heavy coverage of this issue in the press.[125] With the exception of the Slovenian and Kosovan reports, all conference reports advocated renewed worker participation in the LC. This confirms that the LCY's intention, at this time, was to affirm the traditional communist party model with the workers as the vanguard of the party.

Federal reports to promote the image of LCY unity

The LCY conference minutes were published in a different format to the equivalent CPSU and HSWP meetings. Although individuals did voice more personal viewpoints at the conference, only a handful of these appeared in the press. The majority of the press coverage was of Boško Krunić's long speeches and the conference resolutions.[126] There was a summary of the views of a delegates' working group (comprised of fifteen senior party members, mainly from the LCY CC) and reports from the nine individual republics; the LCY and the JNA party organisation each presented a report, and conference resolutions approved were included in the published minutes.[127] Since these reports did not express personal viewpoints but rather constituted statements on behalf of the respective republican parties, speeches were significantly longer than CPSU and HSWP speeches; they were more formulaic and the language was dispassionate.[128] In general, there was significant policy agreement across the reports, republics did not criticise each others' policies and no extreme views were expressed. The fact that few divergent views were published bears out the LCY's intention that the conference should display federal party unity. The choice on the part of the leadership to condense the minutes of these republican conferences into reports in such a way additionally supports this.

As the title of the conference suggests – 'Conference of the LCY for consolidating the political ideology of the party's leading role and for the unity and accountability of the LCY in the struggle to get out of the socio-economic crisis' – the main thrust of the discussion was focused on the need to strengthen the leading role of the LCY in society and to reassert federal control over the republics. With the exception of the Slovenian, Montenegrin and Kosovan republican reports, each report expressed the need to strengthen the leading role of the LCY in society.[129] One of the main purposes of the conference was to introduce directives to modernise the party and thereby help renew party authority over a disillusioned and sceptical society. The most widely discussed topic was economic reform. All conference reports referred to this at length, with the exception of the JNA report, and all expressed the need to liberalise the economy further and open up more to world markets.[130]

Krunić described the pressures from the left and right, within society and the party, that were undermining the leading role of the party and he warned that unless republics started implementing federal directives the LC would lose its leading role in society. He reiterated that the party must remain on a Titoist path:

> The LCY is today especially subject to pressure, on the one hand from citizens on the political right, who are drawing us towards the restoration of capital relations and bourgeois democracy, most often of the social-democrat variety, and on the other pressures and calls for methods of sharing party power. Even within the LC currents have surfaced that aggressively advocate pseudo-liberal and state socialism. The problem of securing the LCY's leading role [in society] begins with the question – what has this to do with self-management in Yugoslavia? Does the LCY have the power to implement its decisions and to overcome the differences within its own ranks and to come together in unity of idea and action in its decision-making? Our unity needs to correspond with the working class criteria and conclusions made at the Thirteenth Congress. ... Unless there is proof and evidence, on a daily basis on a class continuum, along a Titoist path, the leading role of the LC will cease to exist.[131]

Krunić's demand to centralise party policy against the forces of left and right is reminiscent of a similar plea that Gorbachev later made, when trying to reconvene the CPSU conference in April 1991, to maintain the integrity of the CPSU in the wake of growing republican autonomy.[132]

Weak federal authority over republican party policy

Repeated demands to strengthen party unity and revive the authority of federal power sounded like a refrain throughout the conference. All republican reports commanded this.[133] Although all republics sought the greater confederalisation of Yugoslavia, none at this time desired the dissolution of the federation.[134] The Slovenian call, at the conference, to affirm the directives of the Sixth LCY Congress of 1952, was an allusion to the rejected liberal Ðilas reform programme which had advocated greater decentralisation of federal power to the republics.[135] Although in favour of greater devolution of power to the republican level, the Slovenian report at the conference confirmed the LCY position that republics should not secede.[136] Over the months following the conference, however, the Slovenian LC became more radicalised and its disagreement with other republics over this and other issues culminated in Slovenian delegates refusing to endorse the resolutions of the Fourteenth Congress in 1990, having left the meeting before agreement could be reached.[137]

Krunić stressed to Gorbachev during their March 1988 meeting that further decentralisation of power to the constituent republican parties would not be tolerated, and that the conference should act to strengthen LCY power over the republican parties:

> In the country there is a growing mood of radicalisation towards change. There are calls to eliminate deformations in different spheres of social life. Criticism of the CC and presidium resounds whenever serious scandals are uncovered, or when there is a violation of the equal rights of the peoples of the nationalities. We are made very uncomfortable by the tendency towards the federalisation of the party. We are decisively against this and the forthcoming national conference of the LCY should suppress such tendencies.[138]

However, two months after the LCY conference, at the end of July 1988, there was no sign that the republics had begun implementing the federal conference resolutions. The Roman edition of the federal party newspaper, *Komunist*, published an article that questioned when the republics would do so, and made a veiled criticism of those republics and provinces (namely Serbia and Vojvodina) that had failed to hold their own conference, as required of them, to discuss the conference theses.[139] As federal directives continued to go unheeded, by September 1988 many LCY members were demanding an extraordinary LCY congress to affirm and specify how to implement the decisions taken at the LCY conference in May.[140]

The main reason for the demise of federal authority lay in the problem of Kosovo. Although the Serbian republican party approved the 1974 Constitution *de jure*, federal authority was compromised by the fact that a significant section of the party leadership had never accepted these new terms granting Vojvodina and Kosovo autonomous status as separate provinces from Serbia.[141] Indeed, according to Desimir

Tosić, Serbian resentment at the 1974 constitution marked the beginning of the dissolution of Yugoslavia.[142] By the time of the conference, the problem of Kosovo had intensified, and conference resolutions on the matter clearly diverged from Milošević's proposed solution.

Kosovo conflict

Between 1986 and 1987 thousands of Kosovan Serbs, led by Milošević, had demonstrated against the Albanian mistreatment of Serbs in Kosovo. Serbs began petitioning the federal government in 1986, initially receiving limited success with 2,000 signatures; but by June 1988 such petitions were supported by tens of thousands of signatories.[143]

Despite this, the published minutes suggest that the Kosovo question received relatively little attention at the conference. Reference to the topic was made by the Serbian, Montenegrin and Macedonian delegations, and the issue understandably dominated the Kosovan report. Discussion of the topic was very general, and only the Montenegrin delegation referred directly to the murder of Albanians by Serbs.[144] Separatist Albanians in Kosovo were described in the reports as the perpetrators. The Kosovan report demanded an enquiry into the migration of thousands of Serbs and Montenegrins from Kosovo.[145] Both Kosovan and Serbian reports stated unequivocally that Albanian separatist tendencies in Kosovo must stop.[146] The Serbian report proposed leadership change in the Kosovan LC to encourage a more pro-federalist stance as a solution.[147] A few months earlier, in 1987, the Kosovan LC leadership had removed the Albanian Fadilj Hoxha from the CC for inciting Albanian nationalism; this decision was upheld by the Eleventh LCY CC meeting on 7–8 December 1987 when it was decided to expel him from the party.[148] In response to the Serbian delegation's suggestion that a Kosovan leadership be elected, which would be more 'Yugoslav in outlook',[149] there was a plea from the Kosovan delegation that any personnel changes should be nationally representative.[150] Surprisingly, the Kosovan delegation proposed that the matter be dealt with in the same way as the Albanian incident of 1981.[151] This was a clear call for a military crackdown on any unrest, as the demonstrations of 1981 had been dealt with harshly by the federal authorities, resulting in many casualties among

Albanian demonstrators. Since the list of delegates appended to the conference minutes indicates that at least two thirds of the Kosovan delegation were members with ethnic Albanian names, the Kosovan proposal of putting down the unrest in this way appears counter-intuitive, although they may have proposed this as their preferred option over losing their independent status.

Although the Serbian delegation did not explicitly request the subsumption of Kosovo and Vojvodina into Serbia as their proposed solution to the unrest in Kosovo, the Serbian report said as much in its statement that 'for the sake of the republic's unity' and 'for the population's protection' the Serbian constitution should be changed in accordance with the decisions taken at the Ninth Serbian LC CC Session.[152] The Serbian solution to the Kosovo crisis was not endorsed in the conference resolution, which articulated instead the need to defuse the growing unrest but maintain the independent status of the province.[153]

After the LCY conference, on 9 June 1988 the Serbian parliament endorsed amendments to the Serbian constitution which provided that the two autonomous provinces of Kosovo and Vojvodina be incorporated into the Serbian republic.[154] This new provision, however, was not accepted by the Kosovan or Vojvodina LC CCs, nor indeed by the federal CC of the LCY.[155] Needless to say, such autonomous action on the part of the Serbian LC was symptomatic of the impotence of the federal party, which struggled to force the republics to comply with federal directives.

Failure to implement 1986 congress directives

All reports expressed concern at the LCY's diminished authority over society as apparent from the widespread failure to implement LCY decisions. Concern that resolutions from the Thirteenth Congress had not been implemented was reiterated.[156] Jurij Bajec confirmed that this factor had been a problem for some time as reforms long since approved by various preceding republican conferences and federal congresses were rarely *de facto* effected.[157] Krunić had mentioned this to Gorbachev in March 1988 and stated that one of the purposes of the forthcoming LCY conference was to address this failure, especially with regard to economic reforms. Similarly, laws introduced by the CPSU and HSWP (which were then rubber stamped by their respective parliaments) were not always heeded by ministries and enterprises in the Soviet Union or Hungary. As has been detailed, these issues were also central to the discussion at the CPSU and HSWP conferences.[158] Krunić confirmed the LCY's intention to maintain the existing regime and the planned economy. As he remarked to Gorbachev at this meeting:

> We have been planning for a long time now many changes to the political system and economy. The problem is that they are never implemented. But... I am not casting any doubt on the concept of a planned economy. The plan and the market are not necessarily mutually exclusive. Really, the matter is all about the market under conditions of socialism, about socialist production of goods. As far as the forthcoming LCY conference is concerned, we intend to discuss the following basic questions: the strengthening of the leading ideological-political role of the LCY; the primary tasks for the realisation of the long-term programme of economic stabilisation; the overdue reforms of the political system; the future democratisation of internal party life. Like yours, our conference is [taking place] halfway between congresses. Above all the questions which concern us are: why have the decisions of the Thirteenth LCY Congress not yet been implemented? How do you mobilise the entire intellectual potential of the party and the country so as to reduce inflation? What should the role of the state be in economic policy?

Krunić voiced concern to Gorbachev that the LCY had lost its legitimacy in society as people had become used to ignoring party directives and legislation introduced by the party. Although Krunić did not intend recentralising the economy, he did stress the need to consolidate federal power over the republican leaderships:

> After many years of stagnation, we have witnessed increased social discontent in the country, a rise in social tensions and growth in opposition forces. Although we are not panicking, we do acknowledge these factors have become more problematic. We are trying to close ranks in the party, to raise [party] accountability for solving problems that are arising, and to work out how to get out of this crisis. We are very aware that we are in a difficult position; we are looking for a way to perfect our method of self-management. Under no circumstances will we return to centralised control. We will not allow federalist tendencies to grow in the party; we will reach unity of action on all levels. People are above all concerned

by the fact that problems that have arisen in the political and economic systems have remained unresolved for a long time. In the party, in the parliament, in the local organs of power, there are demands that social control be strengthened. These demands are not against the LCY, but are made to improve [LCY] work; they are not against self-management but in favour of it being accomplished more fully and responsibly.[159]

This exchange demonstrates the LCY's commitment to maintaining the one-party state in Yugoslavia. Krunić's words also suggest that the purpose of the conference was to strengthen the party's authority within society and put a stop to inter-republican tensions that threatened federal unity. This issue also concerned Gorbachev with respect to republican unrest and growing republican autonomy in the Soviet Union under conditions of *perestroika*, as Chapter 3 discussed. As the next few sections will discuss, a significant rapprochement occurred between the LCY and CPSU after Gorbachev became General Secretary, which enabled the parties' collaboration over their respective conferences. Moreover, there was a common incentive for this cooperation, in the spirit of socialist internationalism, to help preserve the socialist model.

Yugoslav–Soviet relations

The fraternal parties' economic dependence on the West

As detailed in Chapter 4, Gorbachev perceived the Western exploitation of Soviet economic misfortune as a 'plot' to contrive greater Soviet and fraternal party dependence on the West. In discussion with Krunić at his March 1988 meeting, Gorbachev stated:

An especially important question for us is the reduction of our internal debt. If we stop payment of our debts then we will find ourselves in a very difficult situation. The west never gives the socialist countries their technology, even when they participate in the creation of joint stock enterprises. Concrete analysis has shown that the USA has always given the socialist countries their old technology. Do you remember how they behaved towards Poland? Having provided them with the machinery, they made them dependent on [western] supply of the component parts. All they needed to do was stop the supply and the Polish economy would be paralysed. I understand the difficult situation once you have found yourself in foreign debt. We see a way out, above all in saving yourself – as the academic Aleksandrov has called it – from 'import delirium'. Having evaluated your intellectual, technological and other potential you set yourself the task of making yourself a world leader in machine construction.[160]

This sense that the fraternal parties had been compromised financially by the West to secure Soviet acquiescence to Western policies was openly depicted in the Yugoslav press which, although not free, operated within broader parameters than the press in the other fraternal states of Central and Eastern Europe.[161] A cartoon in the newspaper *Politika* depicted an imposing building labelled 'détente' outside which two limousines were locked fender to fender, one marked 'deficit' with a small stars and stripes flag attached to the bonnet and the other limousine marked '*perestroika*' embossed with a hammer and sickle. In the picture, two officials from the limousines walked up the stairs together towards the building marked 'détente', leaving their chauffeurs glaring at one another.[162] This suggests, anecdotally, that some saw through the façade of the reforms to the economic factors motivating them, namely that rising hard currency debts and globalisation had led to *perestroika* and necessitated greater communication between the Soviet Union and the United States. Another interpretation of this might be that the US had made use of vulnerabilities in the Soviet economy to force the Soviet Union to comply with the West politically and pursue a policy of détente. This suggests there was a widespread – albeit unofficial – view that the Soviet model had run its course. Fraternal states' economies were in crisis, the Western hard currency debt had escalated and the West was calling in the debt, reeling these states in politically. Certainly at this time the cause of the economic crisis in Yugoslavia was commonly perceived as the result of the West's demand for repayment of debts.[163]

Another cartoon in November 1987 implied the CMEA had been destroyed by the IMF's recalling CMEA states' foreign debts. Although not a CMEA member, Yugoslavia had CMEA observer status and, as has been described in Chapter 4, its economy was heavily dependent on trade with the CMEA by the late 1980s.[164] Around the time of the CMEA emergency meeting in November 1987 a cartoon was published in *Politika* depicting people standing in a group, hands clasped in prayer, behind a minister in a pulpit reading from a book entitled 'Anti-inflationary Programme'. In the caption he is saying, 'And finally brothers, let us pray about what on earth the IMF is doing to us! Let us all say together, after me!'[165] This additionally captured the sense of hopelessness in Yugoslav society over the party's inability to extricate the country from economic crisis.

Realigning Yugoslavia: Gorbachev's visit to Yugoslavia, March 1988

As detailed earlier, Gorbachev and the fraternal party leaders were (understandably) resentful of Western economic leverage over the communist economies.[166] This factor and Yugoslavia's need for financial assistance are likely to have helped encourage the LCY to accept the CPSU's offer of sudden rapprochement between the two parties in 1988. Agreements made between Gorbachev and his counterparts in the LCY during Gorbachev's visit to Yugoslavia in March 1988 constituted a significant policy U-turn with respect to Yugoslavia, which had been expelled from the Communist Information Bureau (Cominform) by Stalin in 1948 and refused to join the Warsaw Pact in 1955. The main bone of contention between the CPSU and LCY had been Soviet interference in the fraternal states' domestic policy. Khrushchev had tried to mend the rift by inviting the LCY to join the newly established Warsaw Treaty Organisation (WTO), and emphasised the need for unity of action among the fraternal parties in accordance with Moscow's foreign policy goals.[167] Interestingly, this is how Gorbachev solicited the fraternal leaders' support from 1986 onwards, as detailed in Chapter 4.[168] In November 1957, however, Khrushchev's attempts to court Yugoslavia were rejected when Yugoslavia refused to sign the joint declaration of the World Conference of Communist Parties held in Moscow.[169]

In 1961, Yugoslavia's non-alignment with the CPSU was officially enshrined in the CPSU Party Programme, which described Yugoslavia as 'revisionist' and therefore 'outside the socialist camp and outside the world communist movement'.[170] Tito objected to Soviet interference in the fraternal states; the subsequent invasion of Czechoslovakia in 1968, and the occupation of Kampuchea and invasion of Afghanistan in 1979, confirmed to the LCY leadership that the CPSU had not changed its policy in this respect. Consequently, the LCY stance outside the Warsaw Pact remained resolutely fixed.[171]

However, following Gorbachev's visit to Yugoslavia in March 1988, *Komunist* published an article outlining a new rapprochement between the parties. The first step towards this, the newspaper noted, was the change made in the Party Programme at the Twenty-seventh CPSU Congress in 1986, where the section describing the LCY non-alignment was altered so that the 'LCY and its government were saved from this dogmatic and Stalinist disqualification'.[172]

Gorbachev visited Yugoslavia in March 1988, shortly before the LCY and CPSU conferences. During his visit, meetings were held between the LCY and the CPSU which ratified a new treaty between the two parties that was to apply until 2000. The agreement detailed proposed limited economic collaboration (as the USSR looked to Yugoslavia for experience as a mixed economy) and the founding of a Yugoslav cultural information centre in Moscow. Gorbachev's visit was described in the Yugoslav press as that of a CPSU visit ('by the General Secretary of the CC CPSU') to the 'Yugoslav leadership' and a renewal of bilateral Yugoslav–Soviet relations. Therefore, this was clearly not just considered a state visit, but instead marked the renewal of relations between the parties, relations that had been severed since 1948:

> What was ratified was a political declaration... composed of resolutions and principles regarding two lands and two *parties* that had overcome their mutual disagreements and conflicts to agree on a new basis, agreed in the form of bilateral relations as in the wider international arena.[173]

In a section entitled 'party cooperation' this new-found cooperation between the LCY and CPSU was spelled out by the LCY newspaper, *Komunist*:

> Discussions between the leading members of the LCY and CPSU were held in a friendly atmosphere of comradeship and mutual understanding. Discussions were lively, spontaneous and informal. This wide and extended exchange of thinking embraced the question of cooperation between the LCY and CPSU, and relations were evaluated as having developed very successfully, and opened up possibilities for further growth on recognised and approved principles. In addition there was an exchange of information about

the two parties' activities on the domestic level (the role of the party in the socio-economic development of each country) and appropriate attention was also paid to the issues of the situation and trends in socialism as a world process, as well as to the international workers' movement.[174]

The *Komunist* article in March described Gorbachev's 1988 visit as a renewed attempt to pick up where Khrushchev had failed to bring Yugoslavia back into the socialist fraternity in 1957:

> The Soviet state pointed out that the Moscow–Belgrade declaration, which has established on new grounds the relations between the two countries and two parties, constitutes a major turning point, which was displayed in the wisdom of Tito and Khrushchev in overcoming problems. In his statement, the General Secretary of the CPSU stated that the accusations against Yugoslavia were false and added that the principles adopted had a far-reaching significance, as time had shown. It was stated that these interparty relations were extremely important factors for the complete cooperation between the two countries and that this visit has made a new contribution to this.[175]

The visit was reported as having had a positive impact on economic, political, social and diplomatic relations between the two parties and countries. During his visit, Gorbachev presented LCY leaders with 90,000 documents pertaining to Yugoslavia from the CPSU archives. Interestingly, reportage on this issue was couched in cautious terms, suggesting that the LCY expected that further records would be transferred:

> It was stated that the recently approved programme of international cooperation had made a great impact – also in the realm of party schools, party newspapers, and especially outstanding in the realms of successful cooperation with the party archives. Around 90,000 documents from the CC CPSU archives have been put at the disposal of the CC LCY archives for the sake of Yugoslav research, but at the same time it is estimated that in this respect there is still a good deal more room for the development of cooperation.[176]

During his visit, Gorbachev publicised the forthcoming CPSU conference as a watershed event that would transform the political system. One article described how Gorbachev informed the LCY 'exhaustively' about the preparations for the Nineteenth CPSU Conference; the photograph in the newspaper does indeed show a picture of Gorbachev holding forth before a weary audience.[177]

Statements in the Yugoslav press made about the new-found relations between the two parties described Gorbachev's new political thinking policy towards the fraternal parties and his renunciation of the Brezhnev Doctrine. The new policy was outlined by *Komunist*, which presented a summary of what had been agreed at the International Communist Movement's meeting on 4 November 1987, at which fraternal party heads of state[178] had been present. Yugoslav approval of this meeting's declaration appeared to close the rift that had remained after Yugoslavia had refused to sign the joint declaration of the World Communist Parties held in Moscow in November 1957.[179]

> Within the framework of discussions about the conditions and outlook in the international workers' movement, the two countries praised highly the meeting which was held in Moscow last year to commemorate seventy years since the October revolution. The meeting took new and substantive steps in furthering the cooperation among communists, socialists, social democrats and other progressively orientated parties and movements around the world... Moreover, in practice, foundations have been laid, on the basis of multilateral cooperation within the international workers' movement, that rest on the principles of openness towards all progressive parties and movements and zero tolerance for narrow forms of ideological cooperation. [It stressed] the axiom that all forms of multilateral cooperation stem from the principles of egalitarianism, independence, non-intervention and democracy, which are important for bilateral relations.[180]

Soviet archival sources from Gorbachev's visit to Yugoslavia in March 1988, as discussed in Chapter 4, also detail conversations on the subject of the forthcoming party conferences, which to a certain extent correspond with the official press. These private meetings elaborated on the causes of the problems, identifying the common enemy as 'capitalist' Western powers, uniting these parties in defence of 'socialism' through the convening of their conferences. Transcripts of meetings between LCY President Boško Krunić and Gorbachev during his Yugoslav visit outline the leaders' motives for conference convention and what they hoped to achieve. Krunić openly expressed his concern over the rise in political opposition forces in Yugoslavia, as well as the tendency towards fragmentation of the federation.[181] He stated that the forth-coming LCY conference would be specifically geared towards overcoming these nationalist tendencies and the consolida-tion of LCY power in the wake of growing discontent at the economic situation.[182] Gorbachev's concern that the West was trying to take advantage of the critical circumstances in the Soviet Union and Soviet preoccupation with the economic crisis are apparent in these conversations. He explicitly voiced concerns that the West was trying to gain the advantage by financially compromising the Soviet Union's 'outer empire', thereby reducing Soviet political influence over these states. Gorbachev claimed that the US had taken advantage of its trade relations with Poland and made the country entirely dependent on the US.[183]

As outlined in Chapter 4, Gorbachev claimed that the West was actively trying to undermine the progress of *perestroika* and scupper any chances of economic independence for the Soviet Union. He claimed that the West had been encouraging the growth of opposition groups and ultimately the breakaway of the outer empire from the Soviet Union, in the knowledge that should the Soviet Union retaliate against such opposi-tion groups, it would be accused by the West of reneging on its 'democratic reforms'. Gorbachev stressed the importance of consolidating the Communist Party's role in society as a way of maintaining the federal structure of the Soviet Union and Yugoslavia in the wake of growing republican nationalism and the inevitable growth of opposition cells that accompanied of such 'Western influences'. Gorbachev presented this clearly as a strategy to be worked out at the forthcoming Nineteenth CPSU Conference.[184]

Gorbachev stressed to Lazar Mojsov that the West had been spreading pacifism among army conscripts, thus giving rise to a growth in the number of conscientious objectors. And, as mentioned earlier, Mojsov concurred with this and pointed to alleged incidences of political groups forming in Yugoslavia with Western support to undermine the sovereignty of the LCY and promote the introduction of a multiparty system. Gorbachev clearly stated that combating such 'attacks of Western propaganda' on Soviet and the fraternal parties' socie-ties was within the 'sphere of common policy' shared by these states. Although no evidence was found of discussion between Gorbachev and the LCY leadership regarding the specific measures that the LCY was to take with respect to opposition groups, one week after Gorbachev's visit, the LCY CC met and decided to arrest the editorial of *Mladina*. More generally, however, the NPC was suggested as the forum at which the crisis in the socialist system should be discussed.[185] The exchange strongly suggests that Gorbachev perceived Western economic leverage to be a real threat to the one-party system in these regimes. He claimed that the West had always treated them unfairly, for example, by selling the socialist countries old technology. There is also clear confirmation in this exchange that while introducing some liberalising measures and checks to his own power, Gorbachev never intended relinquishing the leading role of the CPSU.[186]

> **Gorbachev:** We see and feel how the attacks of Western propaganda are growing, even on our army, which unfortunately does provoke a response in our society. This manifests itself in moods of pacifism, especially among the youth. There are incidences of refusals to serve in the army, absences for religious reasons. All this has forced us to take serious measures to deal with the collapse of order in the army. According to our sources, the west has come to the conclusion that it is currently important to agree with the USSR on issues relating to nuclear disarmament in so far as the USSR is experiencing financial difficulties and needs this. It has been reckoned that the west, on the strength of new technology, is modernising its warships, missiles and other weaponry, as a means of establishing its superiority. We consider it important that we discuss this with you in the sphere of our common policy.

> **Mojsov:** I completely agree with you that these are all instances of the strategy of the special war which the west is waging against the socialist countries. I regularly read *Problems of Communism*, and often learn from this about interesting western strategies towards us and especially towards the socialist countries. We also have conscientious objectors against national service and in our country there are certain groups of individuals who adopt a hostile attitude towards socialism and who, with the support of the west, are fighting to found other [political] parties in Yugoslavia and promote the introduction of a multiparty system.[187]

Gorbachev said to Krunić that they shared problems inherent to their regimes' stage of economic development and that collaboration between the parties over possible solutions would be beneficial; he questioned how far decentralisation would encourage greater efficiency without promoting the break-up of the federation:

Gorbachev (to Krunić): The thoughts you have expressed testify that in both our cases we search for solutions to certain questions along the same lines. We need to decentralise the management of our economy and in that respect your experience to us is important. Where do you stop in the process of decentralisation, how do you make sure you are not destroying the dialectic of mutual relations between the centre and the localities, federations and republics, central ministries and enterprises? The centre is without a doubt necessary. Historically [it follows that] situations that form under extreme conditions tend to have been dogmatically transferred from other conditions. Now let's think: perhaps we should give more rights to the republics, protecting and strengthening the role of the centre.[188]

Economic relations between the two states were discussed during these meetings, and a resolution concerning the Yugoslav debt to the Soviet Union, estimated at 1.25 billion dollars in January 1988, was reached. The solution was very favourable to Yugoslavia. Although the country was not a CMEA member, the agreement granted Yugoslavia CMEA rights in exporting goods to other CMEA countries as a way of paying off the Soviet debt while continuing to receive vital Soviet oil imports.[189] The new Soviet treatment of Yugoslavia as a *de facto* CMEA member indicates a realignment of the LCY with the CPSU. In turn this realignment of the LCY was a pledge of support for Gorbachevian *perestroika* at a crucial time for Gorbachev, just five days after the Nina Andreeva letter had been published in *Sovetskaia Rossiia*. The new agreement, made with a large financial package that was very beneficial for Yugoslavia, secured what Khrushchev had sought but failed to achieve: the inclusion of Yugoslavia in the socialist fraternity on the understanding that there was to be unity of action among the fraternal parties in accordance with Moscow's foreign policy goals.[190]

Since the doctrine of Soviet military intervention in the fraternal states had been renounced, the LCY could safely appeal to the CPSU for financial aid as well as political support in its desperate attempt to retain its leading role in society and the unity of the federation. Significantly, perhaps, was the republication, in more glowing terms, of the March *Komunist* article about Gorbachev's visit in one of the May issues; following the discussion of Yugoslavia's previous condemnation of Soviet military intervention in the fraternal regimes, including the Soviet invasion of Afghanistan of 1979, was a short article detailing the withdrawal of Soviet troops from Afghanistan, that had happened that very week. As *Komunist* mentioned, the agreements and treaties between the LCY and CPSU promised to strengthen the international workers' movement by sending a message of LCY endorsement of Gorbachev's *perestroika* to all fraternal states:

> As relations between the LCY and CPSU, as well as those between the SFRY and USSR, have always greatly influenced the trend within the whole international workers' movement and community, there is no doubt that the message of the Belgrade meeting will have wider repercussions in the international community.[191]

Alternatively, the last line in this *Komunist* citation may have been alluding to the Western powers as the 'international community'. In this context the new LCY relationship with the CPSU, and in particular the new Soviet financial support, could have been seen as a way of countering Yugoslavia's economic dependence on the West and a possible antidote to their increasing political influence.

CPSU, HSWP and LCY collaboration over conference outcome

As was detailed in Chapter 4, the LCY and CPSU leaderships collaborated over the convention of their respective conferences and the LCY aligned itself with the CPSU in trying to achieve a Gorbachevian conference outcome. This entailed what was mutually beneficial to both sides: the salvaging of the future of the Communist Party through its modernisation.[192] According to one former member of the Serbian LC CC, conferences were convened across Central, Eastern and South-eastern Europe with a common purpose, which was to allow the 'reform communists' a forum where they could present their policies of modernising their respective parties.[193] Moreover, the Soviet Union influenced these events, and the conferences were convened specifically to promote the cause of the centrists in the party, those viewed as supporting a policy course that aligned with the CPSU.

In the case of Yugoslavia, this centrist course was supported by the JNA.[194] A centrist Gorbachevian line of policy was evident in the JNA report from the textual analysis. It stressed the need for a consolidation of power by the party, the strengthening of the vanguard role of the party in society, and identified as 'counter-revolutionary' those elements perceived to represent republican interests at the expense of federal unity. The army report most closely resembled that of the Serbian LC, which stood against the introduction of a multiparty system and preferred to retain some features of the Soviet-model command economy instead of fully embracing the market. At the same time, the JNA advocated military intervention in Slovenia to suppress the growing opposition groups.

As had been heavily publicised in the Soviet press around the time of the seventieth anniversary in 1987 of the October revolution in 1917, the Yugoslav press also raised the issue of Bukharin's rehabilitation. Additionally the more general issue of the Stalinist–Bukharinist debate was raised, questioning whether a return to the Bukharin tradition would serve as an adequate and viable solution to the economic and systemic crisis of the 1980s. In the wake of *glasnost* the Yugoslav press questioned whether the Soviet model had developed or degenerated, and debated the rehabilitation of those who throughout Soviet history had been condemned as deviators. These newspaper articles reappraised deviators' reform programmes and discussed whether such alternatives might have led to a more equitable and viable model, had Stalinist repressions not choked them.[195] Whether readers would have paid much notice to this is difficult to ascertain. Levels of disillusionment within and outside the party were high, which suggests that this debate would have been of limited interest to Yugoslav readers. On the other hand, there was a sense that the Soviet Union was a highly influential neighbour whose policy changes impacted on the LCY.[196] Reportage by the fraternal parties' press organs at this time of the conferences indicates that the same debates were being considered in the press in preparation for possible future changes to the Soviet model and subsequent application to their own respective parties.[197]

Conference timing as evidence of collaboration between fraternal parties

As Tables 1 and 2 indicate (pp. 41, 117), there appears to be some correlation between timing of conferences and type of outcome. Conferences held earlier, in Albania, Bulgaria and Romania, affirmed the pre-Gorbachev *status quo ante*, whereas conferences held later, in Hungary, the Soviet Union and Yugoslavia, endorsed a more reformist, pro-Gorbachev stance. Originally the LCY conference had been planned for the spring of 1988, and in the press there was an announcement that both hardliners and reformists considered the conference would be of little consequence:

> Following on from the recent announcement that in spring of next year, the conference of the LCY will be held, the public finds before it a strange conundrum. From two different poles, from the circles of two of the fiercest opponents – the party apparatus and the so-called opposition – they have managed to come up with the very same warning: from the LCY conference you should expect nothing substantive.[198]

In accordance with this, by 18 December 1987, just over a week after convention had been approved by the LCY CC, the date agreed for the conference was March 1988, as publicised in *Komunist*: 'The CC of the LCY at its last session approved the idea of convening the LCY conference. It is foreseen that this conference will be held in March 1988.'[199]

However, perhaps following the cue of the HSWP or after advice from the CPSU, the conference was postponed until May 1988. There is a clear pattern that conferences held earlier in the year had less reformist outcomes; instead of proposing a centrist Gorbachevian line, these meetings were normalising events that endeavoured to maintain the *status quo*. Leaderships of these regimes did not liberalise as Gorbachev had. This was the case with Albania (November 1987), Romania (December 1987) and Bulgaria (January 1988). Originally, Kádár's preferred timing for the conference was February rather than May,[200] and centrist Gyúla Horn proposed May or June.[201] On 2 March 1988 Grósz had declared to the media a provisional date of 13 May, before the date had been determined by the CC a few weeks later.[202] The conferences held between May and June 1988, in contrast, represented a consolidation of power for the centrists – the groups that came to be known a few months later as the 'reform communists'. Interestingly, the Nina Andreeva affair – a highly publicised incident which marked a CPSU hardline resurgence against Gorbachev's liberalisation policies and in particular his limited market liberalisation – occurred precisely during Gorbachev's visit to Yugoslavia. Those hardliners opposing Gorbachev's *perestroika* would have been aware of Gorbachev's purpose in meeting with the LCY leadership and that he was seeking LCY support for his reforms.

There is evidence in the press of collaboration between reformist party leaders. Since the press was still the party's propaganda organ, we can assume that what was published had been vetted by the party. Centrist 'Gorbachevian' reformist policies were publicised in the Yugoslav press. Significantly on 7 December 1987 – the date the HSWP CC formally approved the convention of the forthcoming NPC (just one day before the LCY CC approved convention of their conference on 8 December 1987) – an article in *Politika* detailed Pozsgay's request to the HSWP for greater pluralism, increased discussion and toleration of different views within the party. In the article, Pozsgay was cited as advocating interest aggregation within the HSWP as opposed to enforced monolithic unity.[203]

Immediately following the LCY conference, favourable press coverage was devoted to the HSWP and CPSU 1988 conferences. Although six weeks had elapsed between these two conferences, articles in the LC press followed in close succession, in two consecutive issues. A very positive account of the HSWP conference appeared in the weekly *Komunist* six weeks after it had taken place, on 1 July 1988, coinciding with the last day of the CPSU conference.[204] In the following issue, 8 July 1988, *Komunist* took a Gorbachevian stance in their evaluation of the CPSU conference, describing the defeat of *perestroika*'s opponents as creating a 'strong tail-wind' for *perestroika*.[205]

HSWP–LCY relations similarly began flourishing around this time. Significantly, the Yugoslav Foreign Minister, Raif Dizdarević, visited Grósz in Budapest during 7–8 December 1987 (the days on which both respective parties endorsed at CC meetings their intention of holding a conference) for bilateral talks as well as to discuss internal affairs.[206] The HSWP Politburo report of December 1987 stated that in 1988, Károly Németh (a Kádárite; not to be confused with Miklós Németh) would return the Yugoslav foreign minister's visit.[207] In the end, the LCY instead sent a delegation to Budapest and the LCY chairman, Branko Mikulić, met with Grósz from 10 to 11 April 1988, and they forged links between the leaderships prior to their respective conferences in May 1988. The leaders vowed to strengthen economic ties between the two parties. Not surprisingly, the forthcoming conferences were discussed, and future collaboration between the parties over how to introduce market mechanisms successfully and avoid further problems following their implementation was proposed. *Komunist* reported that 'Talking of the domestic circumstances in Hungary, Grósz remarked that the progress of economic development was weak, and that in the life of society contradictions and tensions had begun to appear'.[208] Grósz stated that the failing economy was impacting on the party's legitimacy in society, creating a growing gulf between the party elite and the people that could only be resolved through the modernisation of the party. He stated that these issues were to be determined at the forthcoming party conference:

> The sources of these difficulties, in the main, lie in the weaknesses of the economy, which over the last fifteen years have incidentally also begun impacting on the political situation in society. A condition for the further economic development of the country is the modernisation of the political system, which will be the subject of particular discussion at our forthcoming party conference – said Grósz.[209]

Interestingly, the same terminology as had been used by Gorbachev appeared in Yugoslav documents in reference to the unwanted personnel that needed ousting from the LCY leadership: 'the ballast' needed firing.[210] This term had been used by Gorbachev to denote those hardliners who needed expelling from the party to rid the party of those opposing reform.[211]

Conclusion

This chapter has shown empirically that the LCY conference in 1988 clearly aligned the LCY with the centrist Gorbachevian CPSU policy of *perestroika*. This constituted staging public federal approval for the consolidation of the LCY's leading role in society within the existing framework of the one-party state. As at the CPSU and HSWP conferences, demands were made at the LCY conference to implement the preceding congress's economic directives. Similarly, the democratisation of internal party processes and the modernisation of the party were advocated with a view to re-engaging an increasingly disillusioned and dwindling membership, in particular the youth and workers. These were issues central, also, to the CPSU and HSWP conferences. Most significantly for the future of the LCY at this time was the demand at the conference that federal unity be maintained and that republican nationalist conflicts be put down. As outlined, the conference's informal constraints, institutionalised during the conferences of the 1970s, constituted a reassertion of federal over republican power and normalisation of republican with federal policy. These 'informal constraints' apparently continued to operate in 1988 despite the amendment to the formal rules in 1982 changing the conference as an institution. This supports the argument in Chapter 1 that even when formal rules are changed, informal constraints prove tenacious. However, the change governing conference convention in the 1982 rules suggested a realignment with the fraternal and Soviet party model.

Evidence that Gorbachev actively collaborated with like-minded centrist-reformists in the LCY over conference convention and outcome supports the argument that the conference was a vehicle for the fraternal parties to stage an expression of solidarity with the CPSU and each other, when the need arose, in the spirit of socialist internationalism.

Notes

1   B. Magaš, *The Destruction of Yugoslavia: Tracking the Break-up 1980–92* (London: Verso, 1993), pp. 100–1.

2   'The Socialist Way: Party Conferences, Realistic Renewal', *World Marxist Review*, 31:10 (1988), pp. 45–6.

3   J. Lampe, *Yugoslavia as History: Twice there was a country* (Cambridge: Cambridge University Press, 1996), p. 338.

4   V. Meier, *Yugoslavia: A History of its Demise* (London: Routledge, 1999), p. 71.

5   Lampe, *Yugoslavia as History*, pp. 342–3.

6   Chapter 1, pp. 43–4; 46–7.

7   D. Rusinow, *The Yugoslav Experiment, 1948–1974* (London: C. Hurst for RIIA, 1977), pp. 279–81.

8   R. J. Crampton, *The Balkans since the Second World War* (London: Longman, 2002), pp. 129–35.

9   S. Burg, *Conflict and cohesion in socialist Yugoslavia: political decision making since 1966* (Princeton NJ: Princeton University Press, 1983), p. 83; A. Carter, *Democratic reform in Yugoslavia: the changing role of the party* (London: Pinter, 1982), p. 25.

10   *Borba* 28 October 1970, p. 1, §57.

11   Carter, *Democratic reform in Yugoslavia*, refers to the *preds(j)edništvo* as Presidium; Rusinow, in *The Yugoslav Experiment*, translates it as *Presidency*.

12   Although in the case of the CPSU this was twenty per cent. See Chapter 2, p. 55 and Chapter 3, p. 98.

13   *Borba* 28 October 1970, p. 1, §56.

14   *Borba* 28 October 1970, p. 1, §58.

15   *Ibid.*, §59.

16   *Ibid.*, §60.

17   *Borba*, 28 October 1970, p. 12.

18   Interview with Latinka Perović, Belgrade, 2 November 2003; Interview with Aleksa Đilas, Belgrade, 10 November 2003.

19   Interview with Aleksa Đilas, Belgrade, 10 November 2003.

20   *Ibid.*

21   BBC Monitoring Service, *Summary of World Broadcasts*, 11 December 1972, B/3.

22   *Ibid.*, 2 May 1973, B/10.

23   *Ibid.*, 14 May 1973, C2/2 for Tito's letter presented at the conference.

24   Rusinow, *The Yugoslav Experiment*, p. 281, refers to this as the attempt to create a 'confederation' of Yugoslavia.

25   *Borba* 26 October 1970, p. I-|IV| for the proposed conference Resolution for fuller details of these points.

26   *Borba* 29 January 1972, pp. 5–7.

27   *Ibid.*, p. 1.

28   Rusinow, *The Yugoslav Experiment*, pp. 291–2.

29   *Ibid.*, pp. 276–87.

30   *Ibid.*, p. 323.

31   L. Perović, *Zatvaranje kruga: ishod rasčepa 1971–1972* (Sarajevo: Biblioteka Refleksi, 1991), p. 358.

32   Perović, *Zatvaranje kruga*, pp. 166; 362–3.

33   Carter, *Democratic reform in Yugoslavia*, p. 30.

34   Milka Planinc speaking at conference. BBC Monitoring Service, *Summary of World Broadcasts*, BBC Monitoring Service, *Summary of World Broadcasts*, 11 December B/5, 1972.

35   BBC Monitoring Service, *Summary of World Broadcasts*, 12 December: B/8–9, 1972.

36   *Borba* 10 May 1973, pp. i-vii of Stane Dolanc's report.

37   Carter, *Democratic reform in Yugoslavia*, p. 46.

38   B. McFarlane, *Yugoslavia: Politics, Economics and Society* (London: Pinter, 1988), p. 27.

39   League of Communists of Yugoslavia, *Dvanaesti kongres Savez Komunista Jugoslavije: dokumenty usvojeni na 12. kongresu SKJ, 1982* (Beograd: Privredni pregled, 1982), pp. 213–14, §79.

40   *Ibid.*

41   *Ibid.*

42   M. Palairet, 'The Economic Consequences of Slobodan Milošević', *Europe-Asia Studies*, 53:6 (2001), p. 907.

43   Woodward, *Socialist Unemployment*, p. 253.

44   *Ibid.*, p. 254.

45   League of Communists of Yugoslavia, *13. kongres SKJ, dokumenti, referat, rezolucije, Statut SKJ, završna riječ, sastav organa SKJ, 25-28 lipnja 1986* (Beograd: Izdavački Centar Komunist, 1986), p. 242.

46   *Ibid.*, p. 242, §118.

47   S. Ramet, *Balkan Babel: the Disintegration of Yugoslavia from the Death of Tito to the Fall of Milošević* (Boulder CO: Westview Press, 4th edn, 2002), p. 13.

48   Interview with Jurij Bajec, Belgrade, 14 November 2003.

49   Lampe, *Yugoslavia as History*, p. 339.

50   M. Brudar, *Nada, obmana, slom: politički život Srba na Kosovo i Metohiji, 1987–1999* (Beograd: *Nova srpska politička misao*, 2003), p. 36. Brudar, however, contends whether or not Milošević's comment was taken out of context; Milošević argued that this comment was in response to police brutality towards the crowd.

51   R. Smiljković, *Prelomne godine* (Beograd: Narodna Knjiga, 1991), pp. 5–6.

52   Interview with Ljubinka Trgovčević, 5 November 2003.

53   Stipe Šuvar, *Komunist*, 27 May 1988, p. 10.

54   *Komunist* 27 May 1988, p. 10.

55   Interview with Jurij Bajec, Belgrade, 14 November 2003.

56   *Ibid.*

57   *Komunist* 11 December 1987, p. 9.

58   Magaš, *The Destruction of Yugoslavia*, pp. 100–1.

59   Smiljković, *Prelomne godine*, pp. 89–91.

60   *Komunist* 11 December 1987, p.6.

61   *Ibid.*, p. 9.

62   *Ibid.*, p. 10.

63   *Ibid.*, p. 9.

64   'The Socialist Way', p. 46; G. Schöpflin, 'Political Decay in One-Party Systems in Eastern Europe: Yugoslav Patterns', in P. Ramet (ed.), *Yugoslavia in the 1980's* (Boulder CO: Westview Press, 1985), p. 316.

65   *Komunist* April 15 1988, p. 5.

66   League of Communists of Yugoslavia, *Jačanje vodeće idejno-političke uloge, jedinstva i odgovornosti Saveza komunista u borbi za izlazak iz društveno-ekonomske krize, Konferencija SKJ, Beograd, 29–31 maj 1988* (Beograd: Izdavački Centar Komunist, 1988), p. 127.

67   See Chapter 3, p. 82 and Chapter 5, p. 158.

68   Interview with Ljubinka Trgovčević, Belgrade, 5 November 2003.

69   Crampton, *The Balkans since the Second World War*, pp. 143–4.

70   *Politika* 9 October 1987.

71   *Komunist* 18 December 1987, p. 16.

72   *Politika* 8 December 1987, p. 5.

73   Interview with Jurij Bajec, Belgrade, 14 November 2003.

74   Interview with Ljubinka Trgovčević, Belgrade, 5 November 2003.

75   *Komunist* 11 December 1987, p. 9. The first of these, the Bosnian conference, was referred to as 'the first in the line of this kind of conference to be held in all republics and provinces'. *Komunist* 22 April 1988, p. 16.

76   *Komunist* 22 April 1988, p. 16.

77   *Ibid.*, p. 16.

78   *Ibid.*, pp. 16–17.

79   *Komunist* 29 April 1988, p. 7.

80   *Komunist* 1 July 1988, p. 12.

81   See Table 3, p. 183.

82   M. Balažic, *Slovenska demokratična revolucija 1986–1988* (Ljubljana: Liberalna akademija, 2004), www.mladina.si/tednik/200441/clanek/kul--knjige--bernard_nezmah/ (last accessed 1.12.10)

83   *Komunist* 29 April 1988, p. 7.

84   Crampton, *The Balkans since the Second World War*, p. 153–4.

85   *Ibid.*, p. 152.

86   *Komunist* 29 April 1988, p. 7.

87   *Komunist* 1 July 1988, p. 13.

88   *Komunist* 6 May 1988, p. 8.

89   *Ibid.*, pp. 8–9.

90   *Ibid.*, p. 8.

91   *Komunist* 27 May 1988, pp. 8–9.

92   *Komunist* 29 April 1988, p. 10.

93   *Komunist* 13 May 1988, p. 5.

94   *Ibid.*, p. 5.

95   *Komunist* 3 June 1988, p. 18.

96   See Table 3, p. 183.

97   *Komunist* [Roman edition] 3 June 1988, pp. 4–5.

98   The JNA had its own party organisation. *Komunist* 27 May 1988, p. 11.

99   *Komunist* 24 June 1988, p. 7.

100 *Ibid.*, p. 8.

101 *Ibid.*

102 *Komunist* 1 July 1988, p. 8.

103 *Ibid.*, p. 10.

104 *Komunist* 22 April 1988, pp. 6–7.

105 *Ibid.*, p. 20.

106 *Komunist* 6 May 1988, p. 10.

107 *Komunist* 29 July 1988, p. 8.

108 *Komunist* Press release from Stipe Šuvar, 18 December 1987, pp. 16–17.

109 Gorbachev's fond, 88.Mar.14-18.doc, see present chapter, pp. 211–12 for Gorbachev's comments.

110 *Ibid.*

111 LCY, *Jačanje vodeće idejno-političke uloge*, Krunić, p. 19.

112 *Ibid.*, Slovenia, p. 122.

113 LCY, *Jačanje vodeće idejno-političke uloge*, Montenegro, p. 85.

114 LCY, *Jačanje vodeće idejno-političke uloge*, Krunić, p. 18; Croatia, p. 104; JNA, p. 186; Brigić, p. 27; Croatia, p. 104 (and that SK must get rid of the 'balast') Bosnia and Hercegovina, p. 66; Macedonia, p. 117; Serbia, p. 135.

115 LCY, *Jačanje vodeće idejno-političke uloge*, Resolutions, p. 40.

116 LCY, *Jačanje vodeće idejno-političke uloge*, p. 9.

117 See: CPSU (1988), *XIX Vsesoiuznaia konferentsiia KPSS, 28 iiunia - 1 iiulia 1988: stenograficheskiĭ otchet v dvukh tomakh*, Moskva, vol. 1, p. 79.

118 *Ibid.*, p. 13.

119 *Ibid.*, p. 22.

120 *Ibid.*, p. 28. 'We approve the suggestion that the CC evaluate the importance of cadre changes in the CC, Presidium and working committees.'

121 *Ibid.*, Bosnia and Hercegovina, p. 66; Montenegro, p. 76; Croatia, p. 94; Macedonia, p. 113; Slovenia, p. 124; Serbia, pp. 138–9, 141; Kosovo, pp. 145–6; Vojvodina, p. 158; JNA, pp. 178, 186–7; Federal, p. 190.

122 *Nin* 27 December 1987, p. 56.

123 See Chapters 4, p. 12 and 5, pp. 158; 169.

124 LCY, *Jačanje vodeće idejno-političke uloge*, Brigić, p. 25; Krunić, p. 53; Bosnia and Hercegovina, p. 62; Montenegro, p. 74; Croatia, pp. 92, 104; Macedonia, p. 118; Serbia, pp. 127–8; Vojvodina, pp. 160–1; JNA, p. 187; Federal, pp. 189–90.

125 *Politika* and *Komunist*, 1987–1988.

126 *Komunist* 3 June 1988, pp. 6–17.

127 LCY, *Jačanje vodeće idejno-političke uloge*.

128 In contrast to the 14 reports in the LCY conference minutes, 71 and 52 speeches were published in the CPSU and HSWP minutes respectively.

129 LCY, *Jačanje vodeće idejno-političke uloge*, Krunić, p. 20; Brigić, p. 27; Resolutions, p. 48; Bosnia and Hercegovina, p. 62; Croatia, p. 106; Macedonia, p. 115; JNA, p. 182; Federal, p. 190.

130 *Ibid.*, Krunić, p. 11; Brigić, p. 24; Resolutions, pp. 31–2; Bosnia and Hercegovina, pp. 59–0; Montenegro, pp. 78–9; Croatia, pp. 105–6; Macedonia, pp. 118–19; Slovenia, p. 120; Serbia, p. 130; Kosovo, pp. 146–7; Vojvodina, p. 156; Federal, pp. 191–2.

131 *Ibid.*, Krunić, pp. 20; 22.

132 See Chapter 3, p. 99.

133 LCY, *Jačanje vodeće idejno-političke uloge*, Krunić, p. 16; Brigić, p. 27; Bosnia and Hercegovina, p. 68; Montenegro, p. 86; Croatia, p. 91; Macedonia, p. 114; Serbia, p. 135 Vojvodina, p. 164;

134 Interview with Perović, Latinka, Belgrade, 2 November 2003, p. 8.

135 *Ibid.*, Slovenia, p. 124.

136 *Ibid.*, Slovenia, pp. 123–4.

137 Magaš, *The Destruction of Yugoslavia*, p. 243.

138 Gorbachev Foundation. Gorbachev's fond, 88.Mar.14–18.doc.

139 *Komunist* [Roman edition] 29 July 1988, p. 9.

140 *Komunist* 23 September 1988, pp. 1–2; 30 September 1988, pp. 1–2.

141 Interview with Latinka Perović, Belgrade, 2 November 2003.

142 Interview with Desimir Tosić, Belgrade, 5 November 2003.

143 N. Vladisavljević, 'Nationalism, Social Movement Theory, and the Grass Roots Movement of Kosovo Serbs, 1985–1988', *Europe-Asia Studies*, 54:5 (2002), pp. 774–5.

144 LCY, *Jačanje vodeće idejno-političke uloge*, Montenegro, p. 82.

145 *Ibid.*, Kosovo, p. 148.

146 *Ibid.*, Kosovo, pp. 147–8; Serbia, p. 136.

147 LCY, *Jačanje vodeće idejno-političke uloge*, Serbia, p. 136.

148 *Komunist* 11 December 1987, p. 10.

149 LCY, *Jačanje vodeće idejno-političke uloge*, p. 139.

150 *Ibid.*, p. 145.

151 *Ibid.*, Kosovo, p. 148.

152 LCY, *Jačanje vodeće idejno-političke uloge*, Serbia, p. 134.

153 *Komunist* 3 June 1988, p. 10.

154 *Komunist* 17 June 1988, p. 6.

155 *Komunist* 29 July 1988, p. 13. In a referendum, in late August, Vojvodina and Kosovo both rejected the Serbian claim. See *Komunist* [Roman edition] 9 September 1988, p. 6.

156 LCY, *Jačanje vodeće idejno-političke uloge*, Krunić, p. 10; Brigić, p. 28; Resolutions, p. 31; Montenegro, p. 83; Croatia, p. 102; Macedonia, p. 115; Slovenia, p. 120; Serbia, p. 136; Vojvodina, p. 150; JNA, p. 173.

157 Interview with Jurij Bajec, Belgrade, 14 November 2003.

158 See Gorbachev Foundation, Cherniaev's fond, ch.87.May.10.doc; Németh Miklós: MOL 288.f.4/288–229, 11 November 1987, pp. 154–65; Károly Grósz: MOL KB 288.f.4/230–231, 8 December 1987, p. 107.

159 Gorbachev Foundation. Gorbachev's fond, 88.Mar.14-18.doc.

160 *Ibid.*

161 B. Jelavich, *History of the Balkans: twentieth century* (Cambridge: Cambridge University Press, 1986), vol. 2, p. 394; P. Ramet, 'The Yugoslav Press in Flux', in P. Ramet (ed.), *Yugoslavia in the 1980's* (Boulder CO: Westview, 1985), pp. 100–10.

162 *Politika* 22 November 1987, p. 1.

163 Interview with Jurij Bajec, Belgrade, 14 November 2003.

164 Chapter 4, pp. 134–5.

165 *Politika* 15 November 1987.

166 See present chapter, pp. 205–6; Chapter 4, p. 119.

167 Svetozar Rajak (2004), *Yugoslav-Soviet Relations, 1953–1957: Normalization, Comradeship, Confrontation*, Ph.D. Thesis, LSE, London, pp. 179–81.

168 Chapter 4, pp. 110–11.

169 Rajak, *Yugoslav-Soviet Relations*, p. 333.

170 *Komunist* [Roman edition] 20 May 1988, p. 17.

171 *Ibid.*

172 *Ibid.*

173 *Komunist* 18 March 1988, p. 1.

174 *Ibid.*, p. 18.

175 *Ibid.*

176 *Ibid.*

177 *Ibid.*

178 Kádár was present at this meeting, as mentioned in Chapter 4, p. 132.

179 See present chapter, p. 207.

180 *Komunist* 18 March 1988, p. 18.

181 V. Vujacić, 'Perceptions of the State in Russia and Serbia: the Role of Ideas in the Soviet and Yugoslav Collapse', *Post-Soviet Affairs*, 20:2 (2004), p. 167.

182 Gorbachev Foundation. Gorbachev's fond, 88.Mar.14-18.doc.

183 As referred to above in this chapter, pp. 205–6.

184 Chapter 4, pp. 134–7.

185 Gorbachev's fond, 88.Mar.14-18.doc. For example, during Gorbachev's meeting with the Slovenian LC, Milan Kučan stated: "We need to discuss how we see a way out of the difficult situation, which Yugoslavia currently finds itself, as does the whole socialist world". Gorbachev concluded at this meeting: "You have broadly raised issues that are most central to the party, clearly also with respect to [your] forthcoming party conference. I can see that we have a lot of common interests and policies in maximising the potential of socialism, with respect to specific features of our countries and a common outlook on the world. From this, it is clear that we need each other not just in economic terms, but also politically and ideologically."

186 See, for example, Chapter 3, pp. 75–6; Chapter 4, p. 136.

187 Gorbachev Foundation. Gorbachev's fond, 88.Mar.14-18.doc.

188 *Ibid.*

189 *Komunist* 18 March 1988, p. 19.

190 As described in this chapter pp. 208–10.

191 *Komunist* 18 March 1988, p. 19.

192 See note 185 above; Chapter 4, p. 110.

193 Interview with Latinka Perović, Belgrade, 2 November 2003.

194 *Ibid.*

195 *Politika* 10–11 October; 1 December; 4 December 1987.

196 Interview with Latinka Perović, Belgrade, 2 November 2003.

197 *Życie Partii* 1988; *Rudé Právo* 1988, 29 January p. 1 (BCP conference), 27 May (CPSU conference preparations and CPCZ regional conferences); *Novo Vreme* 1 (1988), pp. 60–71 (describing how the BCP and other fraternal parties were effecting the same changes as the CPSU).

198 *Komunist* 13 November 1987, p. 3.

199 *Komunist* 18 December 1987, p. 16.

200 MOL KB 288 f.4/230–231 8 December.1987, p. 145.

201 *Ibid.*, p. 143.

202 By suggesting a date to the public and publicizing that the conference would aim to solve Hungary's problems, Grósz induced the CC to decide on a date for a conference around that time, see G. Schöpflin, R. Tökés and I. Völgyés, 'Leadership Change and Crisis in Hungary', *Problems of Communism*, 37:5 (1988), p. 35.

203 *Politika* 7 December 1987, p. 3.

204 *Komunist* [Roman edition] 1 July 1988, p. 16.

205 *Komunist* 8 July 1988, p. 4.

206 MOL PB 288.f.5/1014.1.December.1987, p. 80.

207 *Ibid.*

208 *Politika* 12 April 1988, p. 4.

209 *Ibid.*

210 LCY, *Jačanje vodeće idejno-političke uloge*, Croatia, p. 104.

211 Interview with Anatoly Cherniaev, Moscow, 24 September 2002.

7

The PUWP conference, 4–5 May 1989: too little, too late

Introduction

Whereas in Bulgaria, Hungary, the Soviet Union and Yugoslavia, NPCs were convened in 1988 and all served the same function, in Poland the PUWP held their conference in May 1989. Moreover, unlike these other parties the PUWP CC had already committed by 1986 to convene its conference, and this was generally expected to take place in 1988. In the cases of the Soviet Union and Hungary, the CPSU and the HSWP NPCs had not been convened since 1941 and 1957 respectively, and were therefore unprecedented, until 1987 when the leaderships in these parties decided to convene them.[1] The timing of the PUWP NPC, therefore, raises important questions regarding some of the commonalities shared by cases that have been discussed so far.

The PUWP conference took place after the first set of round-table talks in Poland between the party and representatives from the opposition, and just one month before the scheduled semi-free elections to the Sejm of June 1989. With hindsight, it could be said that, by this stage, the party had begun negotiating the terms of regime change with the opposition, and it had become inevitable by this point that the party was in the process of relinquishing its leading role in a one-party state. Strictly speaking Poland's regime had been multiparty (in the same way as, for example, Bulgaria) for many years in that other parties – the United People's Party (ZSL) and the Democratic Party (SD) – also existed and their representatives served in the Sejm. In practice, however, these other parties worked under the close supervision of the PUWP and acknowledged its leading role in both state and society, which certainly remained the case at the time of the conference in 1989, as attested by interviewees Jerzy Urban, who was Speaker of the Sejm until 1988, and former Prime Minister Leszek Miller.[2] As discussed in Chapter 3, this is the kind of 'multiparty' system that Gorbachev envisaged, one where the CPSU would retain the leading role, but where other parties would ostensibly represent interests in society other than those of the Communist Party. As the present chapter shows, this was the type of model the PUWP hoped and expected to retain, and even as late as May 1989, the leadership still believed this.[3]

Returning to the main question of this book, preceding chapters have shown that in the CPSU, HSWP and LCY there was a common initiative at conferences to make *perestroika* irreversible, consolidate the party's power and reassert its leading role. To what extent, therefore, can the PUWP conference be considered comparable with the 1988 conferences in other fraternal parties, in terms of this very special function which they served? Secondly, why was the PUWP conference convened later than anticipated? Had the conference been convened in 1988, would it have served a different purpose than it did in 1989? As mentioned in Chapter 4, Gorbachev would most probably have been aware that the PUWP was due to convene a conference as he had attended the Tenth PUWP Congress in 1986, when Jaruzelski announced this. If this was known to Gorbachev, then what bearing did this have on his own decision to convene the Nineteenth CPSU Conference when he did so?

As in the previous case studies, we need first to distinguish what the NPC entailed as an institution, in the case of the PUWP, and what formalities existed in the organisation of conferences and congresses that might have facilitated or constrained the leadership's control of outcome. This will help to identify any differences between these all-party meetings in terms of a 'policy choice': why the party would choose in some instances to convene a conference rather than an extraordinary congress, between scheduled five-yearly congresses. As discussed in Chapter 1, because actors are aware of the various constraints that institutions impose on them, and which choice of institution is likely to yield their preferred outcome, institutions themselves come to represent a particular policy choice. From this it follows that different actors with different preference are likely to vie with each other over the choice of institution as a means to securing their preferred outcome. In the cases of the CPSU and HSWP, as discussed in Chapters 3 and 5, the CC debated the choice of meeting, and more reformist party factions opposed the leadership's decision to convene a conference, advocating instead an extraordinary congress.[4]

The PUWP conference as an institution and as a policy choice

As in other fraternal states,[5] there was little formal regulation of the conference in the PUWP Party Rules. Until the Ninth Extraordinary Congress in 1981, the Party Rules articulated that 'between congresses the national conference may be convened with the purpose of discussing current issues of party policy'.[6] This provision leaves us none the wiser as to the function of the conference, except that it was for discussing matters of party policy. At interview, Professor Hieronim Kubiak, who was a member of the Politburo in 1988, explained that the conference was not so much a decision-making institution, but rather an organ of party publicity designed to inform the rest of the party or the general public about party activities and policies.[7] Regarding the manner in which individuals were selected to attend, the rules provided that 'the basis of delegate selection to the conference is determined by the Central Committee'.[8] The process of selecting delegates to the congress, however, was statutorily a more decentralised process, as the regional party organisations elected individuals.[9]

By the time of the congress of 1981,[10] these provisions regarding the conference had been removed from the Party Rules, [11] although the absence of relevant rules did not prevent the party from convening conferences in 1984 and then again in 1989. Since there were no provisions in the Party Rules regarding NPC powers and procedure this leaves open to question what a PUWP conference generally entailed, and why leaderships chose to convene these when they did so. To try to bridge this gap, the next section briefly outlines previous conference outcomes and agendas to reconstruct what may be described as the conference's 'informal' constraints, from

patterns common to previous conferences held, to help identify what the institution constituted as a policy choice.

Review of PUWP conferences before 1989

The early tradition of the Polish conference is very similar to
that of other fraternal parties,[12] which confirms that during
the era of the Comintern, before it was disbanded, the conference was convened to purge party factions in accordance with
Comintern policy, which was tantamount to Soviet policy.[13]
This pattern is very visible in the Polish case. During the 1920s
the Polish Communist Party convened four conferences. The
first of these, in April 1920, approved the Communist Workers'
Party of Poland (KPRP) CC's decision to join the Comintern.[14] At the second conference in February 1921, delegates
unanimously approved the twenty-one points that had been
agreed at the Comintern's Second Congress of August 1920,
and resolved in accordance with these to purge leftist factional
elements on the ground that they were a counter-revolutionary
threat.[15] This purge took place at the third conference in April
1922, when a new CC was elected and the resolution stressed
the need for a united front in rooting out left factionalists.[16]
The next conference, the fourth, or the 'first', as the party had
changed its name by then to the Communist Party of Poland
(KPP), was held in Moscow in December 1925. This meeting comprised a small select gathering of members, which
decided that the CC had failed to comply with Comintern
policy and consequently overturned a resolution that had been
unanimously adopted by the Polish Communists' CC, on the
grounds that it was 'factional'.[17] Once again, a new CC was
elected at the conference.[18]

By the time the next conference was convened, the party
had evolved a good deal, and to a certain extent had incorporated social democrat ideals with those of communism. The
PUWP's first and second conferences were in the 1970s under
the liberal leadership of Edward Gierek. He had adopted a policy
of import-led growth, and the Polish economy was becoming
increasingly dependent on Western imports, while at the same
time industrial productivity failed to grow or develop in terms
of quality. Both conferences of 1973 and 1978 were therefore
dedicated to evaluating progress in achieving economic targets
that had been set at the previous Sixth and Seventh Congresses

respectively.[19] The numeration of the party conference began afresh under Wojciech Jaruzelski, and the 1984 conference was not described as the 'third'.[20] Instead it was described as 'The National Party Conference of PUWP delegates' and yet the 1989 conference was described as the 'second'.[21] The rationale for this is not clear. Another more surreptitious change, which distinguished the Jaruzelski-era conference from Gierek's, was the insertion of the word 'delegates': what had previously been described as 'National Conference of the PUWP' became 'National Conference of PUWP delegates'. The change to the institution's name may have been to justify the new leadership's convention of the meeting, after it had been statutorily removed from the Party Rules.

The 1984 conference was the first all-party meeting convened after the period of martial law between December 1981 and the spring of 1983. Jaruzelski was First Secretary during both the 1984 and 1989 conferences (although no longer also Prime Minister by the 1989 conference), so the outcome and 'informal institutional constraints' of this 1984 meeting are particularly salient, as they offer a template of what the party and delegates might have expected in anticipation of the next conference.

A case study of the PUWP conference, 16–18 March 1984

The 1984 conference appears to have been a public reaffirmation of the party's decisions taken at the Ninth Congress, and a restatement of the fact that the unrest following the congress, which had resulted in the introduction of martial law, had constituted a threat to socialism.[22] At the close of the conference a declaration was made which restated the history of the party, and its programme. This document reiterated the importance of Poland's alliance with the Soviet Union and the socialist fraternity as a way to protect Poland's sovereignty and the integrity of its territories.[23]

The conference evaluated party progress since 1981 on the basis of a questionnaire distributed to conference delegates, which indicated a very favourable impression of party work in implementing goals set at the Ninth Congress. According to the questionnaire, around 90% of delegates had the strong impression that central and provincial authorities were endeavouring to implement the party's programme. 63.4% considered that there had been a slight increase in the party's authority since the Ninth Congress, while 23.1% considered that this increase in authority was significant. Of the delegates, 63% definitely believed that 'since the Ninth Congress the party is achieving a leading role in the state through democratic and cooperative means'. Most surprisingly, 55% completely agreed with the opinion that 'the party is entirely subject to the wide control of the working class and society'.[24] These positive appraisals are highly unexpected in the light of events that had unfolded since the Ninth Congress. In the interim, martial law had been introduced for a period of eighteen months, and there had been a very marked reduction in party membership, and an even more significant drop in membership among workers.[25] The party had outlawed Solidarity following the 1981 Congress, which had not had the desired effect of attracting workers to join the party. Instead, worker membership as a proportion of the party had continued to drop from 45.6% in 1978 to 38.5% in 1984. Since overall membership had also plummeted by 26% during this time,[26] it is hard to imagine that the majority of delegates would not have been aware of this, even from anecdotal evidence. We could therefore conclude from this questionnaire that the majority of delegates had a more optimistic view of the party's performance than it merited, or simply that those individuals selected as delegates could be relied upon to convey the upbeat picture that the leadership wanted to be broadcast. The latter explanation appears more likely given that Jaruzelski was keen in advance to broadcast and publicise the event widely, which suggests he was confident beforehand that the conference would yield a favourable outcome. Such confidence could only be guaranteed by the selection of the right delegates, and Jaruzelski issued orders to the Politburo to organise wider dissemination than usual of the results on television and radio.[27] The explanation that delegates were hand-picked for the conference to guarantee the right outcome is confirmed by archival documents from PUWP Politburo meetings in 1984, which indicate that rank-and-file members were concerned that delegate selection for the conference was exclusive, and that people generally felt disconnected from the event.[28]

The conference as a policy choice

The 1984 conference bears out the description of the institution as more of a 'tool for publicity', as advanced earlier,
and one which apparently the leadership was confident that it
could control. Although provisions concerning the conference
had been removed from the Party Rules by the time of the 1984
conference, the 'party leadership' remained in charge of deciding who would attend the meeting. At interview, the former
Prime Minister, Leszek Miller, remarked that the party leadership strictly controlled delegate selection to the conference:
members of the higher central leadership were automatically
selected and all other delegates were party members whom the
upper leadership wished to attend.[29] Mr Miller was a delegate
at the 1989 conference and also at the 1984 conference, for
which he was a member of the organising committee.[30]

The conference was ostensibly an 'all-party meeting', yet one
which the leadership could more easily control than the other
all-party meeting, the congress, because the Party Rules defined
the selection of delegates to the congress in a more decentralised way. The reason why the leadership chose to convene a
conference in 1989 instead of an extraordinary congress was
because they could more easily control the conference,[31] from
which we might infer that the leadership could more easily
achieve their desired outcome at this meeting. According to
George Tsebelis' argument, as discussed in Chapter 1, because
actors are aware of the various constraints that institutions
impose on them, and which choice of institution is likely to
yield their preferred outcome, institutions themselves come
to represent a particular policy choice. As in the cases of the
CPSU and HSWP, more reformist party factions opposed the
leadership's decision to convene a conference and advocated
instead an extraordinary congress.[32] Professor Kubiak described
an analogous situation in the PUWP when a grass-roots party
movement successfully pressured the party leadership to
convene the Ninth Extraordinary Congress of 1981 less than
eighteen months after the Eighth Congress of February 1980.

Debate over choice of conference or congress in 1980–81

Interviewees described the 'Horizontal Structures' movement
(*'Struktury Poziome'*) of 1980–81 as a movement mobilised

horizontally, independent of the CC and leadership, through informal networks of individuals.[33] Stanisław Kania, who had replaced Gierek as First Secretary in September 1980, first conceded defeat to this pressure group in October 1980, and agreed to call an early congress should tensions between the party and Solidarity escalate.[34] Evidently Kania only acquiesced in these demands because he did not believe that such confrontation would arise, and therefore circumstances would not ultimately require an extraordinary congress before the next scheduled congress.[35]

By the end of January 1981, there was growing animosity between the rank-and-file party membership and the leadership, and a common awareness that in the event of a congress the leadership would be 'overthrown'. For this reason, the PUWP leadership were opposed to convening an extraordinary congress,[36] as were the Soviet leadership, who were also concerned any such event would turn into a 'Výsočany Congress'. This referred to the Fourteenth Congress of the CPCZ in 1968, at which the reformist Aleksandr Dubček was re-elected as First Secretary. The decisions of this meeting were later discounted on the ground that the meeting was illegal.[37] At this Czechoslovak congress the delegates rejected the legitimacy of the Soviet invasion of Czechoslovakia, and elected a more reformist CC and Presidium than had been in post before the Prague Spring had begun.[38]

In April 1981, after the PUWP leadership had agreed to convene a congress, the Horizontal Structures movement held a meeting attended by members from across the country. They demanded of their party changes in the leadership, that censorship laws, recently introduced, be repealed, and that they be allowed to elect delegates to the forthcoming congress in a democratic way. They also insisted that the congress should be conducted according to democratic procedures.[39] One of the more reformist of the national weekly newspapers, *Polityka*,[40] took the side of the Horizontal Structures movement, and in the run up to the congress published an article demanding that the PUWP democratise the party's internal structures, because 'only a party which is democratic internally will observe the democratic rules of the game with respect to Solidarity and other social forces'. The article recommended that congress delegates choose a leadership that would represent the different currents within the party.[41] This movement's preferred candidate, Stanisław Kania, was re-elected as First Secretary at the congress, although he had not been proposed through the usual channels, by his own regional party organisation. He was only selected as a candidate when he was invited to stand by another regional committee, in Cracow, which was dominated by members of the Horizontal Structures movement.[42] The reason why the Horizontal Structures movement had supported Kania was because he was opposed to the use of force in the event that relations with Solidarity deteriorated.[43] Since he was one of the more liberal candidates, the outcome of the Ninth Extraordinary Congress was analogous to the 'Výsočany Congress' in that the liberal who had been earmarked for replacement at the Congress was re-elected, but only three months later, in October 1981, was forced to resign and was replaced by the more hardline General Jaruzelski, who was also Prime Minister and head of the army.

According to both Professor Kubiak and Professor Matuszak, the reason why there was no similar pressure, on the same scale, in the late 1980s to convene an extraordinary congress instead of a conference was because the situation was very different.[44] Firstly, by the beginning of 1987, the party had lost more than a quarter of its membership since its heyday in 1978 under Gierek.[45] The introduction of martial law and the outlawing of Solidarity might, therefore, have concentrated the proportion of hardliners in the rank and file of the party's membership, or at least blunted their will to mobilise themselves and act independently of the CC. Many of those high-profile party members, such as Tadeusz Fiszbach and Zofia Grzyb, who had vocally advocated Solidarity's cause at the 1981 Congress, were removed from office after Solidarity was outlawed later that year.[46] Edward Gierek was expelled from the party at the 1981 Congress, and then later placed under house arrest after martial law was introduced.[47]

There is, however, evidence that a large proportion of the rank-and-file PUWP membership must have been to some extent 'reformist', if we define the notion of reformist as synonymous with a liberal or conciliatory attitude towards the Solidarity movement. Before Solidarity was outlawed in 1981, around two million PUWP members had also been members of Solidarity.[48] Since total PUWP membership, at its highest, only reached approximately three million in 1978, we could conclude that a good proportion of the party in 1981 had at some stage been sympathetic to the cause. Moreover among those PUWP members who had never taken up membership of Solidarity, some sympathised with the cause and maintained contact with members of Solidarity even after the independent trade union was outlawed.[49] Until 1985, however, Jaruzelski's regime maintained an actively repressive stance towards members of Solidarity, imprisoned some and placed others under house arrest for their continued involvement in the movement.[50] One particularly high-profile Catholic priest became a cause célèbre for the movement. In October 1984 priest Jerzy Popiełuszko was taken into custody by members of the Ministry of Internal Affairs under suspicion of leading a double life as a priest and secret Solidarity activist. A week afterwards, Pope John Paul II made an appeal to the Polish authorities to release Popiełuszko, but instead of release, his dead body was discovered a few days later.[51]

Although by 1986 policy towards the opposition had relaxed somewhat after the authorities declared an amnesty for members of the underground movement and released those that had been imprisoned, in 1988 the CC remained predominantly 'concrete' hardline.[52] Since the Politburo, in contrast, was described as ninety per cent 'reformist', in terms of their alignment with *perestroika*, we might question how and why more radical decisions were not blocked by the CC. This could be explained by the fact that by the autumn of 1988, when Mieczysław Rakowski replaced Zbigniew Messner as Prime Minister, the authority of the post changed significantly. According to Jerzy Urban, while Messner was Prime Minister he was handed directives from the Politburo which he simply implemented. In the autumn of 1988, when Rakowski replaced Messner, Rakowski began taking decisions more autonomously. Although Rakowski was also in the Politburo, his new authority freed him up from the constraints of a hardline CC, which became powerless to intervene.[53]

Choice of conference or extraordinary congress, 1988–89

Between 1987 and May 1989, the issue of whether an extraordinary congress should be convened instead of a conference did not become a matter for strong debate within the CC or Politburo.[54] Some interviewees did not recall any debate on this question within the party more widely, while a former member of the Politburo, Professor Kubiak, stated that only a small number of members advocated an extraordinary congress instead of a conference between 1988 and 1989. These individuals, however, were not in the central party leadership, and had formed a small group in the summer of 1988.[55] By the autumn of 1988, following the PUWP's first preparatory talks with Solidarity, the prospect of Solidarity's legalisation was becoming more likely.

At a meeting of the first secretaries of all higher education party committees across Poland, on 22–23 October 1988, there were calls for an extraordinary congress and Jaruzelski's replacement.[56] Many speakers at this meeting expressed that they were disillusioned with what was happening and described the system of leadership as diseased. They considered that the party would lose its legitimacy if Solidarity were legalised.[57] At this meeting, Janusz Lipiec, from the Agricultural Academy in Cracow, accused the leadership of 'cowardice' and questioned, 'Will the party find the strength from within to replace the First Secretary?'[58] Following this speech, Marian Urbański, from the Nicholas Copernicus University in Toruń, claimed that neither the Politburo nor the CC were fulfilling their duties as the party expected, and that to solve this problem an extraordinary congress, the Eleventh Congress, should be convened.[59] This was followed by other speeches, which reiterated Janusz Lipiec's views.[60] Since one of these received a standing ovation at the meeting,[61] we might assume that a good number of others present were also in agreement. Whom they would have preferred as a replacement for Jaruzelski is not specified from the notes of this meeting; however, a summary of the overall resolution from this meeting quoted Rakowski: 'citing the words of Premier Rakowski, we need to shake up the country, he also said that we need, in equal measure, to shake up the party.'[62] Other members of the leadership were not mentioned in the report, which could suggest that certainly among party intellectuals, Rakowski was the preferred choice as a replacement for General Jaruzelski.

By the time of the May 1989 conference, one delegate declared that there was a growing view that an extraordinary congress should be held and that a date for this should be set immediately.[63] Although prior to the May 1989 conference, this group did not have the requisite support of one third of the party membership (as provided in the Party Rules)[64] to force an extraordinary congress, Jaruzelski may have worried that events could follow the path they had in 1981, and resulted instead in the convention of an extraordinary congress, by popular demand. Otherwise, why would he have deferred the conference?

The timing and planned purpose of the conference

As mentioned earlier and in Chapter 4, the PUWP had already publicly announced, in 1986, their intention of convening the conference. At the Tenth Congress in 1986, which Gorbachev attended as a guest speaker,[65] Jaruzelski mentioned in his speech that the National Conference of PUWP delegates would be convened during the next five-year period before the Eleventh Congress.[66] Official documents since then indicate some discrepancy over when this forthcoming conference would take place. Jaruzelski told Gorbachev during his April 1987 visit to Moscow that the PUWP intended to hold the party conference at the end of 1988.[67] In December 1987, in Hungary and Yugoslavia, the CCs of the HSWP and LCY decided to convene their respective national/federal party conferences.[68] At the December 1987 Sixth Plenary Session of the CC, Jaruzelski referred a number of times to the forthcoming NPC, although he did not indicate specifically the planned timing for this.[69] One interviewee confirmed that the PUWP would have convened the party conference in 1988, but explained that it was postponed because of the wave of strikes in the summer of 1988, the ensuing impasse with Solidarity and then immediately afterwards preparations began for the round-table talks with the opposition.[70]

There is however, other conflicting evidence which suggests that the date for the conference had already been postponed before the wave of strikes in the summer of 1988. At a meeting with party intellectuals in March 1988, the CC Secretary, Kazimierz Cypryniak, announced that the NPC would be held in the first quarter of 1989, but that this conference was a statutory meeting.[71] A few months later, during Gorbachev's visit to Warsaw in July 1988, Jaruzelski also confirmed that the conference would take place in the spring of 1989.[72] Immediately following Gorbachev's visit, the PUWP newspaper, *Życie Partii*, published an article which praised highly the Nineteenth CPSU Conference and Gorbachev's policies of *perestroika* and *novoe myshlenie*.[73] In the same issue, another article detailed the preparations for the PUWP conference which it stated would be held in March 1989.[74] By March 1989, the conference had still not been fixed, and on 31 March the Politburo finally proposed to the CC that they convene the conference on 4–5 May and that Marian Orzechowski should organise the event.[75]

We see from this picture that between 1987 and 1988, Jaruzelski had informed Gorbachev, three times, of a date for the conference and then subsequently postponed it. As the following section outlines, Gorbachev broached the topic of the conference with Jaruzelski, and although the meeting transcripts do not record that Gorbachev directly asked Jaruzelski why the PUWP had not yet set a date for the conference, this is implied by the way in which Jaruzelski offered excuses for the conference's deferral. During these conversations Gorbachev firmly advised Jaruzelski on how the PUWP should maintain its leading role in the face of opposition.

Soviet influence on the convention of the PUWP conference

In the spring of 1987, Jaruzelski met with Gorbachev in Moscow, and they discussed their respective forthcoming party conferences, as well as the 'blank spots' in the history between the two states, as will be detailed later in this chapter.[76] At this meeting Gorbachev warned Jaruzelski that the PUWP should introduce fundamental reforms to prevent a crisis situation developing in Poland as it had between 1980 and 1981. Gorbachev pointed out the dangers of the 'mood of the masses' influencing party decision making and advised that in all things the party must remain the vanguard, that it must retain its leading role. Otherwise the party would be in danger of becoming the 'brakes'. In other words, Gorbachev expressed concern at the need for repression should a mass popular movement in opposition to the PUWP be allowed to develop, but at the same time was certainly not advising that the Polish fraternal party relinquish its leading role. Gorbachev warned that alternatively, if the party did not initiate change in keeping with public opinion, then there was a danger that 'someone else will'.[77] Gorbachev stated to Jaruzelski:

> I'd like to make a few comments on the topic of the leading role of the party in society. You know from your own experience that one of the main reasons that the crisis occurred in your country was that the party was unable to give timely answers to the questions that arose concerning matters of social development. And in our experience we found how difficult it is to reverse what happens. Now, our party has identified concrete ways out of these difficulties and taken the lead in this process. If it had not done this, then events could have taken a different, undesirable turn. My trip to Czechoslovakia and discussions with our Czech friends about the lessons of crises convinces me still more that if the mood of the masses starts to influence the actions of the party then it could become dangerous. If the party is late in adopting essential reforms then we could turn from being the vanguard to the brakes. To put it the other way round, if the party does not initiate the implementation of essential changes then someone else will do this. That is why we communists must not remain idle.[78]

At this meeting Jaruzelski expressed gratitude for the Soviet Union's generous financial aid via the CMEA, acknowledged that Poland owed the Soviet Union $300 million and requested that repayment be deferred until 1990. Jaruzelski then claimed that the PUWP would convene the party conference at the end of 1988: 'We intend holding our party conference at the end of 1988. We are preparing for elections in the Sejm and in the local party organisations.'[79] Whether Jaruzelski expressed compliance in promising to hold a conference as a way of securing continued financial support from the Soviet Union is not directly attested in this document. It seems unlikely, though, that such a *quid pro quo* would have been explicitly stated. The same theme appears in transcripts of further discussions between the two leaders during Gorbachev's visit to Warsaw in July 1988, a couple of weeks after the close of the CPSU conference.

Portions of the transcript from this July 1988 meeting, according to Russian archival sources,[80] show that Jaruzelski felt a need to explain why the PUWP had not yet convened the conference. This information is conspicuously absent from Polish archival sources.[81] Jaruzelski suggested this by saying that Poland was under fire from internal opposition and propaganda from the West, and that the Seventh Plenary Session of the PUWP CC had acted for them as 'a mini-conference'.[82]

At the meeting Jaruzelski seemed to imply that convening a full NPC was too risky under the circumstances and that the party would hold their conference later in the spring of 1989. Jaruzelski stated that he would not tolerate the legalisation of trade unions, nor the growth of opposition parties. This indicates his commitment to retaining the one-party system. At this meeting Jaruzelski stated to Gorbachev:

> We need to stabilise ourselves. We are under fire from internal opposition and external propaganda. The results of the Seventh Plenary session of the PUWP CC were of great import. For us this acted as a mini-conference. We are striving to make sure that the decisions really are implemented. Then we will start the democratisation of society. Failing to do this would lead to catastrophe. Socialism is inextricably linked to democracy. But in our country there are two bounds beyond which we will not go... We cannot accept the pluralisation of our Trade Union movement. ... The second boundary for us is that the growth of opposition parties is unacceptable. In the West they are trying to persuade us to recognise Wałęsa. We will hold our PUWP national party conference in the spring of 1989. Until then we will just hold individual meetings with PUWP members, which understandably will not take the form of purges.[83]

These extracts suggest that Jaruzelski thought Gorbachev expected him to adopt a policy clearly in line with *perestroika*, which entailed purging hardliners and modernising the party, but that the party would clearly set the boundaries on reform by reaffirming the leading role of the PUWP at an NPC.

By the time this second meeting took place in July 1988, János Kádár had already been persuaded to resign as First Secretary of the HSWP, and had been 'kicked upstairs' to the ineffectual new role of 'President' at the May 1988 HSWP conference.[84] Interviewees confirmed that with respect to other socialist states, Poland only enjoyed good relations with Hungary and Yugoslavia.[85] From this we might infer that some members of the HSWP and PUWP leaderships would have discussed among themselves such momentous events. Jaruzelski may, therefore, have feared a similar palace coup in 1988, and deferred an all-party meeting for that reason. Jaruzelski told Gorbachev that at the Seventh Plenary Session of the CC of the PUWP, held a month before Gorbachev's visit, measures had been taken that were commensurate with a 'mini-conference'. This suggests that Jaruzelski wished to confine the necessary agenda to discussion within the CC, and hoped that this would be sufficient to satisfy Gorbachev.

The Seventh Plenary Session of the CC, June 1988, as a 'mini-conference'

At the Seventh Plenary Session of the CC, on 13–14 June 1988, a number of senior officials who had served during the period of martial law resigned from the CC and Politburo, because of their appointment overseas as ambassador.[86] New personnel that had not hitherto served in the party leadership were promoted, including Stanisław Ciosek (who was later to help organise the round-table negotiations and became an adviser to Aleksander Kwaśniewski), Mieczysław Rakowski and the economist and president of the Polish national bank, Władysław Baka.[87] At this session Professor Zdzisław Cackowski, member of the CC and Rector of the Marie Curie Skłodowska University in Lublin, argued that the most pressing issue for the PUWP was how to define the leading role of the party, which although guaranteed within governing state structures by the Constitution, had in practice lost much of its influence over society. 'The Party... has incurred losses on a critical scale... in terms of Party personnel's loss of influence in the sphere of social influence, but there is no constitutional possibility for [the Party] to lose its power.'[88] The Resolution from this plenary session affirmed the party's commitment to develop further their coalition with other parties in the Sejm, and that individuals from other movements should be allowed to participate in government.[89]

A number of other decisions in the Resolution are also very reminiscent of the main tenets of *perestroika* proposed at the Nineteenth CPSU Conference, as detailed in Chapter 3. These issues include increasing the role of the youth in the party, the elimination of wasteful bureaucracy; greater accountability within the party for non-implementation of directives; the development of a stronger work ethic among the workforce and the practice of meritocracy in appointments, with an additional proviso that there must be at least two candidates in competition for any one post.[90] At interview, Leszek Miller stated that the Seventh Plenary Session of the PUWP CC was, among other things, undoubtedly an expression of

PUWP support for Gorbachev and *perestroika* in advance of the Nineteenth CPSU Conference.[91]

The PUWP conference, 4–5 May 1989

By the time the postponed conference took place, the political situation in Poland was in the process of evolving significantly, but it was still not clear what would be the outcome of the round-table talks and the semi-free elections to the Sejm.[92] Although the CC and the upper party leadership had already in practice lost a good deal of their influence to the Sejm,[93] at the time of the conference, the PUWP leadership did not anticipate that it would soon lose its leading role.[94] Delegates' speeches, though, especially those of rank-and-file members, which were not included in the published booklet of the conference, indicate some apprehension at what the leadership had agreed, and that the round-table talks were conceding too much to the opposition. A number of speakers voiced their concern at 'pluralism' and others demanded that a way be found to consolidate the party's power and that in particular the CC's authority should be increased. Speeches shared the basic underlying assumption that the PUWP would retain its leading role, and simply incorporate portions of the opposition into its ranks, so that these other voices might contribute to decision making but under the firm leadership of the PUWP. According to Leszek Miller, present at the conference, the majority of delegates were 'centrists'.[95] This would chart the PUWP's conference as aligned politically with the CPSU, HSWP and LCY conferences in terms of the concentration of those delegates present who were in favour of policy in keeping with modernising the party but retaining its leading role in society.

Much of what was said by delegates appears anachronistic in the context of 1989. Many advocated changes that were already underway, such as the inclusion of individuals outside the party in the decision-making process, or blindly reaffirmed their right and duty to maintain the party's leading role. Gorbachev's policies were praised a number of times. In terms of content, therefore, the conference certainly adhered to the expected formula of espousing *perestroika*, consolidating party unity and maintaining the leading role of the party.

But in the context of the PUWP in May 1989 this must have seemed somewhat irrelevant. Although the leadership had been refreshed with a number of reformist elements by this stage, the mission statement which the conference approved was hopelessly backward-looking. Discussion of the PUWP's electoral campaign for the upcoming June parliamentary elections – clearly a very pressing issue – received little attention at the conference, which again supports the argument that Jaruzelski was more concerned with (belatedly) convening a party conference to show alignment with and support for Gorbachev's *perestroika*.

The PUWP's electoral manifesto and campaign

In his opening address to the conference, Wojciech Jaruzelski had stressed that the conference was not a 'pre-electoral meeting'.[96] Perhaps for this reason, the issue of the upcoming elections received little attention in delegates' speeches, which provoked a regional party committee representative, Izabella Sierakowska, to begin her address at the close of the first day of the conference: 'Wake up comrades! People are saying one thing in the conference hall, and another thing in the corridors. ... Elections! We are not discussing the elections!' She asked what programme the party would be presenting in their campaign.[97]

A guest at the conference, the Marshall of the Sejm and President of the ZSL, Roman Malinowski, proposed that the three-party coalition embark on their electoral campaign with the aim of attracting voters from the broadest range of society, and that although the ZSL's electoral manifesto would be different from the PUWP'S, the ZSL would state clearly that the parties would remain in coalition.[98] What the PUWP's manifesto would entail, however, was not clear to delegates. The sense of confusion as to who and what the PUWP had come to represent was boldly expressed in one speech by a worker, Krzysztof Abramczuk. He accused the party of selling out its traditional ideals to those of 'social democrats' and the middle classes:

> I think that one of the fundamental sources of our party's weakness lies in our inability to clearly define whose political interests, which class and social strata, we represent in terms of our

practical activities. The PUWP Rules claim that we are the Party of Polish Communists, the vanguard of the working classes, that we are led by the working classes. Everyone is wondering, though, whether we really do just have Communists in our ranks. There are quite a lot of people among us, who could aptly be called Social democrats, rather than Communists. We need to take this into account, that's one suggestion. We needlessly want to be the party of Poland's entire society. This way we will lose the character of our party as class-based. We all know that workers do not currently constitute a majority in our party. We see very clearly that our coalition partners ZSL and SD are much better able to capture the social strata that they want to represent.[99]

Concerned, perhaps, that the PUWP was not directing sufficient resources to its own campaign, and that their opponents were gaining advantage, Jan Ciemniewski, a farmer and member of a regional party committee, remarked that he had been impressed when he saw Solidarity's campaign in the centre of Warsaw during the conference break that day.[100] Although the party had already conceded the need to include representatives from Solidarity in parliament, there was no enthusiasm that Solidarity be legally recognised as an independent trade union, as this was seen as a back door to its recognition as an independent political entity, which would therefore make it a rival to the PUWP.

Consolidating the party's leading role and re-establishing party unity

Some delegates emphatically expressed their disapproval of Solidarity's legal recognition, and equated the notion of political pluralism with anarchy. Ryszard Paluch, a locksmith from the Katowice regional committee of the PUWP, acknowledged that:

> ... Pluralism in politics and trade unions has had a place for a few years now; party activists stand together with other colleagues that have different convictions. They each fulfil their duties as members of different trade unions, and as long as they work together and fulfil their duties in terms of production, then this is fine. When, however, [this pluralism] brings with it an unhealthy political rivalry or rivalry between trade unions, which results in disorganisation at work, then we don't consider this pluralism, but rather common anarchy...[101]

This theme was developed in Antoni Szczuciński's[102] speech when he touched on ideological work: 'We note that heterogeneity can be a source of development, but it can also be a spark to enflame anarchy.' He described the merits of Gorbachev's 'new thinking' and argued that it:

> ... is also a return to the side of individualism, which is defined in Poland by the term socialist personalism... In accordance with what comrade Jaruzelski has said, we have to do something about the political crisis in the Central Committee, and the political crisis with respect to the political programme as soon as possible; we don't yet have a political crisis in the means of operation in the PUWP but it is highly likely...

Szczuciński urged the party to increase the power of individuals as the only possible solution to retaining its leading role in society:

> In wanting to increase the individuality of the citizen within the state and retain the leading role of the party, we not only can, but must, significantly increase the individual voice of party members within the party.[103]

There was a more impassioned plea from the head of the Lenin shipyard in Gdansk, Marian Truszkowski, a member of the CC, for greater discipline in the party and he made a strong statement that the situation was very reminiscent of 1981: 'The situation is analogous to 1981. The political struggle could intensify, which would require of us determination and also force.'[104] This latter statement could suggest that he was literally advocating the use of force in the event that the situation worsened.

Zdzisław Cackowski stated that greater participation by non-party members was essential to increasing social responsibility. At the same time, he stressed that people must not see this 'democratisation' as a panacea, which would guarantee external funding to solve Poland's economic crisis:

> But without participation, without widening freedom there will be no accountability. However, it would be better if we could see that democracy is not a commodity which someone outside is buying for us. I'm hoping that we can do something to banish this delusion not just from within our own ranks, but among others.[105]

Another delegate expressed concern at the split in the party that had occurred over the decisions taken at the Tenth Plenary Session of the CC regarding the legalisation of Solidarity:[106]

> We have come to the point where we need to say that there is no unity within our party. This was especially apparent in rank and file party members' approach to the decisions of the Tenth Plenary session regarding political pluralism and pluralism of the trade unions.[107]

A deputy director of an enterprise and a member of a regional party committee, Paweł Zawadzki, remarked that relations between the factions in the party had become so strained that 'we have in the party today a rather paradoxical situation that we speak of each other within the party slightly worse, than others outside speak of us'.[108]

Although delegates invited to speak at the conference expressed their support for Jaruzelski, those in the audience were not so supportive. We might question whether speakers were selected for this reason. There was a heavy contribution from the central leadership, which comprised just over 30% of speakers. More than half of this contingent's speakers were Politburo members. Approximately another 30% were managers or directors of enterprises. Slightly more than 10% were professionals (school teachers, doctors, lawyers, etc.). About 10% of those that spoke were manual workers or farmers; 5% were editors from local or regional newspapers (rather than from the national press). Regional party representatives constituted about 8%. The proportion of speakers who were academics comprised less than 5%. This was the group, as described on page 237, that had advocated Jaruzelski's replacement and that an extraordinary congress be convened. The large proportion of speakers that were managers or directors of enterprises (30%) would have guaranteed a strong voice against the legalisation of Solidarity. They would have been particularly frustrated over the preceding year by the strike action and the divisive effect of Solidarity on the workforce. Rakowski's speech, in contrast, reaffirmed the importance of the round-table talks and argued that plurality among trade unions would lead to competition, which would be good for the country.[109]

Evidently, delegates did not greet Jaruzelski's speech at the conference with much enthusiasm, and the audience was

sceptical because 'the General does not have the authority
he had a few years ago'.[110] In contrast with this, a number of
delegates expressed praise for the 'Rakowski Government'; the
entire hall fell completely silent as Rakowski delivered his own
speech, and he received praise from colleagues for his work.
Moreover:

> the universal appraisal [of my speech] was that it was very realistic,
> well-judged, and that the kicks were sensibly aimed. In the corri-
> dors there is the opinion, according to Professor Popiela, that if I
> had made [the speech] on the first day, then the conference would
> have taken a different course. Wojciech Jaruzelski was pleased.[111]

What 'other course' the conference might have taken, had
Rakowski made his speech on the first day of the conference,
is left open to speculation. We might wonder (if this account
is accurate) why Jaruzelski would have been 'pleased' with the
conference after having been upstaged by his Prime Minister.
This begs the question whether Jaruzelski had feared the same
fate as János Kádár at the HSWP May 1988 conference, and
was simply relieved he was still in post at the close of the
meeting.

Could Jaruzelski have been replaced earlier with a more reformist actor?

By analogy with the Hungarian case, we might have expected
Moscow to encourage Jaruzelski's replacement with a more
reformist actor, and the conference would have been a conven-
ient place for this. In the case of Hungary, the centrist Károly
Grósz had been groomed by Gorbachev as a suitable alternative to Kádár.[112] However, the dynamic in the HSWP, where
there was a larger contingency of reformists in the leadership,
was quite different to that of the PUWP, where the CC was,
according to interviewees, predominantly hardline.[113] One
interviewee, who was a member of the Politburo in 1988,
described the CC as overwhelmingly 'concrete' in terms of its
hardline propensities and generally more conservative than
Wojciech Jaruzelski and his Politburo. For this reason, the
member claimed, there was no pressure, within the leadership,
to replace Wojciech Jaruzelski with a more reformist actor.[114]
Others concurred with this view, explaining that there was no

obvious replacement for Jaruzelski as his power base straddled both the centrist-reformist and conservative camps.[115] Jerzy Urban stated that the possible replacement of General Jaruzelski had only been an issue during the early 1980s, when a conservative group of the leadership kept in close contact with Moscow in the event that Jaruzelski became unable to maintain control through martial law. Had this been the case, according to Urban, then the Soviet Union would have intervened militarily and this group would have stepped in to take over the leadership. For that reason, they were known as the 'Welcoming Committee'.[116] All these individuals were removed from post between 1985 and 1986, after Gorbachev came to power.

As has been stated, respondents at interview maintained that the relationship between Jaruzelski and Gorbachev had been very close, and that it was therefore highly unlikely that Gorbachev would have wished to see him replaced.[117] However, there is some evidence which suggests that Gorbachev and one of his chief advisers, Georgii Shakhnazarov, would have welcomed a new First Secretary by 1988. During his visit to Warsaw, on 11–16 July 1988, Gorbachev had shown interest in Rakowski, they had spent some time together informally, and they had got on well together.[118] According to Mieczysław Rakowski's own memoirs, Gorbachev indicated his approval at Rakowski's appointment, remarking to a couple of students in a café, 'Well, now you have wise, liberal people in the leadership like Mieczysław Rakowski.'[119] Gorbachev's statement could be interpreted as an implicit critique of some of the existing leadership as illiberal. As will be discussed later in this chapter, Rakowski was a known opponent of martial law in the early 1980s, and as this information had been documented in discussions between Brezhnev and Jaruzelski, we could assume that Gorbachev would have been aware of this at the time.[120]

Georgii Shakhnazarov expressed regret in his memoirs that Rakowski had not been made First Secretary before 1989: 'Mieczysław Rakowski finally became Chairman of the Polish Council of Ministers and First Secretary of the PUWP, but the time for this had already, hopelessly, passed.'[121] This statement suggests that had Rakowski become First Secretary earlier, then the party might have been able to evolve and survive longer. It was only after the first set of round-table talks with the opposition, the May party conference and the party's resounding and unexpected defeat at the first semi-free parliamentary elections in June 1989 that Jaruzelski eventually resigned and Rakowski was elected as First Secretary.[122]

I would argue that there were two issues over which Jaruzelski had become an embarrassment to Gorbachev and the reformist wing of the CPSU leadership by 1988. The first of these was the introduction of martial law in 1981, which Jaruzelski had justified as the lesser evil to an imminent Soviet invasion, and the second was the spectre of the Katyń Massacre. From 1987 onwards, disclosure on both these topics would have been essential as proof that the Soviet Union had renounced the Brezhnev Doctrine and that *glasnost* was genuine with respect to reassessing Stalinist crimes. Also, Solidarity had been vocally pressing for recognition of the truth concerning Katyń since 1980, influenced by the Polish community in London and its government-in-exile that had persistently but unsuccessfully lobbied the British Government to open a new investigation into the Katyń tragedy during the 1970s and early 1980s.[123] As the next two sections will indicate, Rakowski was provided with arguably compromising information about Jaruzelski in 1988, which he could have used with more reformist colleagues to oust the General. We cannot know whether this information was intentionally given for that purpose, but the discussion is interesting from the point of view of charting how Gorbachev sought to distance himself and withdraw CPSU support from the regime that Jaruzelski had so painstakingly tried to align with Moscow since 1981.

That old cherry: the threat of Soviet invasion in 1981

Shakhnazarov informed Rakowski during his visit to Moscow in August 1988 that there had never been any threat of the Soviet Union intervening militarily in Poland during the early 1980s.[124] In his own memoirs Shakhnazarov reiterated this statement, explaining that at the time, in 1980, the prevailing position in Moscow was that military action analogous with the intervention during the Prague Spring in 1968 had been categorically ruled out.[125] Since the unrest in 1980, the Soviet Union started taking a great interest in Poland, according to Rakowski, and had formed a 'crisis committee' that year, which was later referred to as the 'Polish Club'. This group included, among others, all those who after Brezhnev soon, successively, became CPSU General Secretary: Andropov, Chernenko and Gorbachev.[126] Other individuals in this group had begun their careers during the Stalinist era, and for a long time had been involved in policy-making concerning the fraternal states, or had been involved in organising Soviet military intervention into these states.[127] Soon after coming to power, Gorbachev disbanded this group.[128]

According to Shakhnazarov, in Moscow there were only two views as to how to deal with the situation between 1980 and 1981. The majority were in favour of putting pressure on the Polish leadership to introduce martial law and repress the opposition, and advocated freezing relations with Poland to ensure that the 'plague of Solidarity' did not reach the Soviet Union. Others suggested that the Poles should resolve their own problems, and the PUWP leadership should find a mutually acceptable compromise with Solidarity. This group did not view the unrest of 1980–81 as a 'counter-revolution' incited by dissidents but instead considered Solidarity an independent trade union, which was supported by the entire Polish working class.[129]

On 5 December 1980 Stanisław Kania and Wojciech Jaruzelski attended a meeting of the leaders of Warsaw Pact countries in Moscow to discuss the matter.[130] During this meeting they were told that 'Socialist Poland, the PUWP and the Polish people could depend on unconditional fraternal solidarity and support from the Warsaw Pact Countries'.[131] This statement ambiguously leaves open to question whether support would entail military intervention. As discussed in Chapter 5 with respect to the case of Hungary, other published sources suggest that the dynamic of the Brezhnev Doctrine of military intervention was finely balanced between the Soviet Union and the socialist state in question, and that intervention was only agreed when it was mutually acceptable. According to the former Soviet Foreign Minister Andrei Gromyko, in the case of Hungary in 1956, Soviet military support against 'counter-revolutionaries' was only afforded after leaders from 'democratic bodies, including that part of the leadership that patriotically stood for the defence of Hungary's social order' had persistently requested this intervention.[132] Similarly, the invasion of Czechoslovakia by Warsaw Pact troops was only initiated after persistent pleas from within the Czechoslovak leadership.[133] The issue of the possibility of a Warsaw Pact invasion of Poland between 1980 and 1981 is tantalisingly absent from Gromyko's memoirs. Nonetheless, as a member of the 'Polish Club' at the time, even if he had personally been in favour of such military intervention in Poland, which might have been in keeping with his forthright justification of this action in Hungary in 1956 and Czechoslovakia in 1968, the prevailing opinion of the Polish Club was that intervention was impractical in terms of the sheer number of Solidarity supporters, and the anticipated bloodshed this would cause. The Polish Minister of Internal Affairs throughout the 1980s, General Czesław Kiszczak, stated in a published interview in 1991 that the Soviet leaders he met with to discuss the matter, Andropov and Kriuchkov, were both of the opinion that Solidarity's supporters, which numbered some ten million, were too numerous to contain by force and therefore negotiating with them was the only solution.[134] According to this source, Jerzy Urban expressed the opinion that pressure from the Soviets had led to the signing of the August agreement in 1980 with Solidarity.[135] This suggests, therefore, that Andropov, at that time head of the KGB, had advised the Polish leadership to adopt a conciliatory approach towards Solidarity.

In his own memoirs of that time, Rakowski recounted various discussions within the PUWP leadership and his own encounters with Soviet emissaries. The only source during this time that suggested directly to Rakowski that Soviet military intervention was imminent was Jaruzelski, who urged Rakowski in February 1981 that 'it is our historical mission to prevent Soviet intervention' [136] and later in June that 'according to W.J. the Russians have got to the stage of preparing an invasion, now they are just looking for a pretext'.[137] In early August 1981 Jaruzelski told Rakowski that the Soviets were planning an invasion between late August and early September, and that Soviet troops had begun significant manoeuvres on the Soviet Western frontier and in the Baltics.[138] If there was never any question of invasion, or at least this solution had been dismissed by this point in time, we might surmise that these military manoeuvres were helpfully staged by the Soviets as a warning to the Polish general public and also to help convince others in the Polish leadership that martial law was necessary as the only alternative to Soviet military intervention. A number of commentaries have identified evidence in a range of Soviet sources, including memoirs and Politburo documents of 1980–81, that not only did the Soviet Union have no intention of militarily intervening in Poland at this time, but that instead, Jaruzelski had repeatedly requested Soviet military intervention, which the Soviets declined.[139]

During Jaruzelski's meeting with Brezhnev in the spring of 1982,[140] a few months after martial law had been introduced the previous December, Brezhnev expressed his support for the Polish leadership's action:

> During the discussions Brezhnev emphasised that the introduction of martial law was accepted in Moscow with complete understanding. There was no alternative way out of the frustrating counter-revolutionary attempt that would prevent civil war.[141]

The latter statement, if taken at face value, could be unpacked to suggest that Brezhnev himself had renounced the Brezhnev Doctrine, certainly with respect to intervention on the scale that would have been required in the case of Poland. Other evidence confirms this. In December 1981, Brezhnev sent the message to Jaruzelski that Moscow had no plans to send in troops to Poland and that the 'Poles themselves must resolve the Polish question'.[142]

During the period of unrest, 1980–81, the Soviet Union provided considerable financial assistance to Poland of four billion transferable roubles, estimated as equivalent to three billion US dollars, and during the period of martial law promised a further two point seven billion rouble credit for the years 1982–83.[143] In this document there are no overtones of any threat of future Soviet intervention, nor are there any hints of an offer to intervene in the event of any future unrest.[144] However, it could be argued that the timely provision of Soviet financial support, which notably was very significantly higher for the years 1980–81, could have been to equip Poland with the means to deal with the problem internally, as (hypothetically) agreed in advance.

Many believed that the introduction of martial law in December 1981 was a domestic solution to the unrest in Poland, and one chosen to avert Soviet military intervention. Jaruzelski's legitimacy as a leader was founded on this interpretation of events, much as Kádár's legitimacy had been founded on the principle that he had not been complicit with the Soviet Army's invasion of Hungary in 1956.[145] In the same way that the reformist camp of the HSWP claimed to have been presented with relevant compromising material about Kádár, in the spring before the May 1988 conference, to convince him to resign,[146] we might wonder whether Rakowski was similarly provided, in August 1988, with the information that there had never been a threat of invasion. A number of Politburo members, including Hieronim Kubiak, Kazimierz Barcikowski, Andrzej Werblan and then Deputy Prime Minister, Mieczysław Rakowski, had vocally opposed the introduction of martial law, as attested in a Polish archival document of 1982. According to this document, Brezhnev consequently queried these individuals' suitability for the leadership.[147] Since these individuals remained in the leadership and other liberals were appointed after 1986, it seems logical to conclude that Jaruzelski managed to sustain the myth that he had averted Soviet intervention. In April 1987, the US defector from the Polish Army, Colonel Ryszard Kukliński,[148] revealed that Jaruzelski's and Kania's claim that the Solidarity strikes and unrest in 1980–81 amounted to a 'counter-revolution' had conceded the need for help from Warsaw Pact forces and provoked a Soviet response.[149] This revelation was published in April 1987 in a Paris journal.

The CPSU leadership may also have wanted to set the record straight on this issue, or alternatively, maintaining the myth of the threat of Soviet military intervention in 1981 may no longer have been expedient for the Soviet Union. In 1986 Gorbachev attended the Tenth PUWP Congress, and gave a speech to the delegates that cooperation between the socialist states was to be made on an equal footing.[150] A number of speeches at the Congress reiterated Poland's commitment to strengthening ties and developing closer cooperation with the Soviet Union, and a pamphlet of these speeches was separately published under the title 'The Tenth Congress of the PUWP: friendship and cooperation with the Soviet Union'.[151] Gorbachev stressed the need for more intensive cooperation between Poland and the CMEA, warning of the danger of importing goods from the West because of 'the traps that lie on the trade routes leading West... as has been spoken about [at this congress] Poland has already suffered great losses'.[152] In his speech Gorbachev explained that the ' "Polish crisis"... was not a protest by the workers against socialism. It was above all against those deviations of socialism in practice which the working class has most painfully experienced'.[153] This statement was very powerful in that it rejected the notion of this unrest as a 'counter-revolution', and in blaming the PUWP leadership, Gorbachev attributed some legitimacy to Solidarity's actions in 1981.

At the 1984 conference, as mentioned earlier in this chapter, the delegates had produced a document that explained that following the events of August 1980, Poland had prevented counter-revolution by deploying national forces: 'We opposed the threat of national tragedy with our own forces. The road to a counter-revolutionary coup was cut off.'[154] Therefore, Gorbachev's reassessment at the next all-party meeting in 1986, of the 'Polish crisis' as ultimately the fault of the Polish Government, as the result of the malpractice of socialism rather than a 'counter-revolution', was an important signal to Jaruzelski's leadership that the Soviets would not intervene in an analogous situation. Moreover, these statements rather challenged Jaruzelski's legitimacy and must have raised a few questions. We might surmise that this myth was one of the historical 'blank spots' which Gorbachev wished to be brought out into the open and publicly debunked by a new PUWP First Secretary.

The Katyń Massacre of 1940

In April 1987 Jaruzelski visited Moscow and signed a declaration on 'Ideological Collaboration between the Communist Party of the Soviet Union and the Polish United Workers' Party'.[155] In this declaration there was a pledge that both parties highly valued collaborative historical research and that there should be no historical 'blank spots'. 'Above all we must do all that is necessary to strengthen the friendship between our parties and peoples and determine what has brought harm to this friendship.'[156] In discussion with Gorbachev on that day Jaruzelski also stated that the PUWP was considering how best to mark the fiftieth anniversary of the defeat of fascism.[157] Instead of naming outright that the bone of contention was Katyń, Gorbachev and Jaruzelski declared their joint intention was to find the historical source of the problem through collaborative Polish–Soviet historical research. As the 'truth' about Katyń has been variously amended by different political elites, since the 1940s, to support their changing agendas,[158]

Gorbachev's momentous step in addressing the issue when he did, in 1987, deserves some attention.

The issue had received a good deal of publicity in Poland since 1980. A significant source of Solidarity's discontent with the regime was anti-Soviet sentiment, which intensified in 1980. One of the main issues was Katyń, which appeared repeatedly in Solidarity publications and was raised during negotiations with the government.[159] Since the failure of the PUWP to deal with this movement had resulted in the introduction of martial law, for which again, the Soviet Union had been blamed, we can imagine that the CPSU, among others, might have anticipated that anti-Soviet sentiment remained rife in Poland. Commentators consider it highly unlikely that, after taking office as General Secretary, Gorbachev would not have known that the Soviet Union was responsible for Katyń.[160] In Poland, by the mid-1980s, various publications (both official and unofficial) had ascribed guilt to the Soviet security services.[161] The approach taken by Gorbachev and Jaruzelski in their joint declaration of 1987, however, was careful to suggest ignorance of the evidence before investigation.

The research began shortly after the Soviet–Polish agreement of 1987 was signed, and was conducted by a group of Soviet and Polish historians commissioned specially to investigate the matter of Katyń. Finally, a forty-page research report was presented for discussion to the PUWP Politburo in June 1989.[162] This report comprised a brief summary of the different versions of events, and a survey of the official stance the Polish authorities had taken over the decades. The report noted that during the decade following the tragedy, the Polish government had always denied any suggestion of Soviet culpability, and that any such allegations had been rebuffed as anti-Soviet propaganda. The research recorded a slight change in policy regarding the matter after 1956 when, as evidence against the Soviet Union mounted up, the Polish authorities simply maintained a silence, or had used censorship to block information. For example, the research stated there was no entry in Polish or Soviet encyclopaedias on the matter 'Katyń'.[163]

According to the research, only eight per cent of Poles who took part in the survey believed that the Germans had been responsible for the massacre, from which the report concluded that 'the possibility of exerting any influence over social consciousness in this matter is now completely exhausted'.[164]

This latter statement is quite telling of the thrust of the research, which seems to have evaluated the extent to which public opinion might still be open to persuasion of the falsified version of events.

Since Gorbachev had only recently come to power, disclosure on the Katyń massacre would have exonerated his own leadership from culpability and pointed the finger at previous general secretaries (all deceased) who had failed to bring the matter to light. For Jaruzelski, however, who had actively and publicly taken a supportive stance of the original Soviet Burdenko account, contrary to the reported silence adopted by his predecessors since 1956, this revelation could have been harmful. In 1985 Jaruzelski had publicly attributed culpability for the crime to Nazi Germany. In April of that year, a monument commemorating the Katyń victims was erected and inscribed with the words: 'To the Polish officers who were victims of Hitler's fascism on the land of Katyń.' This was interpreted by the majority of Poles as a treacherous action on the part of Jaruzelski.[165]

During the May 1989 NPC, Jarzuelski addressed the topic of the joint reappraisal of history between the CPSU and PUWP rather obliquely when he stated:

> We have a close friend, and although the past has not always been without flaw, our current inter-party relations with the CPSU and state relations with the Soviet Government are genuinely on an equal footing, as partners, and have the character of mutual respect and trust. We are together concluding an honest appraisal of the past and a clear vision of the future.[166]

With respect to this reappraisal of history, a two-page commemorative declaration marking the fiftieth anniversary of the German invasion of Poland and the outbreak of the Second World War was published as part of the conference booklet. This declaration claims that Poland was vulnerable and isolated as a result of the Western policy of appeasement towards Germany and deep mistrust between Poland and the Soviet Union. The expected reference to Katyń in this account is then fudged and only alluded to indirectly, in terms of 'grievous suffering' inflicted by Soviet troops in eastern territory that belonged to Poland before the Second World War. The unfortunate use of the clause 'regardless of the motive' appears to highlight the elephant in the room: the question of Stalin's motive for the atrocity and why the Polish leadership had corroborated with the perpetrators, the Soviet leadership, for so many decades in hiding the truth. The statement simply claims that Poles were offended by the fact that they were presented with a falsified account of events:

> Among other things, the source of our isolation was the Polish leadership's mistaken political and military doctrine of that time. In the face of the threat of Hitler's Germany, the countries of Europe each defended their own interests. As a result of this, a fight to the death began in Poland with Hitler Germany on 1 September 1939 and then the invasion by Soviet troops, on 17 September 1939, on former territories of the Polish state, caused grievous suffering. Regardless of the motive for this decision, what dramatically deepened feelings about this were the erroneous [historical] accounts, phrases which were offensive to Poles, as well as the subsequent repression by the Stalinist-Beria apparatus.[167]

The declaration then briefly outlined that when the Soviet Union fell prey to Nazi invasion in 1941, Poland and the Soviet Union fought together and that 'in this common war grew an unbreakable union'.[168] The address urged at the end:

> Our correct stance and patriotic duty is to strengthen ties with countries of the socialist fraternity, make a contribution to building a common European home, and never stop fighting for a safe and just world. Poland must never again be as weak as it was fifty years ago. It is therefore every Pole's duty to unite around the political, economic and social reforms, so as to build a modern state.[169]

According to Mieczysław Rakowski in 1988, revelations concerning Katyń 'were simply a question of time'.[170] Rakowski recounted a conversation he had had with the Czechoslovak Minister of Foreign Affairs, Bohuslav Chňoupek, on 15 July 1988 at an evening dinner reception held in Warsaw to mark the meeting of the Political Advisory Committee, the main governing body of the Warsaw Pact. Rakowski recounted:

> [Vasil] Bilák [Secretary of the CPCZ CC] was sitting on the opposite side of the table. 'That's the kind of person you can like as much as having your teeth pulled at the dentist,' Chňoupek remarked, and then he said, 'look at the left side of the top[171] table. There are some tough old comrades sitting there,' ([First Secretary of the CPCZ, Gustav] Husák, [Prime Minister of the GDR, Willi] Stoph, and someone else), after which he informed me that the Katyń affair also had implications for them. It turned out that Husák was

also on the [investigating] Commission, which the Germans sent to Katyń. Fancy that![172]

Why Husák, Stoph, and another unnamed individual were referred to in this instance is not clear. One interpretation of this exchange is that all three individuals had been on the German investigating commission into Katyń (and had falsified the evidence in favour of the Soviet Burdenko account), or all had instrumentally taken part in falsifying evidence in some way. If this is true, then revelations concerning Katyń would have been harmful to the First Secretary of the CPCZ, Gustav Husák, the Prime Minister of the GDR, Willi Stoph, and a third person, who was sitting next to them at the dinner. Why Rakowski omitted the third person's name is not intimated.[173]

In April 1990 Gorbachev finally presented Jaruzelski, who by this stage had been made President, with some of the relevant Soviet documentation, and a public statement that Katyń was 'one of the heaviest Stalinist crimes'.[174] Since then, experts researching the matter of Katyń have been disappointed that proper investigation and full disclosure by the Russian authorities is still pending.[175]

Conclusion

This chapter has shown empirically that the PUWP leadership could more easily control delegate selection to a conference than at a congress, and consequently was more able to guide the outcome to a conference. Aware of this, more reformist grass-roots movements developed in 1981 and 1988 in anticipation of the conference, to pressure the PUWP leadership to convene instead an early congress. This supports the argument that these two institutions represented very different policy choices, and that actors vied with each other over the choice of institution as a means to securing their preferred outcome.

At the same time, Gorbachev encouraged Jaruzelski to use the conference in Poland to broadcast publicly the PUWP's alignment with Gorbachev's policies of *perestroika* and modernising the party within the boundaries of the one-party state. The issue of conference timing was one which affected both parties. Gorbachev needed support from the socialist fraternity to help secure his own reformist position against CPSU hardline opposition in 1988, and Jaruzelski's contribution in this respect came rather late. Moreover, the transcripts of conversations between Gorbachev and Jaruzelski indicated Gorbachev's sense of urgency that the PUWP do more to negotiate with Solidarity to include the opposition within the decision-making process. In the case of Poland, the prospect of a conference was complicated by the particularly troubled history between the Soviet Union and Poland, which also had implications for Jaruzelski. Nonetheless, for the PUWP conference to espouse convincingly the new philosophy underpinning relations between the CPSU and PUWP also required adequate explanations of Katyń and martial law. This was ultimately not achieved by the PUWP May 1989 conference, nor could it have been, while Jaruzelski remained First Secretary. In this respect, the conference yielded too little in terms of Gorbachev's agenda. Those that advocated an extraordinary congress also sought Jaruzelski's replacement, and so we might surmise that had a congress been convened instead of a conference, then this would have been more likely to have resulted in Jaruzelski's ouster. By the time the conference took place, in May 1989, the event was overshadowed by more significant developments. If, however, the conference had taken place earlier, in 1988, before the round-table negotiations, it is most likely that it would have been the subject of greater debate within the party, and reformists might have seen the event as an opportunity to mobilise for more sweeping changes.

This chapter has examined, broadly speaking, evidence of Soviet influence over PUWP policy-making at this time. Gorbachev himself, however, had remarked that the fraternal states, including the CPSU, should borrow elements from each other's models when designing their own variant of *perestroika* to strengthen socialism.[176] As noted in the Introduction, the Communist Party of China convened their conference to replace personnel and declare a new era of market liberalisation. While the HSWP conference apparently followed suit in this respect, ousting the old-guard, the CPSU chose not to effect personnel changes at the conference. While Chapter 2 detailed some significant features of continuity since the first conference in 1905, personnel change was more rarely effected at Soviet conferences and the issue of whether or not this would be on the agenda was a matter decided relatively soon before the Nineteenth CPSU conference in 1988. This leaves partially unanswered the question of what ultimately influenced Gorbachev in his design of the conference. We might surmise that effecting personnel change could have signalled the influence of the CPC or collaboration between the two parties, which as mentioned in the Introduction, Gorbachev had stated in October 1985, was to remain secret. When asked whether Gorbachev might have modelled the Nineteenth CPSU Conference on the Polish conference of 1984, one interviewee said that this was certainly possible, because Gorbachev had considered Poland the *polygon* (testing ground) of *perestroika* and had often said that he very much admired the Polish model of socialism.[177] Gorbachev was present at the Tenth PUWP Congress in 1986, when Jaruzelski announced that a conference would take place before the next scheduled congress; this would certainly have acquainted Gorbachev with the idea. Clearly, the conference was designed, in the Polish case, as an organ of publicity rather than a decision-making body, and delegates were selected, for this purpose, to express a particular, united view. There are strong parallels with the Nineteenth CPSU Conference, as seen from Chapter 3. Similarly, the unprecedented decision by Gorbachev to televise the Nineteenth CPSU Conference, and broadcast and disseminate its results in a way that had never been done before, is strongly reminiscent of the example of the PUWP March 1984 conference.

Notes

1   See Chapter 1, pp. 39–42; 46.

2   Interview with Jerzy Urban, Warsaw, 28 September 2010; interview with Leszek Miller, Warsaw, 30 September 2010.

3   Interview with Leszek Miller, Warsaw, 30 September 2010.

4   Chapter 3, pp. 98–101, and Chapter 5, pp. 167–9.

5   See Chapter 1, pp. 43–4.

6   PZPR, *Statut Polskiej Zjednoczonej Partii Robotniczej uchwalony przez III zjazd PZPR* (Warszawa: s.n., 1959), p. 77, §31; PZPR, *Statut Polskiej Zjednoczonej Partii Robotniczej: ze zmianami i uzupełnieniami uchwalonymi przez VII Zjazd PZPR w grudniu 1975 r.* (Warszawa: Książka i Wiedza, 1978), p. 74, §31.

7   Interview with Professor Hieronim Kubiak, Cracow, 29 September 2010.

8   PZPR, *Statut Polskiej Zjednoczonej Partii Robotniczej uchwalony przez III zjazd PZPR*, p. 77, §31; PZPR, *Statut Polskiej Zjednoczonej Partii*

Robotniczej ze zmianami i uzupełnieniami uchwalonymi przez VII Zjazd PZPR w grudniu 1975 r., p. 74, §31.

9   See the Party Rules approved at the Tenth Congress, PZPR, *X Zjazd Polskiej Zjednoczonej Partii Robotniczej, 29 czerwca – 3 lipca 1986 r.: stenogram z obrad plenarnych* (Warszawa: Książka i Wiedza, 1987), p. 928.

10   See, for example, 'Najwyższe władze partii' in PZPR, *IX Nadzwyczajny Zjazd Polskiej Zjednoczonej Partii Robotniczej, 14–20 lipca 1981 r.: stenogram z obrad plenarnych* (Warszawa: Książka i Wiedza, 1983), pp. 721–4.

11   See, for example, 'Najwyższe władze partii' in PZPR, *X Zjazd Polskiej Zjednoczonej Partii Robotniczej, 29 czerwca – 3 lipca 1986 r.: stenogram z obrad plenarnych* (Warszawa: Książka i Wiedza, 1987), pp. 906–10.

12   See pp. 149–51; note 14, p. 177.

13   R. Crampton, *Eastern Europe in the Twentieth Century* (London: Routledge, 1995), pp. 154–6.

14   PZPR, *KPP: Uchwały i rezolucje* (Warszawa: Wydział Historii Partii KC PZPR, 1954–56), t. 1, pp. 86–103.

15   *Ibid.*, pp. 104–26.

16   *Ibid.*, pp. 127–92.

17   J. A. Reguła, *Historia Komunistycznej Partii Polski w s'wietle faktów i dokumentów* (Torun: Portal, Wyd. 3, r. 1934, 1994), pp. 131–42.

18   H. Gruda (ed.), *IV Konferencja Komunistycznej Partii Polski, 24.XI – 23.XII, 1925* (Warszawa: Książka i Wiedza, 1972), t. 1, pp. 5–8.

19   PZPR, *I Krajowa Konferencja PZPR, 22–23 paz'dziernika 1973 r.: podstawowe dokumenty i materiały* (Warszawa: Książka i Wiedza, 1973); A. Dobieszewski (ed.), *PZPR, 1948–1978* (Warszawa: Państwowe Wydawn. Nauk, 1978), p. 315.

20   PZPR, *Krajowa Konferencja Delegatów PZPR 16–18 marca 1984: podstawowe dokumenty i materiały* (Warszawa: Książka i Wiedza, 1984).

21   PZPR, *II Krajowa Konferencja Delegatów PZPR 4–5 maja 1989 r.: podstawowe dokumenty i materiały* (Warszawa: Książka i Wiedza, 1989).

22   PZPR, *Krajowa Konferencja Delegatów PZPR 16–18 marca 1984*, p. 65.

23   'Deklaracja Krajowej Konferencji Delegatów PZPR "O co walczymy, dokąd zmierzamy" przyjęta 18 marca 1984', in Centralne Archiwum Komitetu Centralnego PZPR, *Dokumenty programowe polskiego ruchu rabotniczego 1878–1984* (Warszawa: Książka i Wiedza, 1986), pp. 608–21, 612.

24   Archiwum Akt Nowych. PZPR KC BP, 'Najważniejsze konkluzje i ustalenia badania ankietowego', in *Protokoł nr. 109 z posiedzenia Biuro Politycznego KC PZPR wraz z załączniki 13.03.1984*.

25   Archiwum Akt Nowych. PZPR KC BP. Dr J. Paweł Giorgica, *Reprezentacja polityczna rabotników w Partii i w jej władzach: streszczenie wyników badań prowadzonych w IBKR ANS PZPR*, in *Posiedzenia Biura Politycznego KZ PZPR w dn. 1987.05.12.*

26   *Ibid.*

27   Archiwum Akt Nowych. PZPR KC BP. 'Polecania tow. W. Jaruzelskiego wysłano członkom BP "Uwagi o Krajowej Konferencji Delegatów" 3.3.1984', in *Protokoł nr 108 z posiedzenia Biura Politycznego KC PZPR z załącznikami 6.3.1984* mkf nr 3049.

28   Ibid.

29   Interview with Leszek Miller, Warsaw, 30 September 2010.

30   Archiwum Akt Nowych. PZPR KC BP. 'Polecania tow. W. Jaruzelsk-iego wysłano członkam BP "Uwagi o Krajowej Konferencji Delegatów" 3.3.1984', in Protokoł nr 108 z posiedzenia Biura Politycznego KC PZPR z załącznikami 6.3.1984 mkf nr 3049.

31   Interview with Leszek Miller, Warsaw, 30 September 2010.

32   See pp. 98–101; 167–9.

33   Interview with Jerzy Urban, Warsaw, 28 September 2010; interview with Professor Hieronim Kubiak, Cracow, 29 September 2010.

34   M. Rakowski, Dzienniki polityczne, 1979–1981 (Warszawa: Iskry, 2004), p. 306.

35   Ibid.

36   Rakowski, Dzienniki polityczne, 1979–1981, p. 327.

37   Ibid.

38   K. Williams, The Prague Spring and its aftermath: Czechoslovak politics, 1968–1970 (Cambridge: Cambridge University Press, 1997), pp. 131–3.

39   A. Paczkowski, Pół wieku dziejów Polski, 1939–1989 (Warszawa: Wydawn. Nauk. PWN, 1995), p. 492.

40   This paper ceased publication for two months just after martial law was introduced. The last issue of 1981 was nr. 50 (1293) 25, 12.12.1981 and the next was nr. 1 (1294) 26, 20.2.1982.

41   'List do delegatów', Polityka, nr 28(1271) rok XXV, 11 July 1988, p. 1.

42   Interview with Professor Hieronim Kubiak, Cracow, 29 September 2010.

43   Ibid.

44   Interview with Professor Hieronim Kubiak, Cracow, 29 September 2010; interview with Professor Grzegorz Matuszak, Łódź, 6 June 2010.

45   Archiwum Akt Nowych. PZPR KC BP. Dr J. Paweł Giorgica, Reprezen-tacja polityczna rabotników w Partii i w jej władzach: streszczenie wyników badań prowadzonych w IBKR ANS PZPR, in Posiedzenia Biura Politycznego KZ PZPR w dn. 1987.05.12.

46   Interview with Jerzy Urban, Warsaw, 28 September 2010.

47   M. Rakowski (ed.), Polska pod rządami PZPR: praca zbiorowa (Warszawa: Profi, 2000), pp. 368–71.

48   Interview with Jerzy Urban, Warsaw, 28 September 2010.

49   Interview with Professor Hieronim Kubiak, Cracow, 29 September 2010.

50   Interview with Jerzy Urban, Warsaw, 28 September 2010.

51   Ksiądz Jerzy Popiełuszko: modlitwy, kazania, rozważania: nagrania archiwalne z lat 1982–84 (Warszawa: Agora / 4BNB, 2010) In December 2009 the Vatican decided to beatify Jerzy Popiełuszko, and the public open-air service took place in Warsaw in June 2010 attended by more than 100,000 people.

52   Interview with a member of the Politburo, who served in 1988, Warsaw, 8 June 2010.

53   Interview with Jerzy Urban, Warsaw, 28 September 2010.

54   No evidence for this was found in CC stenographic reports nor in the Politburo archival documents I consulted. I was not granted access to verbatim Politburo records for these years.

55 Interview with Professor Hieronim Kubiak, Cracow, 29 September 2010.

56 Archiwum Akt Nowych, PZPR KC. Wydział Nauki, Oświaty i Postępu Naukowo-Technicznego KC PZPR, *Informacja o przebiegu Seminarium I Sekretarzy komitetów uczelnianych PZPR w Sobieszewie w dniach 22–23 X 1988 r.*

57 *Ibid.*, p. 2.

58 *Ibid.*, pp. 2–3.

59 *Ibid.*, p. 3.

60 *Ibid.*

61 *Ibid.*, p. 6.

62 *Ibid.*, p. 2.

63 Archiwum Akt Nowych. PZPR. II/147. *Krajowa Konferencja Delegatów PZPR 4–5 maja 1989* [stenographic report] speech by Krystian Łuczak.

64 PZPR, *X Zjazd Polskiej Zjednoczonej Partii Robotniczej, 29 czerwca – 3 lipca 1986 r.: stenogram z obrad plenarnych* (Warszawa: Książka i Wiedza, 1987), pp. 906–7.

65 As will be discussed on pp. 254–5; 261 of this chapter.

66 PZPR, *X. Parteitag der Polnischen Vereinigten Arbeiterpartei, 29. Juni bis 3. Juli,* (Berlin: Dietz Verlag, 1987), p. 79.

67 See p. 241 of this chapter.

68 See Chapter 5, pp. 155; 159, and Chapter 6, p. 217.

69 *VI Plenum KC Polskiej Zjednoczonej Partii Robotniczej: Referat Biura Politycznego i Przemówienie Wojciecha Jaruzelskiego; Uchwała* (Warszawa: Krajowa Agencja Wydawnicza RSW Prasa, Książka-Ruch, 1988), pp. 52; 63.

70 Interview with a member of the Politburo, who served in 1988, Warsaw, 8 June 2010.

71 Archiwum Akt Nowych. PZPR II/51 *Stenogram z obrad Zespołu do opracowania propozycji reform modelu socjalistycznego Państwa Polskiego w dniu 11 marca 1988 roku.* Kazimierz Cypryniak.

72 Gorbachev Foundation. Gorbachev's fond, 88.July.14.doc.

73 *Życie Partii*, 13 July 1988, p. 3.

74 *Ibid.*, p. 9.

75 Archiwum Akt Nowych. PZPR III/192 *Stenogram XI Plenum KC PZPR 31 marca 1989. r.*

76 See pp. 255–6.

77 Gorbachev Foundation. Gorbachev's fond, 87.Apr.21.doc.

78 *Ibid.*

79 *Ibid.*

80 Gorbachev Foundation. Gorbachev's fond, 88.July.14.doc.

81 Compare Gorbachev's fond, 88.July.14.doc. with, for example, 'Wstępna informacja o wizycie Sekretarza Generalnego KC PZPR M.S. Gorbaczowa w Polsce 11–16 lipca 1988' in Stanisław Perzkowski, ed. (1994), *Tajne dokumenty Biura Politycznego i Sekretariata KC: Ostatni rok władzy 1988–1989*, pp. 5–8.

82 Gorbachev Foundation. Gorbachev's fond, 88.July.14.doc.

83   *Ibid.*

84   See Chapter 5, pp. 157–8; 166.

85   Interview with a member of the Politburo, who served in 1988, Warsaw, 8 June 2010.

86   Marian Woźniak was made ambassador to China; General Józef Baryła to Syria and Jordan; Włodzimierz Mokrzyszczak to Czechoslovakia and Stanisław Bejger to Austria.

87   Archiwum Akt Nowych, KC PZPR, III/186. VII Plenum KC PZPR 13–14 czerwca, 1988.

88   *Ibid.*, speech by Zdzisław Cackowski.

89   PZPR, *VII Plenum Komiteta Centralnego PZPR 13–14 czerwca 1988 r.: podstawowe dokumenty i materiały* (Warszawa: Książka i Wiedza, 1988), p. 68.

90   *Ibid.*, pp. 66–74.

91   Interview with Leszek Miller, Warsaw, 30 September 2010.

92   *Ibid.*

93   Interview with Jerzy Urban, Warsaw, 28 September 2010.

94   Interview with Leszek Miller, Warsaw, 30 September 2010.

95   *Ibid.*

96   Archiwum Akt Nowych. PZPR. II/147. *Krajowa Konferencja Delegatów PZPR 4–5 maja 1989* [stenographic report], introductory speech by Wojciech Jaruzelski.

97   *Ibid.*, Izabella Sierakowska.

98   *Ibid.*, Roman Malinowski.

99   *Ibid.*, Krzysztof Abramczuk.

100 *Ibid.*, Jan Ciemniewski.

101 *Ibid.*, Ryszard Paluch.

102 Member of the CKKR and academic at the Institute of Philosophy, Adam Mickiewicz, University in Poznan.

103 Archiwum Akt Nowych. PZPR. II/147. *Krajowa Konferencja Delegatów PZPR 4–5 maja 1989* [stenographic report], speech by Antoni Szczuciński.

104 *Ibid.*, Marian Truszkowski.

105 *Ibid.*, Zdisław Cackowski.

106 Krzysztof Abramczuk, a member of the Central Control-Revision Commission (CCRC) and factory lathe operator.

107 Archiwum Akt Nowych. PZPR. II/147. *Krajowa Konferencja Delegatów PZPR 4–5 maja 1989* [stenographic report], speech by Krzysztof Abramczuk.

108 *Ibid.*, Paweł Zawadzki.

109 PZPR, *II Krajowa Konferencja Delegatów PZPR 4–5 maja 1989 r.: podstawowe dokumenty i materiały* (Warszawa: Książka i Wiedza, 1989), p. 83.

110 M. Rakowski, *Dzienniki polityczne, 1987–1990* (Warszawa: Iskry, 2005), p. 425.

111 *Ibid.*, pp. 425–6.

112 See Chapter 5, p. 133.

113 Interview with a member of the Politburo, who served in 1988, Warsaw, 8 June 2010.

114 *Ibid.*

115 Interview with Leszek Miller, Warsaw, 30 September 2010.

116 'Komitet Powitalny'. According to Mr Urban this group comprised Stefan Olszowski, Mirosław Milewski and Albin Siwak from the Politburo, and General Eugeniusz Molczyk, who headed the united forces of the Warsaw Pact countries until 1984.

117 Interview with Leszek Miller, Warsaw, 30 September 2010; interview with a member of the Politburo, who served in 1988, Warsaw, 8 June 2010.

118 Rakowski, *Dzienniki polityczne, 1987–1990*, pp. 209–10.

119 *Ibid.*, p. 209.

120 See this chapter, pp. 250–4.

121 G. Shakhnazarov, *S vozhdiami i bez nikh* (Moskva: Vagrius, 2001), pp. 144–7.

122 PZPR, *XIII Plenum KC PZPR, 30 czerwca i 28–29 lipca 1989: podstawowe dokumenty i materiały* (Warszawa: Książka i Wiedza, 1989), p. 7.

123 G. Sanford, *Katyń and the Soviet massacre of 1940: truth, justice and memory* (London: Routledge, 2005), pp. 180–6. The matter was dropped after pressure on the UK Government from the Soviet and Polish Governments.

124 Rakowski, *Dzienniki polityczne, 1987–1990*, p. 213.

125 Shakhnazarov, *S vozhdiami i bez nikh*, p. 144.

126 M. Rakowski, *Jak to się stało* (Warszawa: BGW, 1991), p. 22.

127 *Ibid.* According to Rakowski the group 'Pol'skiĭ klub' also included Mikhail Suslov, Andrei Gromyko, Dmitriĭ Ustinov and Konstantin Rusakov.

128 A. Kemp-Welch, *Poland under Communism: a cold war history* (Cambridge: Cambridge University Press, 2008), p. 264.

129 Shakhnazarov, *S vozhdiami i bez nikh*, pp. 144–5.

130 Rakowski, *Jak to się stało*, p. 23.

131 Rakowski, *Dzienniki polityczne, 1979–1981*, p. 301.

132 A. Gromyko, *Memories*, trans. by Harold Shukman (London: Hutchinson, 1989), p. 231.

133 *Ibid.*, p. 232.

134 W. Bereś and J. Skoczylas, *Generał Kiszczak mówi... prawie wszystko*, (Warszawa: Polska Oficyna Wydawnicza BGW, 1991), p. 117.

135 *Ibid.*, p. 106.

136 Rakowski, *Jak to się stało*, p. 25.

137 *Ibid.*, p. 27.

138 *Ibid.*, p. 29.

139 For a review of these, see Kemp-Welch, *Poland under Communism*, pp. 325–7.

140 Archiwum Akt Nowych. PZPR XIA/1399, pp. 42–53. This archival document contains notes and the partial transcript of a meeting held between János Kádár and the Soviet Ambassador to Budapest, Vladimir Bazovs-

kiĭ, in March 1982, which outlined discussions that had taken place
between Jaruzelski and Brezhnev during the first official Polish state visit
to Moscow on 1–2 March 1982, following the introduction of martial law
in Poland the previous December.

141 Archiwum Akt Nowych. PZPR XIA/1399, p. 42.

142 Kemp-Welch, *Poland under Communism*, p. 326. A similar argument is
made in M. Ouimet, *The Rise and Fall of the Brezhnev Doctrine* (Chapel
Hill NC: University of North Carolina, 2003), p. 255.

143 Archiwum Akt Nowych. PZPR XIA/1399, p. 47.

144 *Ibid.*, pp. 42–53.

145 See Chapter 5.

146 See Chapter 5.

147 Archiwum Akt Nowych. PZPR XIA/1399, pp. 49–50.

148 In the summer of 1980, Jaruzelski established a secret military advisory
group, the 'Anti-Crisis Operation Staff', which made contingency plans
for the introduction of martial law. Colonel Kukliński was appointed
to this body, but began leaking details of their plans to the US intelligence authorities in the hope that a military solution would thus be
prevented.

149 R. Kukliński, 'The crushing of Solidarity', *ORBIS*, 32:1, Winter (1988),
pp. 7–31.

150 According to Jaruzelski, in his discussion with Gorbachev in April 1987
in Moscow, this speech made a significant impact on delegates at the
Tenth Congress. Gorbachev Foundation. Fond Gorbacheva. 87.Apr.21.
doc.

151 PZPR, *X Zjazd PZPR o przyjaźni i współpracy ze Związkiem Radzieckim*
(Warszawa: Wydawnictwo TPPR Współpraca, 1986).

152 *Ibid.*, p. 11.

153 *Ibid.*, pp. 9–10.

154 'Deklaracja Krajowej Konferencji Delegató PZPR "O co walczymy dokąd
zmierzamy" przyjęta 18 marca 1984', in *Centralne Archiwum Komitetu
Centralnego PZPR (1986), Dokumenty programowe polskiego ruchu
robotniczego 1878–1984* (Warszawa: Książka i Wiedza, 1986), p. 612.

155 Archiwum Akt Nowych. XIA/1413. *Deklaratsiia ob ideologicheskikh
sotrudnichestve mezhdu Kommunisticheskoĭ partieĭ Sovetskogo Soiuza
i Pol'skoĭ ob˝edinennoĭ rabocheĭ partieĭ* 21.04.87

156 *Ibid.*

157 Gorbachev Foundation. Gorbachev's Fond. 21.04.87.

158 Sanford, *Katyń and the Soviet massacre of 1940*.

159 *Ibid.*, p. 214.

160 *Ibid.*, p. 198.

161 *Ibid.*, p. 215.

162 Archiwum Akt Nowych. PZPR XIA/1440. *Ekspertyza. Kommunikat
komisji specjalnej do ustalenia i zbadania okoliczności rozstrzelania
przez niemieckich najeźdźców faszystowskich w lesie katyńskim jeńców
wojennych – oficerów polskich – dokonana przez profesorów: J. Maci-
szewskiego, C. Madajczyka, R. Nazarewicza i M. Wojciechowskiego,
zgodnie z wnioskiem radzieckiej części komisji uczonych ZSRR i PRL d.s.*

historii stosunków między obu krajami [heading on document: received by Politburo 8 VI 1989].

163   *Ibid.*

164   *Ibid.*

165   F. Kadell, *Kłamstwo Katyńskie* = *Die Katyn Lüge* (originally publ. 1991), (Wrocław: Wyd. Dolnośląskie, 2009), pp. 210–11. Although German sources may be considered partial on this issue, it seems logical that Jaruzelski's action would have provoked a widespread and strong reaction from the Polish population.

166   Archiwum Akt Nowych. PZPR. II/147. *Krajowa Konferencja Delegatów PZPR 4–5 maja 1989* [stenographic report], introductory speech by Wojciech Jaruzelski.

167   PZPR, *II Krajowa Konferencja Delegatów PZPR 4–5 maja 1989 r.: podstawowe dokumenty i materiały* (Warszawa: Książka i Wiedza, 1989), pp. 98–9.

168   *Ibid.*, p. 99.

169   *Ibid.*, pp. 99–100.

170   Rakowski, *Dzienniki polityczne, 1987–1990*, p. 208.

171   I have translated *prezydialny* in this context as 'top', although it literally means 'presiding' or even 'presidential', which could suggest that the table was exclusively for the Warsaw Pact leaders.

172   Rakowski, *Dzienniki polityczne, 1987–1990*, p. 211.

173   Since these were diary entries, however, we could assume that if Rakowski knew the person, then he would have remembered it in the context of such a serious topic. Furthermore, since the three individuals concerned were at the table where the Warsaw Pact state leaders were seated, we could infer from this that the third person was equally senior.

174   Sanford, *Katyń and the Soviet massacre of 1940*, p. 199.

175   *Ibid.*, pp. 218–19. In April 2010, a Polish–Russian Katyń commemorative service was hosted by the Russian authorities. Tragically, the plane carrying Polish President Lech Kaczyński, the Ombudsman, some of the victims' relatives, dozens of MPs and members of the military crashed en route to this service. Regarding the adequacy of the Russian authorities' investigation of the 1940 tragedy, a number of applications have been filed by the 1940 victims' relatives (against the Russian Federation) at the European Court. On 6 October 2011 there was a (European Court) hearing of some of these, *Janowiec and others v Russia Federation* (55508/07 & 29520/09), during which the Polish Government intervened to provide evidence in support of the applicants' cases.

176   Gorbachev Foundation. Fond Gorbacheva 87.Apr.10.doc Zapis' osnovnogo soderzhaniia besedy M.S.G. s chlenami Prezidiuma i sekretariiami TSK KPCh.

177   Interview with a member of the Politburo, who served in 1988, Warsaw, 8 June 2010.

Conclusions

The conference as an institution

A good test of the theoretical model developed in this book is whether the model holds generally beyond 1988–89. With the fall of communist regimes, the conference, together with the one-party state models in Central, Eastern and South-eastern Europe, ceased to exist. Naturally, therefore, we are confined to examining the conference within a limited time frame. As the CPSU and HSWP case chapters showed, with the attempted convention of conferences by Gorbachev and Grósz in 1991 and 1989 respectively, the conference was the preferred forum for General/First Secretaries seeking to consolidate their power, and stage all-party endorsement of policies, which might not be welcomed at a congress. Moreover, as discussed in Chapter 1, the fact that the conference's powers were not explicitly defined in the Party Rules meant that dissenters in the party could not effectively object *post facto* that the conference had not been held according to protocol. Therefore, those who anticipated their preferences would not be taken into account at a conference could only resist the outcome of a conference by objecting beforehand to the choice of institution and lobby instead for an extraordinary congress.

As detailed in Chapters 3, 5 and 7, acrimonious debate between reformists and centrists over which forum be convened to work out their respective parties' futures indicates that reformists considered the conferences too circumscribed by the centrist leaderships, and therefore incapable of yielding a reformist outcome. Only extraordinary congresses could empower a more representative sector of the party to express their preferences and shape outcome. Party leaders' insistence, instead, on a party conference from 1987 to 1989 demonstrates that they sought to set clear boundaries to the reform process, which they anticipated the majority in the party would not endorse. For this reason, leaderships selected an ostensibly 'all-party' meeting at which they could manufacture all-party support for their commonly agreed reform package. In relative terms, therefore, this factor indicates that the congress as an institution must have served, certainly to a greater degree than the conference, some genuine function of interest aggregation among members. It also shows the extent to which one-party regime leaderships, even those of Stalin and Ceauşescu, were genuinely constrained by institutions.

Applying the theoretical model beyond 1988

As was shown in the cases of the CPSU and HSWP, this model applies beyond the conferences of 1988. Evidence in both cases indicates that the conference was considered a more pliable forum where General/First Secretaries could shore up their power, as borne out in Chapters 5 and 6, in that both Gorbachev and Grósz tried to persuade their respective parties to reconvene the conference. Significantly, both tried to convene a conference when under pressure to resign: Gorbachev in 1990–91, and Grósz in 1989 after his opponents had demanded his resignation. In both cases they were defeated by opponents in their respective parties who instead insisted on an extraordinary party congress, as a forum where the outcome could be determined by a genuine party majority rather than a stage-managed pseudo plebiscitary directed by the General/First Secretary. At the subsequent congress, Grósz lost his position, whereas before the extraordinary Twenty-ninth CPSU Congress, scheduled for November 1991, the August Coup took place. Gorbachev, having stood out against the putschists, could have regained some popularity in the wake of the Coup. Instead, Boris Yeltsin stole the limelight.

In terms of a common policy, however, the convention of conferences across the fraternity at this time was in essence a retrograde step, which did little (if anything) to further the process of liberalisation, as party members, aware of the conference dynamic and how they had been orchestrated, became more vocal in their demands for extraordinary congresses. Ultimately, demands for these congresses could no longer be resisted across the fraternal parties of Central and Eastern Europe, and when they did take place, factions within each party crystallised, which engendered the end of party unity. At the Twenty-eighth CPSU Congress in 1990 the party split, although at this congress Gorbachev managed to appoint a large number of conservatives to the top leadership, which helped put a rein on the reformists, allowing him an extra (albeit troubled) last year in office. The Fourteenth LCY Congress in February 1990 marked the end of the LCY as consensus among the republican parties could not be reached at the meeting.[1] Free elections were held very shortly after in March 1990 in Slovenia and Croatia. In Hungary and Poland the next (and final) party congresses occurred around the end of the round-table talks with the opposition, which were negotiating the terms of power sharing, and, as it was becoming clearer, regime change. By the time of the Fourteenth HSWP Congress in October 1989, Kádár had died, the majority of the party had outgrown Grósz and support galvanised around Imre Pozsgay, Miklós Németh and Rezső Nyers, which formed from this party majority the HSP. There was, however, a small conservative contingent which remained the HSWP, although this party has enjoyed little popular support since then. In the case of Poland, at the Eleventh PUWP Congress in January 1990, again there was a split, and the majority of the party founded the Union of Left Democrats (SLD).

Interestingly, the choice of the extraordinary congress as the preferred institution for reformists seeking the ouster of the party leader has continued to apply in the case of the reform-communist successor party to the HSWP, the HSP. In the summer and autumn of 2004, in a bid to improve the party's image, the young reformist wing of the HSP, the 'Mozaik Klub', demanded in the summer of 2004 that the HSP Prime Minister, Péter Medgyessy, be replaced. Just as the reformist wing in 1989, of which Medgyessy, had been a member, demanded an extraordinary congress, in 2004 the Mozaik Klub demanded the convention of an extraordinary congress as the forum at which Medgyessy's future be decided. At the congress in September 2004, Medgyessy was replaced with Ferenc Gyurcsány, who served as Prime Minister until 2009.

This could suggest that within the Hungarian reform communist successor party, such institutional traditions persisted. Conversely one could argue that the actors themselves may have been decisive in influencing outcome, as a significant number of the same personnel were in power in both 1989 and 2004. However, in defence of the institutional explanation of outcome, one could argue that the members of the Mozaik Klub, as youngsters, were newcomers to the party (post-1989). However, some may have been members of the young communist organisation KISZ in 1989 and therefore may have been aware of the conference/extraordinary congress debacle at the time. Nevertheless, this does support the argument that perceptions of institutional choice as crucial to outcome persisted between the 1980s and 2004 in the case of the HSWP/HSP. In the case of the HSP in 2004, we may surmise that the Mozaik Klub borrowed the 'reformist' institution of the extraordinary congress to purposely signal their final break with the party's past.

Does the model generalise beyond the four cases?

Within the context of 1987–91, however, there are other cases that could equally have been examined beyond those chosen for in-depth study. As discussed in Chapter 4, this research concentrated first on three regimes, those of the Soviet Union, Hungary and Yugoslavia, that each held their conferences within the same time frame between May and July 1988. These cases were limited to *like cases only*, which inevitably queries the explanatory force of the results of the research, as case selection was made on the dependent variable – those parties that held conferences with similar Gorbachevian reformist outcomes. Research into the additional case of Poland, which was unlike the others in terms of timing (held a year later), but similar in that we would expect a reformist outcome, also indicated CPSU influence over the PUWP conference in 1989, and some evidence that centrist-reformists in the CPSU would have welcomed a new first secretary. Yet there was apparently insufficient support within the top leadership to secure this change at the conference, although as discussed in Chapter 7, there is evidence that suggests the Prime Minister, Mieczysław Rakowski, had the support of Moscow and party intellectuals as a replacement for Jaruzelski.

The results of the research into these four cases have implicitly raised a number of questions. By analogy with the factor of collaboration between the centrist-reformist leaderships of the CPSU, HSWP and LCY, was there similar collaboration between leaders in those regimes, where conferences did not yield a reformist outcome, or no conference was held? Similarly, did fraternal parties, other than the CPSU, influence each another's decisions to convene conferences? For example, was Grósz's decision to reconvene the HSWP conference in March 1989 influenced by communication with the PUWP leadership as they prepared for their conference in May 1989?

Other archival material discussed in Chapter 4 throws some light on the other regimes' responses to Gorbachev's request that conferences be convened to modernise the fraternal parties, oust the old guard, and stage a show of solidarity for *perestroika*. This at least indicates that fraternal leaders were in communication with Gorbachev about such issues, and that they were encouraged to convene their respective conferences for this purpose. We might anticipate, therefore, that similar debates took place within the Bulgarian, Czechoslovak and GDR parties, and yet the centrist-reformist wing of these parties was simply too weak to secure the desired outcome, in the case of the BCP, or too weak to pressure the leadership to convene a conference, in the cases of the CPCZ and SED. In the case of Poland, a conference was in any event 'due' around 1988, which might have made it more difficult for Jaruzelski to 'cancel' the event, leaving him the only other option of deferring it. The Romanian conference was also due around this time, as it had been institutionalised to occur regularly every five years between congresses, and Ceauşescu convened the RCP conference precisely according to schedule, in December 1987. Ceauşescu had successfully shaped the conference since the 1970s to facilitate his construction of an unassailable power base, which suggests that he would have been relatively confident in convening another such meeting without fear of being ousted.

Liberalisation or democratisation?

The research demonstrates that leaderships across these fraternal parties were initiating 'reform from above' at these conferences, 1988–89 in response to a demand by Gorbachev in the spirit of socialist internationalism, to preserve the one-party state model. What these leaders hoped to achieve, therefore, was economic liberalisation and modernisation of their regimes, so that they could rebuild the party's legitimacy and make their economies sustainable. Their conferences indicated alignment with and support for Gorbachev's *perestroika*. Although in the case of Poland this came so late that it had very little, if any, impact in this respect. The fraternal leaderships achieved these goals in so far as they were able to support Gorbachev's *perestroika* and modernise their respective parties. But, since the main purpose of these conferences was to some extent a hidden agenda, not disclosed to the public, and only made available in some cases to the upper leaderships in the respective parties, these conferences were perhaps bound to fail in transforming the fraternal parties. Inevitably, confusion arose over the new trajectory these parties were embarking on and the best way to reform the Communist Party. Holding a conference to show solidarity with the socialist fraternity and in particular the CPSU's new reform agenda, was unpalatable to some members of the fraternal party leaderships, as it challenged the political autonomy of these regimes. In any event, the one-party regime across the bloc was very soon discredited, and a multiparty system developed in all states. The reform-communists in a number of fraternal states (for example in Bulgaria, the Czech Republic, Hungary and Poland) engaged in round-table discussions with emergent opposition groups to negotiate the terms of regime change. The reform communists, many of whom had served during the 1980s, thus became credible competitors with the new emergent opposition parties and have since formed governments operating under the constraints of liberal democratic institutions.

In Russia, however, there has been no such democratisation, in the main because the necessary conditions for free and fair elections have not been developed, and instead, to some extent the one-party state appears intact. Some consider that under Yeltsin democratic practices were slightly more promising, although given the chaotic nature of the situation during his presidency, the fact that there was relatively more pluralism is likely to have been the result of Yeltsin's need at that time for more liberal advisers in his administration during the early privatisation process, and to satisfy international observers as part of the conditionality pact between Russia and world financial institutions at this time, as a means to secure foreign funding.

The kind of polity that Gorbachev apparently wanted was one where the leading role of the party would be maintained. To do this required establishing a viable economic system – that is, introducing a market economy, shedding the economic burden of CEE, and garnering public support for the party through quasi-pluralisation, much in the vein of Communist-era 'multiparty' systems in the fraternal regimes, where *de facto* the Communist/Socialist Party retained its leading role. During the Gorbachev era those other parties that were allowed to flourish after other political parties were legalised in 1990, such as Zhirinovsky's Liberal Democratic Party, were those that supported the Communist Party's policies.

To some extent, therefore, Gorbachev's vision has been realised during the post-Communist era, in that a market economy has been established and the 'party of power', under Yeltsin, and in particular Putin, has institutionalised a leading role for itself, which is supported by quasi-independent parties and only those parties which United Russia allows to flourish. Although we might assume that Gorbachev envisaged this leading role would be filled by the Communist Party, Yeltsin outlawed the party in 1992. A year later, the Communist Party of the Russian Federation was re-established, after the Constitutional Court issued an ambiguous decision regarding Yeltsin's right to outlaw the party.[2] Although the Communist Party, like the successor parties in Central Europe, split into reform-communist and those conservatives that adhered to previous traditions, the reform-communist branch quickly grew to become the most popular party in Russia by the run-up to the 1995 elections. Yeltsin overcame this competition by throwing in his lot with a new centre-right party, 'Our Home is Russia', on the eve of the elections, purposely created to splinter the opposition to engineer his victory.[3] His subsequent annihilation of the Communists in the 1995 elections undermined the reform-communist movement, and instead created a system where a predominant centre-right party (Unity and then United Russia), with the greatest control of resources, presided. Yeltsin's first significant confrontation, as President, with those who adhered to Communist ideals was in the Parliament over the issue of privatisation in 1993, and after he unconstitutionally dissolved Parliament to side-step the problem, his opponents mounted a coup against him, which Yeltsin had put down by force, resulting in the death of more than a hundred people. This failure to aggregate interests characterises how Russia has followed a different trajectory to the new liberal democracies of Central Europe, which success-fully negotiated regime change allowing the successor socialist parties to compete in free and fair elections. Instead in Russia the creation of pseudo-parties during the Gorbachev era has led to a confusing 'floating party system', where all is not what it seems. Under Yeltsin, this developed into a system where those with control over resources, the 'Party of Power', engineer the capture of a majority. It could be argued that Gorbachev's legacy, in this respect, has been very damaging to the develop-ment of party democracy in Russia.

Other parallels with the system under the CPSU may also be drawn. During the period of privatisation under Yeltsin's presidency, to a large extent the power that the ministries enjoyed over the control of resources was channelled towards individuals who would similarly support the 'Party of Power' through a series of mutually agreed (but informal) conditions with the President. These included the 'loans for shares' deals from 1995, whereby certain favoured individuals were in essence invited to purchase huge state enterprises at cut-price. The development of oligarchs under Yeltsin may be seen as the 'Party of Power' securing its power base through the anticipated future political control over resources. When in 2003 some oligarchs, such as Mikhail Khodorkhovsky, a major share-holder in and board member of the Yukos oil company, began to break rank and offer support to liberal opposition parties, Yabloko and the Union of Right Forces, and the Communist Party rather than the 'Party of Power', Putin quickly moved in to close these oligarchs down.[4] Putin disclaimed the informal agreement through which Yukos had provided free energy resources to support the state during the 1990s in exchange for a waiver on payment of taxes. Khodorkovsky was subsequently prosecuted for (among other things) tax evasion.

In theory, we might expect that Gorbachev would have been more supportive of a system where the party of power had better control over its resources (or oligarchs), such as that of the Putin era, rather than the Yeltsin era, by analogy with his strong belief that the Communist Party should control the ministries, and not vice versa.

Although Gorbachev has since claimed that media freedoms are under threat in Putin's Russia, there is little evidence to suggest that he himself completely embraced such a policy of media freedom during his time as General Secretary and President (1985–91). The media was directed to criticise particular opponents to Gorbachev, in support of *perestroika*. Gorbachev was keen to portray the 1988 CPSU Conference as a forum of free debate, which, as evidence in Chapter 3 demonstrates, was not the case. Moreover, significant historical revelations that were made during the Gorbachev era, which have been described as the fruits of *glasnost*, were all carefully chosen, and the timing of disclosure was also carefully orchestrated. As Chapters 4, 5 and 7 discuss, disclosure concerning Stalinist-era crimes relating to CEE was timed to undermine incumbent old-timers and their power bases, both in the Soviet and CEE leaderships, as a way to sweep the decks of hardliners to improve the Communist Party's reputation, and to try to secure the public's support for the party across the fraternity. The only incumbent leaderships that did not suffer from the revelations of Stalinist-era crimes and those concerning the Brezhnev Doctrine were, of course, Gorbachev and his new cohort in the CPSU and non-aligned Yugoslavia. On the strength of Gorbachev's change in stance regarding Yugoslavia, a significant albeit short-lived agreement was made between the two states and parties, which brought it back into the socialist fraternity, though only temporarily.

In light of this reappraisal of *glasnost*, Gorbachev's *post facto* defence of democratic structures and ideals during the subsequent Yeltsin and Putin eras appears disingenuous, or at the very least a significant transformation in his own thinking since 1991, which should perhaps be viewed with some scepticism.

Similarly, there appears to be some continuity between the Gorbachev and Putin era in the area of attitudes towards the West. The 2006 law on NGOs, which was geared in large part to prevent foreign funding for Non-Governmental Organisations (NGO) activity to safeguard against any foreign support for any potential democratising movements in Russia, indicates that Putin shares with Gorbachev a similar preoccupation with 'Western political infiltration'. With respect to the relationship between Russia and the fraternal states following the collapse of the Communist model across the region, needless to say, the integration of most of the fraternal states of CEE into the European Union has restructured the dynamic between these states and Russia. While dependence on energy resources in particular continues to act, to some extent, as a centrifugal force, this factor also affects other Western European states. Whether there is any common political vision behind such collaboration is questionable, and any sense that such cooperation operates within the framework of the shared ideals associated with socialist internationalism or any other ideology appears completely anachronistic.

Notes

1   O. Ibrahimagić, *Bosna je odbranjena ali nije oslobodena* (Sarajevo: Vijeće Kongresa bošnjačkih intelektualaca, 2004), pp. 153–4.

2   R. Sakwa , *Russian Politics and Society* (London: Routledge, 4th edn, 2008), pp. 135–6.

3   L. Shevtsova, *Yeltsin's Russia: myths and reality* (Washington DC: Carnegie Endowment for International Peace, 1999), pp. 134–7.

4   D. White, *The Russian Democratic Party Yabloko: Opposition in a managed democracy* (Aldershot: Ashgate, 2006), pp. 170–2.

Index